A Charmed Life

By
Peter Steward

DEDICATION

To my grandchildren Elliot, Poppy and Lyla and bump in the hope that one day they will take a dusty tome from a bookshelf and be keen to find out about the life of their grandfather.

Also, in memory of Oliver.

Any proceeds from the sale of this book will be donated to charity.

Please feel free to copy or reproduce any part of this publication without gaining further permission. If you do wish to use or quote from this, I would appreciate it if you would attribute it to the publication and to myself.

Peter Steward 2025.

Please note that no ghost writers were used or harmed in writing this book.

Other Books by Peter Steward:

"Hell in Paradise" – The story of a massacre at Le Paradis in Northern France in May 1940 during the Second World War which saw 97 soldiers, mainly from the Royal Norfolk

Regiment and others, massacred by the Nazis. Published by the Le Paradis Commemoration Group and written by Peter Steward and John Head. Available for £15 including postage and packaging from petersteward@sky.com.

Journalist – A keeper of a journal, a recorder of life.

		Introduction
PART ONE - TEASERS		
Chapter One		Talks
Chapter Two		The Answers
PART TWO – MY LIFE		
Chapter Three		The Early Years 1952-1962
Chapter Four		The Formative Years 1963-1970
Chapter Five		Off To College 1970
PART THREE – OUT TO WORK		
Chapter Six		Lowestoft
Chapter Seven		Norwich
Chapter Eight		Cromer
Chapter Nine		Beccles
Chapter Ten		The Midlands
Chapter Eleven		Return to Norfolk
Chapter Twelve		Norfolk Constabulary and Beyond
PART FOUR – OTHER ASPECTS OF LIFE		
Chapter Thirteen		A Sporting Life
Chapter Fourteen		Awards and Press Coverage
Chapter Fifteen		Samaritans
Chapter Sixteen		School Work
Chapter Seventeen		Parish Council and Publications
Chapter Eighteen		Wedding Day
Chapter Nineteen		Happy and Sad Days
PART FIVE – ODDS AND ENDS		
Chapter Twenty		Bits and Pieces From a Life
APPENDIX		Birth Chart
		My Timeline
		Places I Have Lived
		My Community Involvement
		My Favourite Things
FINALE		
		An Open Letter to Mum
		A Return To The Beginning

INTRODUCTION

Go to any bookshop and you will see the great and the good have written about themselves and their lives.

Well, this book isn't by a member of the great and good. It's about me – an unknown and at times a frustrated author. So, I must start with the obvious question.

Why a book about me when I'm an unknown who nobody is going to be interested in?

Well, it is and it isn't about me. But I must admit that mostly it is. But I hope that my readers see something more in it than just a catalogue of the mostly mundane things that have made my life what it is.

Overall, I have had a happy life, although, of course, there have been times of great sadness too. But it's life experiences that make our lives what they are. I am much taken by a lovely song by The Divine Comedy, one of my favourite rock/pop bands and so I have called my autobiography "My Charmed Life" after one of their songs written by the excellent frontman Neil Hannon, a man who certainly does have a way with words and is probably one of the few people that has ever included the town of Cromer in one of his song lyrics! It's almost as though he knew how important Cromer is to me, both in the past and in the present.

With the advent of self-publishing, it has become much easier for Mr, Mrs and Miss Every Person to burst into print on any known subject.

I have seen friends publish books of poetry, books of short stories, novels and autobiographies. So why not join them I thought?

But do I have anything to say? Well hopefully yes. I hope that I have written it in an entertaining way, but I guess you the reader will have to be the judge of that.

When COVID lockdown struck, I decided to start writing a daily blog. At first, I blogged two or three times a day about my walks and subjects that were important to me. Gradually this dropped down to one entry each day. I was very surprised that people enjoyed and wanted to read what I referred to as my ramblings and dribblings on many different subjects including my family life.

Readers contacted me to say how much they looked forward to the daily blogs. One even went as far as to say it was the reason she got up in the morning – all of which was very humbling.

As I write this I have almost 700 members of my blog. So, I look upon this my autobiography as just an extension of those blogs. It is written roughly in the same style. Just look upon it as one long blog of well over 100,000 words.

In addition, the year 2022 marked 50 years of writing a daily diary. On December 23rd, 1972, I wrote my first real diary entry. I had tried to start a regular journal before but had always given up. But a few days before Christmas that year I got going and I have been going ever since. That's over 19,000 entries in numerous diaries and notebooks.

Many of those entries have proved to be the basis of this work which includes lots of asides and plenty about things that interest me. In other words, as I've already said, an extended and very long blog that I hope at least some people will find interesting enough to read or just dip into. I particularly enjoyed writing the chapters on my early years as they brought back many memories.

Like my blogs, this autobiography goes from the serious to the amusing, the important to the trivial. I know from thousands of comments how people enjoy what I write and that gives me a very warm, fuzzy feeling. So, I have decided to turn my experiences into the book that you now either have in your hands in physical form or which you are reading on a Kindle or other device.

My life has been a relatively ordinary one. I have few real talents, but something has happened that means people enjoy my writing. So, if I have been given any skill, it is the ability to write and through this to entertain people in a way that I still find difficult to understand. And for that reason, I have decided to write about my life and the little incidents that have stayed in my memory over many decades. Whilst writing the book I have had periods of joy, periods of laughter and periods of sadness (in other words gone through all the emotions that people regularly feel during their lives).

I adore writing. I would spend my entire life writing (and my wife would probably say that I do). I find it therapeutic, and I can scarcely do anything without writing about it. I find writing comes easily and naturally just as mending cars and making things, comes naturally to others but which to me is almost a foreign country,

*   *   *

I love the word vignette. I have no idea why, but it just seems an appropriate word for what I do. I write vignettes.

A dictionary definition of the word vignette is: "A brief evocative description, account, or episode."

What follows is in some ways a series of vignettes that I hope come together in an interesting way to give you a little insight into the kind of person I am. I even have a section at the end which is a series of vignettes or incidents that haven't been included in the main part of the book. At times things will be in chronological order, but at others I will dot around somewhat, but I hope that if you stay with the book you will end up feeling that you have been entertained and know a little more about the person I am and what makes me tick and what sometimes only comes out when I'm faced with a pen and a blank piece of paper or, in most cases nowadays, with a computer screen, a Word document and a keyboard.

Thank you very much for purchasing this book. Any proceeds from its sale will be donated to charity. You will see from the front pages that I haven't copyrighted the material and that is deliberate. I find it a huge compliment when people want to use things I have written or photographs that I have taken. I am not precious about keeping control of the material. So, if you are reading this and want to quote any part of it, I would be delighted. All I ask is that you mention where the passages are taken from to help me sell a few more books and raise a little more money for charity.

I finish this introduction by pointing out that this is no aggressive kiss and tell biography. It's meant to be much gentler. In fact, closer to a kiss and gel work.

Peter Steward

Hethersett,

Norfolk: 2025

PART ONE – TEASERS

In which I tease the reader with some aspects of my life, most of which are true and one that isn't. Your task is to decide which is the untrue, made up one.

CHAPTER ONE – TALKS

I'm quite often asked to give talks to local groups.

Now there could be two reasons for this. Firstly, I might be looked upon as an interesting person who has something to say. Alternately the groups might be desperate to fill their calendar and they know I will always say yes.

I always say yes because I enjoy talking to groups. I have no idea why. Ask me to walk into a room of strangers and I panic, not knowing what to say or how to behave and feeling decidedly out of place. Ask me to sing in front of an audience in a karaoke session and I run a mile.

Ask me to talk to a group and it's another matter, however. Just ask me and I'm there. And I never charge for this. I don't know anyone who would want to pay to hear what I have to say. If asked, however, I will always accept a donation for charity. As I write this, I have just completed a 1,500 mile walk in aid of the East Anglian Air Ambulance and you can read about this in the end section of this book.

I give talks about my career (such as it was/is), my village, myself, or virtually any other subject that I am remotely conversant with. Many years ago, I was momentarily a member of a debating group in a town in the Midlands. Their evenings were split into two sections. In the first we had to give a 10-minute talk on a prepared subject of our own choosing. In the second we had to talk about a random subject picked from a hat. I remember on one occasion I got the subject "Tractors."

I know absolutely nothing about tractors, but the skill was to start talking and see where the subject took you. So, I talked about coming from Norfolk where there is a proliferation of tractors and how dangerous they made the roads and that morphed into road safety and many other subjects.

I was beginning to think laterally, to be able to talk on any subject, even if I knew less than nothing about it. And I guess that has passed into my writing. The same thing happened to me many years ago when I studied for a master's degree in professional development from the University of East Anglia. On one occasion we were asked to write 1,000 words about a brick wall opposite where we were meeting. Whilst the other pupils panicked and became stressed, I found the challenge easy, talking about all the people that had climbed the wall over the years and the reasons for putting it in place. Anyway, I digress, and you will find I digress quite a lot over the course of what follows.

One of my talks revolves around things that have happened to me in my life. This is a light-hearted presentation which features seven scenarios – six of which happened and one which is completely made up. The audience is asked to vote for the one they feel is untrue.

My reason for doing this is twofold. Firstly, it involves those present in a bit of fun and secondly it gives me the chance to talk about some of the zanier and more unusual things that have happened to me.

I do genuinely believe that my life has been a very ordinary one (but as I've said in the introduction A Charmed One). It has followed the tried and trusted paths of being born, going to school, going to college, getting a job, getting married, having children and then grandchildren, retiring and undertaking voluntary work (more about that later). There is nothing remarkable about my life. Indeed, it has been singularly unremarkable. But along the way I hope I have contributed to society in a useful way. I'm going to start with my seven scenarios and ask you to work out which is the made up one. I find in my talks that many people are stumped, although some guess the answer almost immediately.

I am taking a risk by doing this as never again will I be able to use this idea for a talk in case some of my readers are in the audience. I will just have to think up some brand-new scenarios. Anyway, here goes. I will give you the basic scenarios and once you have made your choice, you can read about each scenario and how and where it took place and of course find out which is the one made up.

Scenario One – I ran onto the pitch at the end of a Football Association Cup Final and was hugged by members of the winning team.

Scenario Two – I swore under my breath when I virtually walked into Queen Elizabeth II.

Scenario Three – My mother and grandmother didn't talk to each other for three years after disagreeing about my taking piano exams.

Scenario Four – I went into a Norfolk pub dressed as an anarchist to stop a vicar from drinking.

Scenario Five – I was dressed as Father Christmas in a town centre when a group of drunk young ladies decided to rip off my robe and beard.

Scenario Six – I am related to King Charles III and the Royal Family through an illegitimate ancestor.

Scenario Seven – Whilst running a marathon an ambulance pulled up by my side and offered me a lift to the finish line.

There are your seven scenarios. You might need a slight pause now to work out which one is made up and which six happened. In fact, I will leave it until the next chapter before giving the answers. You might like to make a cup of tea.

Time for a pause.

CHAPTER TWO – THE ANSWERS

So, did I catch you out with my scenarios? I hope you took a little time to think about your answer.

You might even like to write it here, so you don't forget. See this isn't just an autobiography but an interactive puzzle book as well:

My answer is
_____

Warning – spoiler alert – the answer follows.

The made up one was probably the most believable. My mother and grandmother didn't fall out over my piano playing. The scenario I give to people on this one is that my grandmother wanted me to take piano exams and my mother didn't as she felt it would put too much pressure on me. This never happened. I did piano lessons from about the age of six, but I never took any exams and never wanted to and was certainly not pressurised into doing so. My grandmother was kind enough to buy me a seemingly never-ending amount of piano sheet music. I still have it all and still enjoy playing most of it. I have no idea how she chose the music, but I have songs by the likes of Frank Sinatra, Abba, the Beatles, Adam Faith, The Seekers, Billy Joel, the Simon May Orchestra and much more – some of which is ultra obscure but was quite well known at the time.

So, let's return to the scenarios that were true. Well, they are all vignettes from my life. So here goes.

Scenario One: I ran onto the pitch at the end of an FA Cup Final and was hugged by members of the winning team.

You probably assumed this was the men's FA Cup Final at Wembley. It was actually the Women's FA Cup Final played at Carrow Road in Norwich in 1986. At the time I was sports editor on the Norwich Mercury Newspaper (this newspaper no longer exists, and I will mention that again later). I had covered and followed the Norwich Ladies team through the competition. In the final they faced Doncaster Belles who were one of, if not, the best team in the country at that time. Before the game the Doncaster team had cast slurs on the Norwich players' sexuality in the News of the World Newspaper. It was the kind of story that wouldn't happen today in our more enlightening times, but which at that time was something of a big deal as was the News of the World which is no longer in existence but at the time was quite influential in certain areas.

With just 10 minutes to go the game was level at 3-3. Norwich broke away to score what turned out to be the winner. As you can imagine at the final whistle there were great celebrations, and I was pulled into them from the side of the pitch. There was a team hug which I was involved in along with much champagne.

Scenario Two: I swore under my breath when I virtually walked into Queen Elizabeth II.

One of my jobs working for Norfolk Police was to look after/manage/facilitate the Media at Royal visits. This meant being part of the planning team for events which included Police, Royalty Protection teams and much more. Each visit was planned to the nth degree. It was almost like a dance being choreographed. Obviously, the Royal visitor wasn't included in the planning stages but would know exactly what they would be doing. I had my plans as to where the Media should go and from where they could get their best photographs without "getting in the way."

This particular visit involved the then Queen opening a new facility at Lynn Sport in King's Lynn in Norfolk. At one point I was likely to get very close to Her Majesty. She was due to peel off to her right and I was also due to peel off to my right. In other words, we were due to go our separate ways. Now the important thing to mention here is that I had free rein (a slight wordplay on the word reign there) of where I went as I was known to the armed police officers and the protection officers. I claim to this day that it was the Queen that took the wrong course. I went to my right and she went to her left and suddenly there I was staring straight at her. This probably took less than a second before I scurried away, but it's one of those things that seem to be frozen in time.

Under my breath I believe I uttered the immortal words "Oh Shit." I do hope she didn't hear me otherwise I might have ended up in The Tower.

And so ends scenario number two.

Scenario Three was the incorrect one as I've already explained.

Scenario Four: I went into a Norfolk pub dressed as an anarchist to stop a vicar from drinking.

This is true as well. When I moved to Cromer to work on the North Norfolk News newspaper in the early 1970s, I had a number of bucket list things I wanted to do. One of these was to appear in a play with an amateur drama group. So, I joined the Sheringham Players or it might have been the North Norfolk Players as time has misted my memory.

In retrospect that might have been a bad move as I didn't enjoy my time with them greatly. The main reason for this was they took it all so seriously and I just wanted to have fun and cross something off the bucket list. It's rather like going to a ceilidh (country dance) where you just want to have fun and mess around whilst the caller wants everyone to take things so seriously.

We had many rehearsals for the play in a rather grand house in Sheringham which was owned by a rather posh couple. I remember the man's name was Rex Bateman but can't remember his wife's name – maybe I just called her Mrs Bateman. I think they had retired to Sheringham from London. I do remember the producer was a lady who claimed to have been involved in drama in the West End. This may or may not have been true, but she ran this voluntary Am Dram group as though it was a top-notch drama group. She took no prisoners. To her it was work. To me it was meant to be fun.

We used to rehearse in quite a spacious bedroom where those not involved in a scene would sit on a single bed in a line. We would also do this when this producer was busy telling us we wouldn't be ready for the performances which would run over two or three nights at Sheringham Little Theatre. This theatre still exists, but I'm not sure it ever really recovered from my performance.

The play was "Lord Arthur Savile's Crime" by Oscar Wilde. It was a period piece and for some reason I was cast as Septimus Podgers an anarchist. I was supposed to play this part with a German accent. What came out of my mouth was more akin to Japanese. I have never been able to do accents. I recently found on the internet a review of that show and I'm not even mentioned which rather suggests just how bad I was because in most local media reports everyone gets mentioned, even if they only made the tea.

The other problem was Podgers was a man in his forties and at the time I was in my early 20s and looked like I was in my early 20s and so posing as a middle-aged anarchist just didn't work. Goodness knows why they gave me one of the biggest parts, particularly when it was obvious, I couldn't learn lines. I have never been able to learn lines. I can remember irrelevant facts about things like who was prime minister of Iceland in 1932 but not lines from a play. I struggled to get them into my brain and on stage I must have been totally wooden. It didn't take me long to realise that I wasn't going to be an actor any more than I was going to be a concert pianist.

A couple of weeks before the play was due to go on, I was taken aside by the producer who told me quite straight that she didn't think I was up to playing the part. Now this didn't make me angry because she was quite correct in her assessment. I was nowhere near right for the part. I would have been better employed as a bell boy with no lines who just brought the tea in. Perhaps that way I would have warranted a mention in the local media.

But there we were a few days from lift off and they were concerned that I couldn't pull the part off. For me it was just too late to back out. So, I told said producer that "it would be alright on the night" although in my heart of hearts I wasn't sure it would be.

But it was. I got through it. Two people forgot their lines, but neither was myself. I needed no prompt. It always amazes me how a simple prompt breathes new life into an Am Dram actor. What would happen if that prompt just didn't hit home, and the actor forgot all their subsequent lines? But I didn't forget mine. The two ladies of a certain age on stage with me forgot theirs though and I had to give them a hint through the corner of my mouth that I hoped the audience didn't hear.

Anyway, I got through it. So, it's time to explain how I came to be in a Sheringham Pub (the name of which escapes me) dressed as an anarchist and why I was pulling a vicar out.

Podgers (ie me) was in both acts of the play. The man who played the vicar wasn't on until the second half. But we were all made up and wearing our stage clothes before the start of the play. In my case that meant a Dinner Jacket or as I refer to them – a Penguin Suit. In the dressing room was an intercom system so we could hear what was happening on stage and we would know when to make our entrance. The guy who was playing the vicar decided to pop off to a local hostelry even though he was dressed as a vicar, along with all the make-up and wearing a dog collar.

The interval arrived and he was nowhere to be seen. The producer panicked; we all thought it funny. Two of us were dispatched to visit pubs. I can't remember whether he had said which one he was visiting but thankfully we found him and dragged him back to the theatre in time for the second half. I have no idea what would have happened had we not found him. The show would have been short of an anarchist, a vicar and another player and I can't remember for the life of me how he was dressed. At least I didn't take my home-made bomb prop out into the streets with me. That was the big black thing with a fuse and the word BOMB written in large letters on it just in case the audience didn't quite grasp what it was. I think it was meant to be a joke!

Well appearing on stage at the Little Theatre was another thing ticked off the bucket list. I have never had the slightest inclination to tread the boards again. My thespian days are long gone.

Scenario Five: I was dressed as Father Christmas in a town centre when a group of drunk young ladies decided to rip off my robe and beard.

Again, this is absolutely true. If I looked like the youngest anarchist in town for the previous scenario, I probably looked equally too young to be Father Christmas in the main street of the shopping area in Long Eaton in Derbyshire.

It was all to do with the charity organisation Round Table. I became a "Tabler" whilst working in Beccles in Suffolk. Round Table I believe still exists but back in the 1970s it was a real deal in the charity world. Round Table was an organisation for young professional men (there was a ladies equivalent which was known as Ladies Circle). Round Table started in my home city of Norwich. It was founded by Louis Marchesi and to this day there is a pub in the city named in his honour where the elitist Norwich Number One Club meets. I will talk more about my time in Round Table later in this book, but for now I will tell you how I came to be disrobed as Father Christmas.

Father Christmas is supposed to be rotund, of a certain age and jolly. I certainly wasn't rotund, old and probably not particularly jolly in the usual ho ho ho kind of way.

When I left Beccles to take up a job in Nottingham in the Midlands (more about that later) I transferred from Beccles Round Table to Long Eaton Round Table because that's where we bought a house.

Christmas approached and the Round Table asked for volunteers to dress up as Santa for a variety of gigs in and around the town. I was asked to do the town centre on a Saturday just before Christmas. So, there I was dressed as Santa, collecting money for our charities and giving out presents to youngsters who were probably not much younger than me!

Everything was going well. I was trying to look old and jolly and wishing the whole thing was over and I could get some fish and chips, when a gaggle of ladies came out of the pub close to where I was. Let's just say they had enjoyed a few pre-Christmas drinks and suddenly I became their target.

They ran towards me. Now of course Santa wouldn't run away from anything and so I stood my ground and that was probably a mistake.

"Hello Santa. Bloody hell how old are you? Here girls Santa's shed some years," one of them shouted.

That was the cue for them to tug at my robes.

"Let's have his f-----g beard off," another shouted.

And they did. I was left standing in a shirt and trousers whilst all around had a laugh at my expense. I grabbed my robe and beard and made a hasty retreat into the nearby pub's toilet where I was able to regain some of my composure before wending my weary way home, making a mental note never to dress up as Father Christmas again, something I have kept to despite now probably being the right age and the right shape to really be Santa.

Scenario Six: I am related to King Charles III and the Royal Family through an illegitimate ancestor.

This is also true. King Charles III is the third great grandnephew of the husband of my fourth great grand aunt, which probably makes me 3,756,889th in line for the throne (of course I actually made that number up).

But we are related. It's all down to a young lady (who eventually became an old lady) by the name of Keziah Edmonds who was my fourth great grand aunt (don't these relationships take some understanding?)? Put in simple terms that means she was the sister of my 4x great grandfather John Edmonds. I won't bore you with details of how that line comes down to me as that will be included in a subsequent book on my family and my ancestors which will include stories about a very rich Londoner and the owner of a major Australian shipping line.

But for now, let's concentrate on Keziah Edmonds. Keziah met and married a man by the name of Ormond Smith. Ormond Smith had a major claim to fame. He was the illegitimate son of Richard Wellesley who was the brother of the Duke of Wellington (The Iron Duke). It was well known that dear old Richard, how should we say, put it about a bit. Well at some point in his putting it about a bit career he fell in with a French actress by the name of Hyacinthe Roland.

Their liaison led to some illegitimate children and several legitimate ones after they eventually got married and came to the United Kingdom where she didn't get on very well with polite society, mainly due to the fact that she spoke very poor English and made very little attempt to learn the language. Back in France she had been quite a famous actress and something of a femme fatale.

Ormond Smith was born in Great Yarmouth in Norfolk. I have not been able to find out what a French actress was doing in Great Yarmouth but there is no doubt that Ormond was cast aside and adopted by a Great Yarmouth couple who I only know as Mr Smith and Miss (or Mrs) Howard. I'm afraid adoption records in the 18th century are virtually non-existent.

My relation Keziah married Ormond and they had 10 children and were responsible for setting up and running one of the biggest and most famous shipping companies in Australia, after first trading in Europe. This is something I have already alluded to.

To find my relationship to the present King you have to go back and sideways and for now you will just have to take my word for it as the actual tree will unfold in my coming volume.

Finally, we come to scenario seven and this one is true as well.

Whilst running a marathon an ambulance did pull up by my side and offered me a lift to the finish line.

Obviously, this was very embarrassing.

I have never been great at long distance running. At school it was always the sprints for me. I was pretty handy at 100 and 200 yards (now that has gone metric of course but, in my day, it was just yardage). I also loved sprint relays.

I was reasonably fast and always got through the heats for sports day, only to always finish outside the top three. But at least I could claim that I was in the top six sprinters in my year. Cross country running was a different story, however. I have never had the lung capacity for long distance running. I wish I had.

At grammar school we used to have sport on Tuesday and Thursday afternoons. That largely meant rugby in the winter, hockey in the spring and cricket or tennis in the summer. I tolerated rugby although I had a problem when everyone else seemed to grow and I stood still, and the game became more and more physical. But I loved hockey, cricket and tennis. One of the hardest decisions in my life came the day when I had to decide whether to continue playing cricket or turn to tennis. It may not sound like much of a decision in the great scheme of things, but I agonised because I loved playing both.

At the age of 11 I played up a year and represented the school at cricket at Under-12 level and then at the age of 12 I again played up a year and represented the school at cricket at Under-13 level. But I also loved playing tennis and I felt I would stand more chance of playing for the school's senior teams at tennis than at cricket.

And so, it proved as I represented the school firstly in the junior tennis team and then in the senior team. I still play tennis but have long given up cricket after I realised that two quite serious ligament injuries were caused by the fact that I could no longer see the ball properly.

Back to school. On days when pitches were waterlogged and we couldn't play rugby or hockey or cricket, you might think we got an afternoon off (bearing in mind we had school on Saturday mornings). But no, we had to do a cross country run around Mousehold, which is a wooded part of Norwich made famous by the 16th century Kett's Rebellion. If you want to read about that rebellion, try the novel "Tombland" by C J Sansom.

Like so many others before and after me, I didn't like running through muddy pathways around the woods and so took the opportunity mainly to walk and chat with my mates. Occasionally I would run the course which was probably only about three miles.

There was one occasion, however, when I did prove I had the ability to run longer distances. We all entered the school's cross-country championship with over 90 taking part. I came in sixth and was the first non-athlete to finish. By that I mean I was the first runner to finish who didn't do athletics as their major sport. I was quite chuffed by this.

But as I got older, I realised I didn't have the lung capacity for long distance running. It's one of those "you either have or haven't got it" things and I always have trouble with my breathing. Some of it is psychological – running long distances hurts, but much of it is down to genes and an ability you are born with. I often wonder whether my poor lung capacity is due in part to passive smoking. Both my parents smoked (my mother cigarettes and my father a pipe). I must have inhaled so much smoke from others in pubs, on buses and in various other places. I can remember coming home many times from a night out with my clothes smelling of smoke.

My bucket list of things I wanted to do (along with appearing in a play as I've already mentioned) also included running a marathon and I realised that would take some serious training. So, at the age of 29 or so I decided to enter the Black Dog Marathon which was run around a circuit between the twin metropolises of Beccles and Bungay in Suffolk. I chose this because I had previously worked in these towns on the local newspaper.

I started my serious training around my adopted village and home of Hethersett and everything was going pretty well until I hit an unexpected snag. When I say an unexpected snag, I actually mean an expected unexpected snag. I started with short three or four mile runs which was just about a circuit of the village and then built this up to eight to ten miles and then more and, on a particular evening which would have been February 23rd, 1982, I was aiming to hit 20 miles for the first time. I will explain how I remember the exact date of this, and it has nothing to do with looking back at my diary entries.

I completed the 20 miles and, feeling rather fatigued, retired to bed only to be woken up a few hours later by a wife in serious agony. Yes, she was about to give birth to our first son. Chris wasn't due for a few days but there was no way of not realising what was happening. Anne was in labour.

So off we went to the hospital and up to the delivery floor and it was confirmed that the baby was on its way. Several hours later we had our first son. Now I kept very calm. I hardly said anything and just provided moral support. After it was confirmed that everything with baby was A OK, I was told I had been one the calmest husbands they had had for a long time. After the baby was born, they said: "would you like a cup of tea and piece of toast?"

"Yes please," I replied.

"Not you, your wife," they said.

I believe I did get a cup of tea.

The reason I remained so calm was simple. I was absolutely knackered from running 20 miles. But to cut a long story short, after that my training regime went to pot – along with the possibility of a good night's sleep of course. So come the day of the marathon a few weeks later and I realised I was very much under-trained. I struggled big time and had to walk quite a bit of the way, but I was determined to finish.

I must have looked rough as I tried to jog the last couple of miles to the finish at Maltings Meadow in Bungay. I must have looked so bad that an ambulance that was driving round the route to ensure that all those taking part were in rude health, stopped alongside me and offered me a lift to the finish.

Of course, I turned it down. The ignominy of arriving at the finish line in an ambulance would have been too much to bear. I soldiered on and managed to stagger over the line. They were giving out bottles of milk for those finishing. It was the sweetest milk I have ever tasted, and I got a commemorative medal as well. Unfortunately, somewhere along life's path I have misplaced that medal. It was very small, but I treasured it until I lost it.

I still drove home feeling elated. I had achieved something else off my list of things to do and another thing, like appearing in a play, that I never ever want to repeat.

*   *   *

There you have my seven scenarios, six of which happened and one which was totally made up. I think you will probably agree that the made-up one was possibly the most likely to have happened.

But there's no resting on any laurels in this story of a life. It's onwards and upwards and I will now take you back to the day of my birth – October 9th, 1952. After all any autobiography has to start with a birth even if the subject can't remember anything about that momentous event.

PART TWO – MY LIFE

CHAPTER THREE – THE EARLY YEARS 1952-1962

I could be trite and silly here and use stupid phrases such as:

"I was born at an early age," or

"Let's start at the very beginning because it's a very good place to start".

But I won't.

I will start with the facts. I was born at about 6 am on Thursday, October 9th, 1952, at 157 Reepham Road, Hellesdon. Hellesdon is a suburb of Norwich that in those days had many fewer homes than it has today. It was a Thursday and the old rhyme states that "Thursday's Child Has Far to Go." Many years later I found out I was born on the same day as Media personality Sharon Osborne. I'm not sure whether that says anything about me or not – probably not.

A number of notable people were born on October 9th including one of my favourite singer-songwriters Jackson Browne, former Prime Minister David Cameron, one of my great heroes John Lennon and George Smallman. If you want to learn just who George Smallman was, you will have to continue reading as all will later be revealed.

Of course there's nothing special about being born on October 9th. I love maths and working out probabilities. If you take the fact that there are approximately 67 million people living in the United Kingdom and there are 365 days in a year (as this is a rough approximation, we will forget about leap years) it means that on average 175,342 share a birthday on any given day. I get wrapped up in these mathematical puzzles. You will find out later as you read through this that I regularly attend football matches at Carrow Road, the home of Norwich City. The ground holds about 27,000 people. That means that on any match day there is likely to be 74 people with a birthday. The ground has four sides and so in our stand there will be 18 people with birthdays.

But enough of this rubbish I hear you say. I want to read about your beginnings and not your obsessions and I will admit I'm getting a little ahead of myself. So, let's wind the clock back to October 1952.

These were the days of home births, and I believe I was born in an upstairs room of a house that was also a greengrocer's shop. The only thing I'm not sure of is which room but I suspect it would have been my parents' bedroom. My family had been in local business for some time with my paternal grandparents owning the greengrocers at 157 and for a time a dairy just two doors down at number 161. My maternal grandparents also owned a fish and chip shop just over a mile away on the way towards the city centre of Norwich. My ancestors in Great Yarmouth were also shop owners and so the retail trade was in the blood. Having said that I have never had any urge to follow in the family way.

I always think it sad that babies don't remember anything about their first couple of years, although I do have flashbacks where I am in a playpen. I know for a fact that I used to live in this playpen for part of the day, presumably whilst my mother served in the shop. She never had an assistant, and my father was a television engineer working for Rediffusion.

I do vaguely remember that the playpen was in the lounge. As I grew it became natural for me to be part of the shop and so I also remember some of the customers from those days in the mid-1950s before the terror of school burst upon my scene. There was Mrs Watson (also known as Elsie) from number 155 who had prominent front teeth that were fused together. She had a son Donald who always promised that he would do a length of the local swimming pool with me on his back to illustrate what a strong swimmer he was. He never did. I didn't really want to go anyway as swimming never really interested me and it still doesn't.

As I got older, I regularly smacked a tennis ball or a football against the side of our house. There were no windows to be broken on this side and so I hammered balls against the brickwork for hours on end. As a result, tennis balls and footballs often found their way into Elsie Watson's garden. She never complained and I had a free run for retrieving my balls (if you'll pardon the expression). Some of the greatest sportsmen to have played tennis or cricket or football honed their skills by smacking balls against a wall. Sadly, I wasn't destined to become one of them.

Now let's move forward a few short years to the terror of school. I use the word terror wrongly to describe school because the terror lasted only for a few days when I thought I was being ripped away from my mother. Then of course I found out that I was. I realised that this new place I was being sent to called school wasn't just for one day, although I had no idea what I was doing there in the first place. Nobody had mentioned it to me. Nobody had prepared me for it.

I can't help thinking about this without recalling the following joke.

A small boy comes home following his first day at school.

"Did you learn lots?" asked his mother.

"No because they say I've got to go back again tomorrow," replied the little boy.

Of course, today it's all very different when it comes to preparing young boys and girls for school. Youngsters often go to nursery or playgroups well before they start school, so leaving parents is nowhere near the wrench or cataclysmic event that it once was.

Life in 1952 was quieter and much simpler, although the end of the Second World War was just a handful of years in the past and rationing was still a thing of present-day memory and in many ways still in place. Of course, none of that remotely concerned me in my early years. The fact that my teachers in those first few years would all have lived through the Second World War either as adults or children themselves never occurred to me until much later in life when I gained a great interest in history. Some of them may have lost relatives in the war although they never talked about this, and it never featured in any lessons. I don't think we would have understood it anyway.

I must digress here to have a musing about the war. A couple of years ago I went back to my old grammar school for their open day. This is held every year and I pop along every few years. It usually involves a tour of the school followed by a lunch in a marquee. On this visit we were told that the war shelters/tunnels would be open and had been completely renovated and cleared out. I had absolutely no idea what this referred to. There had never been any mention of war tunnels during my time at the school which ran from 1963 through to 1970.

You can imagine my surprise when we found that the war tunnels were accessed from the main playground and via a fenced off area. In my day the playground was just a playground, there were no fenced off areas or anything like that.

Down some steep steps we went to end up astonishingly in a maze of tunnels running underneath the school. These had been cleaned up and lighting put in. Apparently during the war much of the school was evacuated to these tunnels during air raids on Norwich. Norwich was bombed on a number of occasions during the Second World War in what became known as the Baedeker Raids – so called because Hitler decided to bomb historic and cultural cities mentioned in the German based Baedeker travel guides to the UK. As I write this, the city of Coventry is commemorating 80 years since its Cathedral was virtually destroyed by enemy bombs.

During these raids, Norwich would have been in great peril from the Luftwaffe whilst young boys recited Latin declensions underneath the playground of the Norwich School, probably not aware of what was happening but possibly feeling very frightened.

But before I talk more about school let's return to my beginnings. I haven't mentioned that I was (am) the only child born to Arthur William and Phyllis Margaret Steward. For the first 10 years of my life my parents owned the greengrocer's shop which was known locally as Northgate Fruit Stores. The business had been given to my parents by my grandparents who lived directly opposite at number 122 Reepham Road. Reepham Road is a very long one, stretching a good two miles from the Boundary Roundabout into the countryside and eventually onto the small but very picturesque little town of Reepham which is well worth a visit if you are ever in the area. The street numbers were rather irregular with number 122 being opposite 157. That was due to large commercial factories at the city end of the road which skewed the numbers on one side but not the other which was exclusively housing.

Legend has it that my grandfather was one of the first residents in Hellesdon when it was a village and before it grew out of all recognition and became primarily a suburb of Norwich. There are actually two parts to Hellesdon. Upper Hellesdon is the one I'm talking about. There is also a Lower Hellesdon about a mile away and along the side of the river. I don't know how true it is about my grandfather being one of the first residents of Upper Hellesdon. What I do know is that by trade my grandfather - also named Arthur - was a painter and decorator. He was a jovial extrovert who had a great influence on my early years, and I loved him dearly. My grandmother was a typical Norfolk lady, speaking with a strong Norfolk accent. There have been many suggestions on genealogy sites that my grandmother came from Leicestershire. I know for a fact that this is untrue. She was born just outside the Norwich city centre and lived in or close to Norwich all her life. One correspondent informed me that my grandmother had actually emigrated to the USA for a time before coming back to the UK. He told me he had photographic proof and sent me a copy of a photograph that looked nothing like my grandmother.

My father went out to work as the shop didn't bring in enough money to keep a family of three. I suspect that was much to do with my mother's kindness and determination to keep prices down for her customers – most of whom she looked upon as friends and many of whom just came into the shop for a chat and probably left with a quarter of sweets from a line of jars that were kept on a shelf behind the counter and which I was often allowed to raid in the evenings. I still remember the sherbet lemons which were my particular favourite. They seemed to be much more lemony and sherbetty than they are today. I can remember making a hole in the side of the sweets with my tongue and trying to suck the sherbet through it before cracking the sweets open.

I still remember the day someone stole my mother's purse. I think that was the only time I ever saw her cry, although she did cry on the telephone many years later when she told me she had Cancer, a disease that killed her when she was only 61.

I would like to think that my mother's generous spirit, friendliness and honesty have rubbed off in some small ways on me. One of my greatest regrets (although it shouldn't be a regret because it's something I couldn't do anything about) is that she died without seeing her grandchildren. They would have loved her as much as I did.

My mother was a good listener and maybe that's why many years later I became a Samaritan councillor – something you will be able to read about in a later chapter. Many is the time that customers unloaded their problems onto my mother as she listened to them in the shop.

The shop struggled along for many years and was a focal point for my pre-school years. I still vividly remember Friday afternoons when my mother would divide the week's housekeeping money into various tins to help meet the bills. I still have the small brown case she used with the initials P.M.D on the top (these represented her maiden name of Phyllis Margaret Dew). Friday was also the afternoon when local deliveries came, and I happily spent time sorting through oranges and apples. There was Russell from Pordages. He would arrive in a large vegetable laden lorry which he would park on the road outside and then bring in massive amounts of fruit and vegetables in wooden boxes which he would then take back. I can't remember where the sweets came from but there must have been deliveries of them as well.

The produce was displayed on the right-hand side of the shop as you viewed it from behind the counter and also in both windows, but I cannot remember the prices of any of the goods, although there must have been price labels attached to them. That kind of economics was well beyond me but looking back it was an immensely happy time and I suppose at that time I thought it would go on for ever.

A number of particular memories flow from those times - all very ordinary in the great scheme of things but all of which left their imprint on a toddler and young boy. I remember my father coming home at the end of the working day. He got to work on a very old fashioned motorbike and wore a green crash helmet. I particularly remember him coming home one day covered in cuts and bruises. He had been knocked off his machine. I can't remember there being much fuss made over the incident. He just got up the next day and got on his motorbike and went into work as usual.

On another occasion I remember him promising to bring me home a couple of walkie talkies from his work. I waited and I waited but they never came and that taught me an important lesson. Never promise someone something that you cannot deliver.

My father wasn't particularly strict, but we were never close. In my early years I remember that he kept a stick up the corner near his chair in case I misbehaved. I can't remember him using it, but it was always there as a threat. I don't think there was anything sinister about this, it was just a sign of the times in which I was growing up and which I would meet with again when I went to grammar school and more about that later.

I do remember being carried screaming up to my bedroom after supposedly misbehaving, but I don't remember exactly how I misbehaved although I probably could be cheeky at times. Somebody once called me precocious. I remember shouting "I'll be good. I'll be good" and I guess this could be construed today as cruelty. But as I keep saying those were different times.

But back to the description of the home. The shop was at the front of the property. Outside in the front was a large piece of tarmac that today would have been used as a car park. I can't remember any cars ever parking there. I guess most of our customers lived very locally and would walk to the shop. Most only seemed to buy a small number of goods as I have already pointed out. At the edge of the tarmac was a wooden fence and behind that fence was a gravel front garden leading to a shed that kept all kinds of rubbish including much of my sports equipment as I grew up. I seem to remember old papers being in the shed as well. The shed was also the picking up point for the distribution of newspapers and was used by somebody we knew who owned a newsagent shop further along the road which just didn't have the room for the papers. Each Christmas this man, whose name I believe was Leslie, would visit us and bring me an annual (Beano or Dandy or such like). This was for me a special visit and it never occurred to me that what I was being given was probably left over Christmas stock that he couldn't shift (cynicism was a long way away at that point).

At the other end of the drive was a glass noticeboard and I have tried to remember without any success what was put in this. The front garden led along a path to the back garden which was long and relatively thin. My father and my grandfather were both keen gardeners (something I haven't inherited) and my father grew vegetables and flowers. I have no idea whether these would be sold in the shop although I suspect it would be missing a trick if they weren't.

My father and grandfather were leading lights in Hellesdon Horticultural Society, and both had cups named after them. They often won their own cups. My father was particularly adept at growing cucumbers, lettuces and tomatoes – which was amazing because he never ate any of them and, after we had left the shop, gave most of the produce away. He actually made the National Media for growing hundreds of pounds of produce, winning cups for it but never eating any of it. In fact, it was worse than that. If he ate a tomato, he would immediately be sick. This hatred of tomatoes has been handed down although I don't have a problem with them, and nothing is nicer than a colourful Greek Salad with those lovely large, sliced tomatoes. But other members of our family have this problem with tomatoes. It's quite an irrational thing.

There was a small area of grass at the back of the shop where I had my photograph taken on a number of occasions with friends or relatives who came to visit and some of those are included in this book. This is also where I would sit on a blanket on a Sunday afternoon and listen to the top 40 music charts on my transistor radio. Sometimes this would be on my own and sometimes with friends. I also undertook something cruel that I became ashamed of. This took the shape of hitting butterflies with my tennis racket and killing them. I have no idea what made me do this horrible thing but as this is a warts and all autobiography, I guess I have to have a few warts.

At the bottom of the garden was a chicken coop which supplied us with eggs. Again, I can't remember whether these were sold in the shop or not. I particularly remember we had a bantam which I adopted as something of a pet. For those readers not up with the chicken world, a bantam is a small chicken. I seem to remember this little chap was bright red. We must have got rid of the chickens when we moved and that would have been when I was 11 or 12 years of age around 1964.

There were three entrances to the house – One was through the shop door where a bell would announce your arrival. Another was through a side door from the front garden. I still have flashbacks where I enter the shop with a cheery "it's only me" to let my mother know that it wasn't a customer, and she needn't come into the shop.

Entering the house via the side door led you into a hall where I regularly played football with a balloon. Yes, I played football with a balloon with furniture as the goals. For some reason I particularly did this around Christmas time along with regularly designing, drawing and writing a special Christmas publication. This was something also done by John Lennon and, as we have already found out, I share a birthday with him. Now over 60 years later I'm still writing and designing publications (more of this later as well). I was well known for being able to "occupy myself" and this is something I can certainly still do. I used to make up games and competitions which included how many times I could hit a tennis ball onto the wall of the house without it bouncing. I also devised games on the large pieces of white paper that you got from the butchers. These would often be racing games. I was also known for never asking for anything. There was never any "can I haves" in my life. I always waited to be asked whether I wanted a specific thing and I believe that continues to this day.

But more about the home layout. As you entered, stairs led to the upstairs. Upstairs on the immediate left was the bathroom which consisted of a toilet and a bath and little else other than a wall cabinet. Then moving along the landing we had my parents' bedroom, a guest bedroom where I occasionally slept when my maternal grandmother came to stay at Christmas and finally my bedroom which was quite small and which looked out onto the main road. I can't drive past today without pointing to it and saying: "I slept in that bedroom." Of course, today it's no longer a bedroom but, once again, more of that later. At night the stairs scared me. The only bathroom was upstairs and that meant trying to get there in the dark in the evenings. The lights were at the end of the hall and so you had to get to them from the lounge in the dark. I can remember thinking I was being chased by ghosts or Red Indians and I'm sure many people of around my age suffered the same fears.

The third entry to the house was via a greenhouse which led to another door into the kitchen. These were usually kept locked. The greenhouse got very hot in the summer as it was almost exclusively made of glass. Equally in the winter it was cold.

Behind the shop downstairs was the lounge which was set-up like all 1950s lounges seem to have been set-up with armchairs either side of a coal fire and in sight of an old-fashioned television and radio. Over the other side of the room was a settee and I believe there was a writing bureau up one corner where I once found a secret copy of Lady Chatterley's Lover by D H Lawrence which was notoriously banned back in the day, but which is now readily available for download from any number of websites, and which is now looked upon as classic literature. But I mustn't mention websites as trying to describe them to a boy from the 1950s would have been an impossible task. There was also a small wooden dining table although we always ate in the kitchen. Sometimes I sat at this table and watched the wrestling on a Saturday afternoon on television. I particularly did this when it was cold and there was some warmth coming from the sun through the greenhouse glass. I believe the wrestling was on a programme entitled World of Sport which featured strange sports like hill climbing and motorbike scrambling which was very popular. More about this later in this chapter.

The only other two rooms in the house were the already mentioned greenhouse at the back of the lounge and a kitchen which I have also mentioned. Notice I haven't mentioned central heating for one good reason – there wasn't any.

The kitchen was small. It was a bog standard 1950s kitchen with table and Formica chairs, a sink and a stove. No washing machine, no dishwasher and no modern appliances. I can't exactly remember what the conservatory was used for. Maybe my father propagated plants there. I seem to remember a lot of wooden boxes around and then there was the wind-up gramophone which played 78 rpm records.

Anyone younger than a certain age won't understand the word gramophone or know what 78s were. So here's a description. The gramophone had to be wound up via a kind of crank lever. This had to be done on virtually every play. The 78 rpm records were made of Shellac which made them very brittle. They had to be handled with care. Drop one on the floor and it was likely to shatter into a number of pieces, particularly as the floor of the conservatory was made of concrete with no matting.

The record would be placed on a turntable which was turned by a belt which was what was wound up. The records were played by a large arm which was brought over onto the record, and which had a needle at the end point. These needles had to be replaced regularly as they became blunt. I remember having a very small tin of replacement needles. I also remember that sometimes a record would slow down, and the machine had to be wound up again mid record.

I have no idea where this gramophone came from (or where it went to) or from where the records came. I remember there was a record of Edward Elgar's Pomp and Circumstances March (better known as Land of Hope and Glory which to my mind should be our national anthem). But it was two others that caused a stir.

My parents weren't greatly interested in music although my father did regularly mention Miki and Griff and Slim Whitman. I thought he had made both of them up until I realised that they did exist and sang some kind of dreadful country music. It's the kind of music you will find today in remainder bins in charity shops or hear walking down Regent Road in Great Yarmouth where everyone seems to be a country and western music fan. That comment might instantly lose me some readers!

How we came to have a couple of 78 rpm records by Little Richard, I have no idea. My maternal grandmother (Selina Maud Dew) thought that the music was so bad it would destroy the record player. She didn't understand that there was no difference between playing classical music like Elgar and this new rock n roll music and that neither would destroy the gramophone. She was convinced that "Good Golly Miss Molly" would make the gramophone explode. Obviously, I played them deliberately every time she came round just to annoy her. I did other things to annoy her like trying to get her to say Czechoslovakia, a word she just couldn't pronounce. Today she might have had a better stab at Czech Republic providing we told her that Czech was pronounced Check.

Being Norfolk born and bred and coming from a certain age, she showed definite signs of racism. This wasn't deliberate but a response to the way she had been brought up. This included not wanting to be treated by black doctors because, in her words, they had "dirty hands," that kind of thing. My aunt (my father's sister) lived until she was 105 and had similar prejudices. She knitted dolls to be sent to the "little black children in Africa" but got very angry when she thought a black family were going to move in next door (they didn't). I have come across racism in many forms during my life and remember an incident when we lived in the Midlands. We got on very well with our neighbours who had a young son. When we put our house up for sale to move back to Norfolk we sold to an Asian family and our neighbours completely ignored us, despite the fact they had always been very friendly up to that point.

Our greengrocer's shop was next to a large ironmonger's and hardware store called Dixons and not surprisingly named after the Dixon family of whom I particularly remember Michael and John. They always had a line of dustbins and other items outside on the forecourt. These effectively cut the forecourt in two. I used these to make a racing circuit for my pedal car and subsequently my small four wheeled bikes. Years later Dixons turned into a number of individual franchise stores and the forecourt was turned into a car park. It still exists and you can read about my return to visit it towards the end of this book. But back to my pride and joy – my little red pedal car. I used to ride this round and round and must have been a rather strange sight for anyone going to Dixons. I can't remember growing out of that pedal car, but I must have otherwise I would still be riding round in it now.

I remember that on the wall of the shop was a chewing gum machine. You popped in a penny, turned a handle and chewing gum came out. Sometimes at night we could hear these machines being hit in an attempt to get the chewing gum out. My mother had to regularly re-fill them so they must have been popular. On the chewing gum machine dial was a small arrow and when this got to a certain point it would dispense two packs of chewing gum – a kind of BOGOF offer (Buy One Get One Free). I always waited for that arrow to get round to BOGOF before popping my penny in. I have mentioned the banging on machines and sometimes in the evenings we would hear youngsters using the forecourt for biking but I can never remember the shop being broken into or any acts of vandalism.

As I grew, I became more and more interested in the left-hand window of Dixons as that's where they had an Airfix section. Airfix models played quite a part in my growing up. I would watch for new ones to come in and then shop with my pocket money which I kept in a tin in my bedroom. I remember making the obvious airplanes but there were also figures such as Beefeaters etc. I loved gluing them together and then painting them. To this day I can still remember the unique smell inside Dixons store and particularly the part where the Airfix models were kept. I have long forgotten how much the models cost but the cost was met by my pocket money if I saved up.

Memories of those early days include stand up washes in a tin bath by the fire because it was too cold to go upstairs for a real bath, I also remember having measles and being made to take disgusting strawberry medicine where the strawberries didn't mask the bitter taste. Kind Doctor Cowan came to see me (yes there were home visits in those days) and remarked on my model soldiers on the mantelpiece. Isn't it strange how such a small thing can make such a lasting memory? Dr Cowan probably thought nothing of it, but I remember it over 65 years later. I also thought he was Jewish until relatively recently when I saw him mentioned on a history website and realised his name was Cowan and not Cohen.

I also remember going to visit friends at the age of four when I thought I was really grown up.

We must have been friendly with a family named McGintey because I remember visiting a girl of my own age by the name of Lesley. When I started school, we found ourselves in the same class and, when it came to country dancing (which we seemed to do quite a bit of), Lesley always picked me as her partner. Or perhaps I picked her, I really can't remember.

I suppose I could claim that Lesley was my first girlfriend. I wonder what happened to her? Perhaps she is still out there somewhere.

Obviously as I grew up, I began to assimilate more and more information and I have quite vivid memories of the ages between five and 11. Below are just some of those memories. I am sure others will come to mind after this memoir is published and I would like to point out here that this is all my own work and no ghost writers have been employed. I've always thought that being a ghost writer is a wonderful job. You get to interview famous people and help them tell their story whilst staying in the background yourself but knowing that the final product is primarily your work. But then there's the other side of it. You might think the person you are writing about is a real jerk, you might disagree with his/her comments or views, they might not be as co-operative as you would like, the interviews might go all over the place (a bit like this book) and of course you will get little or no recognition for writing it with the celebrity taking all the plaudits and getting all the publicity. But once again I digress as I'm likely to do numerous times throughout this narrative.

Back to the memories. I particularly remember Wednesday afternoons when the shop was closed (early closing) and my mother and I would take the bus into the city. Wednesday was always known as Wednesday Half Day. Again, this must have been when I was younger than five as after that I would be at school, unless my mother waited for the end of school which I think unlikely because I remember shopping with her. This would obviously also happen during the school holidays.

When I say shopping what I mean is my mother went shopping while I just tagged along. Same thing happened when I got married. I call it the shopping shuffle and many men reading this will know exactly what I mean. You go into a particular shop (usually in my case a ladies clothes shop). You have no interest in what's on display (being ladies clothes they won't fit you anyway). You then proceed for what seems like hours, but which in reality is probably only a short time, to shuffle round in a square or circle, always ending up at the place where you started. The only rule to this is that nothing will be purchased. Then you widen you square or circle and keep going round and round while the person you are with pulls clothes off the display, examines them and then returns them. You are just waiting for those golden words "it's time to go." Sometimes they may cut short the shuffle by actually buying something and nine times out of ten when they get home, they will immediately decide they don't like the item and so back you go the following week to return it and do the shuffle again.

I recently saw an American cartoon that summed this up nicely. It featured the Pickles family - Earl and Opel Pickles and their daughter Julie.

Earl is lounging in a chair when Julie comes in.

"Dad you look tired out, Are you ok?"

"I've been shopping with your mother for eight hours."

"But dad you've only been gone for an hour and a half."

"Yes but shopping hours are much longer."

Same thing happens with restaurants when you are in a new town or city. You see a nice place to eat but then decide to check what other places are available before you end up at the first place anyway.

My mother used to take me into a department store by the name of Curls, which later became Debenhams, and which, as I write this, is empty and decaying and could become student accommodation thus inserting another nail into the coffin of city centre shopping. I can't remember going into toy shops with my mother or any other shops which would hold my interest. I do remember queueing up at a butchers' shop by the name of Craske's which was famous in Norwich and which is still remembered with fondness. Nobody (and I mean nobody) made sausages or pork cheese like Craske's and that's why they always had queues. At Christmastime, the queues ran round the block, but it was always worth it when you had those sausages in your mouth.

Nobody has ever made sausages like Craske's. For a number of years they had a sausage competition in Norwich (yes seriously). You get to try sausages from different butchers and then you have to vote for your favourite. The winning sausage is crowned sausage of the year. There have been some good ones over the years but nothing, absolutely nothing, to compare with Craske's. The only reason for really taking part in the competition is to get free samples which basically amounts to a free lunch (yes there is something akin to a free lunch although you do have to vote).

I have no idea what made a Craske's sausage so special, but eating one just made you feel hungry and wanting more if that makes sense. Pop on some Colman's mustard and you were immediately transported to sausage heaven. Local people will know exactly what I mean. Craske's sausages from Norwich spread with Colman's mustard from Norwich. A true Norwich delight.

And their pork cheese was also remarkable and has never been equalled. Some parts of the country call this delicacy brawn. It's basically pigs' trotters boiled up and turned into a strange kind of jelly product that also contains bits of stringy pork or beef. Now that doesn't sound very appetising, but I can assure you it was/is, particularly on toast. My dear wife makes pork cheese and it's good – no it's better than good, but even that doesn't reach the standards of Craske's. Another thing I remember about Craske's was the sawdust on the floor, but above all the long, long queues. I don't think we ever had anything else other than sausages and pork cheese so I have no idea what their lamb chops or steak was like, but queueing up at Craske's was like a Christmas ritual and a rite of passage for all youngsters. Sadly, it's no longer there, but every time I pass where the shop once was, I am immediately transported back to the 1950s and 1960s and can again remember the smell of the place.

But back to the Wednesday bus trip with my mother. From the city we went to visit my maternal grandmother who was a widow and lived in a terrace house at 97 Rupert Street. Selina Maud Dew was another kind woman who I was very close to. We would either catch the 89 bus to Unthank Road or walk through Chapel Field. It wasn't a great distance. After having tea, we would wait until about 8 pm and then walk to the bus stop in an area of Norwich known as St Giles to get the bus home. Today that part of Norwich is a dead end but in those days the buses wound their way through the city centre and took us home. I was often so tired by the time we got on the bus that the journey home was tough even though I did, as so many youngsters have done, pretend that I was driving the bus. I often suffered from travel sickness on buses and was very glad when I got back home and fell into bed.

Before catching the bus home from St Giles, we usually watched Coronation Street. That helps me to date when this took place as Coronation Street began in December 1960 when I was eight years of age. So we would be talking about the early 1960s here.

I spent quite a bit of my childhood staying with my grandmother. She lived in a typical post war terrace house. I later found that Rupert Street had suffered extensive damage from bombs in the war but 97 must have been spared. Say the following to anyone of a certain age and they will nod along as they recognise bits of their own youth. So here goes.

The house was a two-storey building. A tiny front garden led to the front door which opened into the special or front room. There was nothing special about this room apart from the fact that all the furniture looked and felt new because it was never used. The special room was for what was termed "high days and holidays." In other words, it was only used on Bank Holidays, at Christmas and Easter and on special occasions. Problem is I can't remember my grandmother's front room ever being used. The ironic thing is neither can I remember taking my shoes off when going through the door. So, everyone walked through the special room to get to the main room with their shoes on. This could lead to mud prints on the special carpet.

The main room was pretty much the same size as the special room, but this was where the day unfolded. There was a coal fire, a table against the wall with a couple of chairs round it, a television on an antiquated stand, a couple of armchairs and for some unexplainable reason a Singer sowing machine. When I visited, I spent most of my time sitting or lying on the floor. This is something I took into my adult life as I often prefer sitting on the floor to sitting in a chair.

This main room led to a very old and long kitchen that I only ventured into when I wanted to go to the loo. And here we have the crux of the whole thing. The word loo hadn't been invented and there was no inside toilet or bathroom. The toilet was out in the yard (I have a photograph of myself in that yard dressed in a cowboy suit – boy how I remember that cowboy suit). On one side was the toilet and on the other another door led to the coal shed. There was a very narrow passageway at the back of the house so the coal must have been brought to the coal shed in sacks and carried from the main road.

Being outside, the toilet was absolutely freezing in the winter. I still remember the shiny toilet paper that looked cheap and nasty and had a particular smell even when it didn't have any deposits on it. If my grandmother ran out of this toilet paper (and the name Izal springs to mind), she would use pieces of newspaper cut into squares with a hole punched through and tied in place with string. I never worried whether using this would leave a newspaper imprint on my bum because I was too keen to get in out of the cold.

Can you imagine what it was like in the middle of winter? You wake up. Suddenly you have a toilet pain and need desperately to wee. You are faced with two options – outside or inside. Outside is where the toilet is but inside is where any small amount of warmth is. Going outside involves going downstairs, unlocking the back door and going halfway down the yard in the freezing cold, doing your business and then making the return journey. In other words, it takes some effort and not a little bravery and of course you might be followed by Indians of ghosts. The only alternative to going out into the cold is peeing or pooing into a chamber pot kept under the bed. That's not a very healthy proposition and could lead to nasty smells for the remainder of the night and then the chamber pot has to be emptied in the outside loo anyway. I believe these chamber pots were known as gazunders as in "goes under."

Towards the end of the yard was a miniscule patch of grass and I do mean miniscule. It would have taken about a minute to cut. Then there was a gate leading to a narrow passage that led onto the road.

Back inside the house there were three bedrooms upstairs, but the set-up was rather strange. On your left was a double bedroom which looked out onto Rupert Street (so far so good). On your right was another double bedroom with a small window looking out into the yard. The third bedroom was a single room that you could only access by going through the double bedroom on your right. Consequently, I never remembered this room being used as a bedroom. It was purely used as a junk room and so, at the time, held no interest for me. My grandmother used to keep newspapers and other things in there. I wish I had them today.

Now I've mentioned that there was no bathroom, so to have a wash you had to use a hand basin with hot water drawn from a boiled kettle. This used to be known as a strip down wash. My grandmother used to supplement her meagre pension by having lodgers. They must have shaved and washed in the kitchen. The first of these was Brian whom I liked because he used to take me to the nearby sweet shop and buy me sweets. That sweet shop is now a private home. The second was a Mackem by the name of Ken who was very charismatic and whom I came across many years later as I will explain further on in this epistle. Ken worked with my father and so he often popped round to Reepham Road as well. My father never forgave him for borrowing money for a new tyre and never paying it back. It was something my father mentioned regularly but which he never mentioned to Ken.

I probably need to explain here what a Mackem is. If I had said Ken was a Geordie you wouldn't have had a problem understanding me. A Mackem is simply somebody who comes from Sunderland. Geordies come from Newcastle. People from Sunderland feel insulted if they are referred to as Geordies. The term Mackem is slang for Make Them and refers to the shipbuilding that went on in Sunderland. We got a question in a quiz about where Mackems come from, and I was able to give a full answer. Mind you Ken was always referred to as Geordie anyway.

My maternal grandfather died before I was born. He was apparently an accomplished musician, and I am sure that is from where I inherited my love of music. I was told that he could hear a piece of music once and then play it on the piano. I have reason to believe that we have his piano today. It is certainly well over 100 years old and went to our shop before being passed onto me. I also inherited the middle name of Owen from him. I have in turn passed this on as the middle name of my eldest son and asked him to include it if he has a boy. For many years I believed that I had

Welsh blood and that this Christian name had been handed down to underline Welsh ancestors. Research established this not to be the case, however, as Owen was the maiden surname of my 2x great grandmother Susan Owen who, like so many of my other Ancestors, was born in Great Yarmouth. This in itself is intriguing as this ancestor must have been dearly loved and respected to have her surname turned into a Christian name and handed down through the generations.

I mentioned Wednesday afternoon visits to my grandmother, but we also visited her on Bank Holiday Mondays when there always seemed to be motor racing or motorbike racing on the television. This must have been a staple diet of the TV coverage. We would get to my grandmother's mid-morning. I think that by this time we had a Volkswagen Beetle car, so we were able to park outside her door. We would then walk to the Garden House Pub. Those were the days before children were allowed in pubs. So we would sit in a shed like contraption by the bowls green and I would drink my Vimto (it was always Vimto), eat my packet of crisps and watch the bowls.

Growing up I did a lot of watching bowls. Whenever I went to Great Yarmouth with my parents we sat and watched bowls. I never got to play bowls, we just sat and watched other people playing. My father eventually took up the game with a vengeance, but I steered clear, although I did enjoy visiting the World Indoor Championships at Potters Holiday Camp a few years ago to watch how the game should be played.

After the Garden House we would return to my grandmothers for a Bank Holiday roast dinner. Isn't it strange how you remember roast dinners from various places? My maternal grandmother used to make massive Yorkshire Puddings. My paternal grandmother used to make massive roast potatoes.

Which brings me onto the question of Yorkshire Puddings (always remember the fat must be piping hot to make them rise properly – sorry I digress again). Yorkshire puddings are wonderful things whether you are in Yorkshire or not. They are very versatile. You can have them on their own as a first course with onion gravy (the thicker the better and its gravy and not jus or any of that nonsense). Apparently, gravy contains flour and jus doesn't, making the latter thinner but to me it's all gravy. Then you can have them as part of the main meal and finally you can have them for dessert with jam or honey or treacle or stewed apple. And yes, I have on more than one occasion had a meal containing all three Yorkshire Pudding elements.

In Norfolk and in Yorkshire it used to be quite normal to have them as a separate first course. This may still be the case as far as I know.

After the Bank Holiday meal, we would stare aimlessly at the television until it was time to go home. I seem to remember ridiculous sports like motorcycle scrambling and hill climbing as I have already mentioned (you will know by now that I am prone to repeating myself). I will probably address the subject of World of Sport later in this book as well. Hill climbing used to consist of specially made cars/vehicles taking a run up and seeing how far up a mud heap of a hill they could get. If ever there has been a pointless sport this was probably it, although it was hugely entertaining.

After all the day's excitement of watching bowls and television sport we set off for home. One thing I did enjoy was playing with a box of old postcards that were in my grandmother's pantry (I forgot when I was giving you a tour of the house to mention the pantry). They were there specifically to keep me amused. Many were picture postcards of Great Yarmouth where both my grandmother and my grandfather came from (and many more ancestors as well). For a time, I thought my mother was born there but I later confirmed that she came from Norwich. Some of the postcards were of the saucy seaside kind. I can't remember what specific games I played with these but there was a large boxful of them. When my grandmother died, I imagine they were thrown away which is a great shame as I wish I had them today. I have always been a collector and some might say a hoarder although I am trying to break this habit.

Sometimes when I went to stay with my grandmother, she would take me with her to a large house in Unthank Road, Norwich, where she had a small cleaning job. The lady of the house was Swedish and went by the name of Mrs Cully. She was very pleasant. I was no trouble as I would sit at the kitchen table and amuse myself by making up games. There's that theme of amusing myself again .I have played entire cricket test matches and football leagues using just a bog-standard dice. I remember one day when Mrs Cully bent over in front of me to pick something up off the floor. Let's just say she was a large lady and the view I got was a bit more than I bargained for. I somehow managed to survive this but it might have taught me that I was going to grow up as what is traditionally referred to as "a full-blooded male.". I think originally, we went to her house in Branksome Close before she moved to Unthank Road. Both are quite upper-class areas of Norwich.

The other thing I remember from those days were pea soupers. Today I love eating pea soup but these pea soupers were very unpleasant. They were thick fogs where misty conditions mixed with the muck from chimneys to produce what became known as smog. We would never stay overnight at my grandmothers, and I remember my mother, who didn't drive, walking in front of the car with a torch which must have been a dangerous occupation. Thankfully there were very few cars on the road. I just sat in the back feeling travel sick and it seemed to take hours to get home, but we always made it much to everyone's relief.

I have always been a great collector of things as I mentioned before. My father on the other hand wasn't. I rescued an old photo album from his and many of those photos are included with this biography. Unfortunately, before he died, he must have thrown away boxfuls of memories because when we went to clear out his bungalow we found no memorabilia at all. I remember having numerous board games and quiz games. All were obviously thrown away. Again, it would have been good to have had these. Something tangible certainly gets the old memory juices flowing. I would probably have thrown them away, but it would have been nice to have had the choice. In those days virtually every television programme had a spin off game. I remember "Bootsy and Snudge," "The Army Game," "Concentration," "Criss Cross Quiz," "Double Your Money," "Take Your Pick" and many many more. All turned into board games.

I haven't really thus far talked much about school – Kinsale Avenue Infant and Junior School to give it its full title. It was so named because, not surprisingly, it was in Kinsale Avenue. I went there from the age of five until 11 and, apart from the first day, have pretty happy memories with just a couple of unhappy ones.

The school was about 10 minutes' walk away although in later years 10 minutes turned into an hour as my friends and I played games on the way home. It is amazing how the imagination can extend time. In those days nobody told us to hurry home. We were free to take our time, unworried about being attacked or anything nasty happening to us. In addition, there was a lot less traffic on the roads and my way home was through very quiet areas. I walked along Links Avenue and through a pedestrian cut to the school. It was probably not much further than half a mile away. I don't greatly remember walking to school but I do remember coming home at the end of the day.

At this point I must apologise if I get anybody's names wrong in what follows. Memory can play tricks - particularly 60 years on, but I am going to mention by name some of the people I remember.

I believe that my first teacher was Mrs Thaxton - a kindly lady as I recall. I seem to remember a beehive hair style. My first reaction to school was one of confusion similar to that of generations of children both before and after me. Of course, like all children as I have already said, I believed I only had to go for the one day and that when I returned home in the afternoon it was a part of my life that had finished. It was a part of my life that wouldn't finish for another 15 years. I couldn't understand what I was doing in this large brick building with other children in a room dominated by a complete stranger who was neither my mother nor the mother of any of the others there. Why had we been left with this stranger? The tears flowed - it was a difficult time and as I've already said, I can't remember anyone preparing me for the shock of it all. I can't remember my mother ever mentioning school to me. It would never have occurred to my father to mention school. It was the same when we went to the doctors if I was ill or had a problem. I was never told we were going to the doctors. I just went along and suddenly found myself in the waiting room. This happened once when I had a "problem with the waterworks" as my grandmother put it and which was obviously a urinary infection. It also happened if I had to have an injection. The first thing I knew about it was almost when the needle was poised to strike.

In those days I think parents were less open and honest with their children. I still remember something that marked me for life (not really). I disliked chicken (still do). I disliked chicken gravy (still do). But when I was obviously given chicken gravy, I was told it was "beef tea". I knew it wasn't but never said so and just became part of the deception.

I knew it wasn't "Beef Tea" because when I stayed with my grandmother, she often gave me some proper Beef Tea which was beef extract and tasted nice and certainly not the Beef Tea that was chicken gravy. The word tea in this connection was a loose phrase. It was pretty much like the drink made with Bovril.

Mind you my grandmother had some pretty awful concoctions that she swore by. If I had a cold or a sore throat, she insisted on giving me what she referred to as "Butter Sugar Pills." These consisted of a wedge of butter rolled in vinegar and then coated in sugar. I can still remember the taste. They provided a little relief for a few moments as the vinegar cut through the soreness of the throat but only for a short time.

But back to school. After that initial angst, I settled in quite quickly and soon those early days at home themselves became a memory. Obviously, my mother still divvied things up on Fridays, fruit and vegetables were still delivered, people still came in for a chat but all that had taken a back seat to my learning to read and write. I guess I still witnessed those things during the school holidays but can't recollect them.

Isn't it strange how new and very difficult skills like reading and writing can just come naturally? The question of why am I doing this or what's the point of this never came into play. I only vaguely remember learning to read and write. I don't remember starting to talk at all. I suppose that suggests that it all came reasonably easy to me. Little did I know what a massive part both would play in my life and how they would become the starting point for what you are reading now. I believe I started like so many others with the Janet and John series of books. Over the years we have come across a number of couples named Janet and John and it always makes me laugh.

I must have made good progress as, by the age of 10, I was starring as Dick Whittington in the school Christmas play. I still remember the luxury of being able to eat a buttered crust of bread on stage (another one of those minuscule events that stand out in the mind). I remember that my friend Violet Nieve played my trusty cat. I also remember the school Christmas parties with the sandwiches with that awful salad dressing spread which seemed to be full of bits of peas and other rubbish. It didn't detract from the importance of these events. They were looked forward to weeks ahead. There was tea, there were games and occasionally we got extra play time in the playground. One time we played cowboys and Indians (yes really) virtually all afternoon. I suspect the teachers were having a meeting of some kind but that didn't bother us. I think I was a cowboy which meant we got to kill all the Indians. I think we had been watching too many cowboy films on television. My father certainly enjoyed them.

I seem to remember coming home at lunchtimes. I must have done this as I have no memories of enjoying (or suffering) school dinners until I went to grammar school. My father came home for lunch as well and he gave me a lift back to school in his van. All this must have been done very quickly as I never remember being late back.

In fact, being on time has been an obsession with me and I wonder whether that comes from those times. I am always more likely to be 10 minutes early than 10 minutes late and I try to never keep anyone waiting. Keeping them waiting to me shows a lack of respect, although there are times, of course, when you can't help being late because you have been let down by transport, let down by others or any other number of events outside your control.

I progressed through school very nicely thank you until I came across a gorgon of a teacher, Miss Q. I believe this brought me my first personality clash. For some reason we did not get on, although I have no idea why. I did nothing whatsoever to provoke her. I have learnt in my life that at times people take to you and at others they take against you. It has taken me many years to realise that this is due to their own personality rather than mine. But back to Miss Q. Other teachers had been kind and supportive.

With Miss Q, I worked hard but continually got shouted at for no apparent reason. My work suffered and on at least two occasions I was accused of something I did not do.

There is nothing worse for a young person than to be accused of something they have not done. No protestations of innocence works. Nobody listens to them because they have all made up their minds. Nowadays if I am in confrontation with anyone (and that is now a rare occurrence) I just say to myself "I know I did or didn't do it and that's all that matters to me."

But at that early age I realised how frustrating life could be. I was accused of knocking a balsa wood model over. I never touched it, but my protestations of innocence were wasted on Miss Q who had decided I did it. This all seemed unfair and unreasonable. I knew I had done nothing wrong but was being punished for it. I think she told me I had to rebuild it, but I had no ability to undertake such a task.

I began to understand that teachers could be unreasonable and not the wise and fair people I had thought. The matter was sorted out when my parents went to school to complain, although I still believe Miss Q thought me guilty. I never did find out who knocked the model over, but it was the kind of senseless piece of vandalism I would never become involved in or with.

The next year couldn't have brought a bigger contrast. I idolised Miss Sloane (I believe this was her name). She treated me like an adult and helped me to understand throughout my life that if you treat people with respect and understanding they usually respond. I remember the pride I felt at coming top of the class. Miss Sloane told the class that there was a surprise over top place. I couldn't understand that as I expected to be top. That was not arrogance but just a culmination of the effort and work I had put in over the year.

My confidence, which had taken a knock, returned and I beat my arch-rival Malcolm Stokes to top place. Malcolm and I were best friends - thus proving that rivals can be mates as well. We saw our friendship as part of the rivalry between us. I remember I was given a bright blue pencil case for coming top. I valued this greatly and still remember how it looked and I used it for many years. Its value to me far transcended the fact it was a bog-standard pencil case. Prizes such as this seem to come from some mythical place and never from Woolworths where I suspect it came from. You must remember Woolworths on the High Street.

Another of those irrelevant memories comes from those days when I went out collecting census forms with Malcolm and his father. We drove some considerable distance in their car and at the end I felt extremely travel sick. I suppose that must have been the 1961 census. Midway through the next year Malcolm and his family moved away. I can't remember where to, but I did manage to track down his sister a few years ago, but never heard from Malcolm. I guess I never will but the fact that I still remember him and can picture him as I write this shows what good friends we were.

Returning to Miss Sloane. She really was one of the kindest people I had ever met. It mortified me the one time when she raised her voice to me. And this time, unlike with Miss Q, I deserved to get my knuckles rapped. I was caught red handed spraying water around the boys' cloakroom by placing fingers over the holes of the water fountain. I do not know what made me do it. It upset me that I felt I had let the teacher down. I still hate letting people down and feel guilty when I do.

Sometime during the year Miss Sloane got married. I don't recall her married name. It might even have been that Sloane was her married name and it's her maiden name that I cannot recall. What I do remember is her coming to our shop to show my mother her wedding photos. I think she must have liked me and my family as much as I liked her. Probably a number of the teachers came to our shop, although I have no memory of these visits. I probably would have hidden with embarrassment if I had.

I have other vivid memories of these times - memories of playing conkers and marbles in the playground and of moving into the junior school where I was thought to be intelligent and able enough to move up a year with older children.

Consequently, my handwriting suffered as I went from a class which printed its letters into one which had already learned to join them up. I never learned this art and even today my writing is disjointed and uneven and at times resembles a spider's scrawl. One of my favourite presents from my parents was a portable typewriter which I spent hours with, typing up stories, football results and much more. It was certainly better than writing stuff out. You can imagine my joy when keyboards and computers came along, and I didn't have to use Tippex fluid to overwrite mistakes.

But back to school. Happy years were spent in the classes of Mr Spinks, the wonderful Mr Potter and then my second Bette Noir Miss W.

Her class was the top one at the school and I was probably struggling to keep up with students a year older than myself. At this point I was approaching the dreaded 11 plus exam which would decide which senior school I would go to. A pass meant grammar school, a fail meant secondary modern. It was as much a class thing as an academic. Secondary Modern scholars were losers consigned to the scrapheap of life or that was how it seemed. The secondary modern school was on the same piece of land as the junior school, so it wouldn't have meant much of a transition and certainly no further to go than the journey I was already used to.

To say Miss W didn't like me was an understatement. Why does success in life come down so much to people's opinions of you? I consider that I have been the same person throughout my life with the same values and beliefs. As I have already said, at times I have forged ahead and at others have been completely stuck depending on what people thought of me at any one time.

As far as Miss W was concerned, I couldn't do anything right although I was the same person who previously came top of the class and was promoted ahead a year. The class was lined up in columns of desks according to perceived ability. There were five lines with the "brightest" pupils in line one and the "stupidest" in line five. Thankfully this kind of thing is from an educational past.

I started off somewhere in line three which probably was a fair reflection of my ability. I then dropped down to line five after once again being wrongly blamed for something inconsequential and something I certainly didn't do.

This time I was accused of writing a rude message in my homework book. My parents were summoned and apparently the dreadful sentence turned out to be totally harmless. It read "This is Miss W's writing" - scarcely a hanging offence. The teacher was obviously paranoid about something or other. I did not write that message and to this day do not know who did. Once again, I felt the hurt that young children do when being wrongly accused of something.

So, I sank without trace until the day when fate took a hand. Miss W moved home. She didn't just move house, she moved next to my grandparents and opposite our shop.

When I heard about this I was appalled and unhappy to say the least. It turned out to be sunshine on a cold day, however. Miss W took immediately to my grandfather who helped her in many ways, particularly with the garden and odd jobs. Suddenly my success at school began to increase in direct proportion to the help he was giving her.

Messages in books were forgotten. I was on the way up through lines five, four, three and two and yes into the top line. I don't remember how this was justified but practically overnight I turned from a bad pupil into one of the tip-top elite. This inconsistency was almost mind numbing. It was certainly something I would experience again in later life. It was a case of on Monday morning being incompetent and useless but by Friday being a shining beacon. And of course, I claim that all the while I had not changed.

Suddenly teachers were talking about what would be in my best interests. It was decided that I shouldn't take the 11 plus a year ahead and that I should stay another year in junior school and go back to my right age group. This brought more disruption, but I enjoyed the extra year under the teaching of Mr London who, despite sarcastic outbursts at times, was a reasonably solid teacher. I notice that on the friends re-united web site there are many reminiscences regarding Jack London and I'm not referring to the writer of White Fang who had the same name. I particularly remember his times table tests in an afternoon when he fired 50 questions at you in ridiculously short time, so you had no time to think and only time to write down the answers. I rarely got any of these wrong unless I had misheard the question. I believe that was where I got my ability to do mental maths. Often at a supermarket check out I can add up shopping before the person on the till can input it into their computer. This has come in handy on many occasions and today I will always add up a restaurant bill in my head to ensure I am being charged the correct amount when the bill comes along.

I eventually breezed through the 11 plus. I found it very easy. Probably nobody told me how important it was, so I looked upon it as just another school test which I always viewed as a challenge anyway. The result was that I won one of only a handful of free places (scholarships) available in the county for what was regarded as the top school in Norwich. At King Edward VI (The Norwich School) I found things very different. I have tried desperately to remember taking that test but cannot which suggests I took it all very much in my stride.

As part of my research for this book I found a typical 11 plus exam on the internet and were delighted to score 96% showing that my little grey cells are still in place.

Before I end this chapter, I would like to mention reading and writing again. I have already mentioned how important the two skills have been to me and this has been since the age of five. I remember joining my local library and regularly taking books home and reading them. I was particularly fond of the novels of Geoffrey Trease and Henry Treece. Their names were so similar that I probably got them mixed up but can still remember both of them. I loved the Jennings Books of Anthony Buckeridge, the Billy Bunter books of Frank Richards, the Dr Doolittle books of Hugh Lofting and many others. One of my favourites was a book named "The Gauntlet" by Ronald Welch which I believe is still available. It is interesting for me now to see that I was already developing an interest in historical novels.

I wasn't aware as such of my love of the written word. It's probably something that crept up on me. I do remember writing a very involved story about a dinosaur who terrified a town. It rambled on and on but I was very proud of it. I also remember doing a project about Cliff Richard which included photographs cut from magazines along with text. For me an early day writing project and perhaps also an early indication that I would further develop my love of music which started with those old 78s.

Little did I know that these small beginnings would lead to a lifetime of involvement with the written word.

I have searched my other memories from those early years and they include

Meeting Father Christmas for the first time on Norwich Market. I can't remember whether I was overawed or scared. It just happened. I do remember being given a present by Santa. It was a small blue plastic gun. You put table tennis balls in the front and squeezed the plastic and the balls shot out. I probably played with this for all of an hour before it became unusable.

I have already mentioned watching wrestling on television as part of the World of Sport on ITV. There were baddies like Mick McManus and Jacky Pallo. There were wrestlers who seemed to bound around the ring such as the brothers Bert Royal and Vic Faulkner who were siblings despite having different surnames and then later on there was Big Daddy whose real name was Shirley Crabtree. He was large and I bet nobody took the Michael out of him for having a girl's name. Then there was Giant Haystacks who made Big Daddy look small. When Big Daddy and Giant Haystacks were in the ring together the bout seemed to consist of their running at each other to see if one of them would fall over. Once they were over it took a long time for them to get up again. Then along came Kendo Nagasaki who pretended to be a Samurai Warrior despite the fact that his real name was Peter Thornley. He wore a striped mask and all the other wrestlers tried to take his mask off – without any success because that would have destroyed the gimmick. Underneath that mask of course he was just an ordinary British guy. We all wondered what he looked like. Did he have two heads? Today you can check out what he looks like on the internet. But no internet in those days.

All that wrestling was of course the precursor of the multimillion-dollar entertainment that became the World Wrestling Federation and then World Wrestling Entertainment and many other American offshoots where the bouts were carefully choreographed and where stories surrounding the wrestlers were worked out. I "enjoyed" these with my sons many years later.

I remember being on holiday at a caravan park in Northumberland when we had our sons and taking them to some wrestling where there were goodies and baddies who seemed to loathe each other. My boys couldn't work out what they were doing all getting into the same minibus at the end of the evening.

I will always remember the first ever episode of Coronation Street in December 1960. I was eight years of age. My parents I believe had gone out to get immunisations (injections) and my maternal grandmother came round to sit with me. It was 7.30 pm and that signature tune for Corrie came on. I can remember my grandmother saying:

"What's this then?"

I hadn't got a clue, but we sat and watched it and I'm still watching it over 60 years later, although it has changed a bit. There were a lot less serial killers in those days. A fight in the pub was big news like the day Len Fairclough lamped Harry Hewitt.

I have mentioned my grandmother bringing me sheet music. She also bought me packets of small cheese biscuits as well. I often ate them as I tried out the new music.

I remember visiting my grandmother in hospital when I couldn't wait for my mother to say "well I think it's time we were going." Often this was after the bell was rung to indicate visiting hours were over. In those days beds were lined up in a long ward and I found the whole atmosphere horrible. I still hate hospitals today. I seem to remember visiting my grandmother when she broke her ankle and on a few other occasions as well. It was in the old Norfolk and Norwich Hospital in the centre of Norwich. It's now flats but you can still see the outline of the original buildings.

I can't finish this chapter without mentioning the weather. It's a great British pastime to talk about the weather but in the late fifties and the early sixties the winters were very cold and I mean very cold. Without central heating in Reepham Road we had to rely on a coal fire for our warmth but this only warmed the lounge. The rest of the house could be icy and the walk from the relative warmth of the lounge up to the bedroom could be almost painful and it wasn't unknown to have ice on the inside of the windows as well as the outside in winter. The winter of 1963 was particularly memorable for cold. Snow, snow and more snow and ice. I remember they had places on the streets where you could draw water. Pipes at homes froze and it was all very unpleasant.

But enough of these reminiscences. If you want to read more just pop along to my website at www.peterowensteward.weebly.com where you will find articles on my television heaven and my television hell.

Perhaps I should stop a while at this point to give the website and my daily blogs a plug. The website has lots more memories of my years growing up and my daily blog covers my views on many different subjects along with more details of my life.

If you want to read the blog just go to Facebook and search for "Peter Steward's Daily Blog."

CHAPTER FOUR – THE FORMATIVE YEARS 1963-1970

I started the Norwich School as a boy of well above average intelligence and someone with a bright future. Over the next few years, I put that in jeopardy with a refusal to put in much effort. Whether it was something inside me or the appalling standards of teaching at the school I have never been sure. Certainly, there was very little motivation from within the teaching staff. You could say I lost my way and even lost my love of maths. But first, let's go back to the day I heard that I would be going to the Norwich School.

Before taking the 11 plus exam my parents had to put their choice of schools down in order of preference. They put Norwich School at number one, the City of Norwich School (CNS) as number two and Thorpe Grammar School as number three.

The result of the exam was notified during the summer holidays via the mail (no internet in those days of course) and was expected to arrive on a certain day, so anticipation was high. If you received a very thin letter, it meant you had failed the exam. A fatter letter told you that there had been a pass as it included information on the school you would be going to.

So, on this morning which would have been in the summer holidays of 1963, a brown package thudded onto the doormat. It was sizeable. Yes, I had passed. But to where had I passed? I got my parents number one choice. Not sure that I was greatly pleased as all my friends had opted for my second choice. That indeed did mean that for a while I felt a feeling akin to "homesickness" and it took me quite some time to settle until I made new friends at the new school.

Only a certain number of free places were given to the Norwich School with the majority being fee paying pupils. But I had been awarded a scholarship. As I've already said, I can't remember whether I was happy or not about this – I guess I just accepted it and there was the rest of the summer holidays to go before I had to think about such things.

But that turned out to be a busy period. We had to go to the school for an interview with the headmaster Andrew Stephenson. Then there were school uniforms and sports equipment to buy. Looking back, it must have been a huge drain on resources for my parents and something I have never fully appreciated. Money meant very little to an 11-year-old and I never heard my parents discussing it or the lack of it although the fact that my father had to work as well as having the shop suggested that there wasn't a huge amount of spare cash around.

I don't remember a lot about the interview. I do remember the head telling my parents that I would be in Coke House (that's pronounced cook), and they genuinely thought I would be working in the kitchen. I soon found out that Coke was one of about six houses named after famous Norfolk people which also included Nelson. There was only one house not named after a person and that was School which was for borders. I often wondered what it would be like to live at school and sleep in dormitories and have enforced periods in the evenings to do homework (prep). I should imagine that after the initial novelty the whole thing would have worn a bit thin. Too much school just couldn't be good for you.

Next on the list of things to do was a visit to Rumsey Wells outfitters in Charing Cross, Norwich. The shop is no longer there but it has been replaced by a pub aptly named the Rumsey Wells. The blazers were bright blue, the tie was red and blue, the trousers were short (never long until you had been at the school for three years). Then there was the cap which had your house badge on it. Shoes had to be black and tie ups (no slip ons), raincoats had to include a belt and socks had to be long but finish just below the knee. Yes, there were rules and there were rules and there were more rules. And when you had learnt the rules, there were more rules to learn about which doors you could go in through and which you exited by.

The tailor who served us at Rumsey Wells (perhaps it was Rumsey Wells himself) was stern and business like. He needed an address to send the bill to and so he said NR meaning he wanted the postcode. I thought he was asking me how to spell Norwich. So, I said N O R W I C H. That didn't seem to please him as he probably thought I was trying to be clever whilst I was just feeling confused.

It would be in September 1963 that I started at King Edward VI which is better known as The Norwich School with the emphasis on the word THE. Strangely I remember quite vividly my first day at school when I was five years old but don't remember my first day at Grammar School. I suppose they all merged into one. I don't even remember what day of the week it was, although there was a tendency at the school to start with a very short week in order to get pupils used to new years and new forms before starting in earnest the next week. So, on those grounds it may well have been a Thursday or Friday which would be followed by a Saturday morning school.

Let me say at this point that over the past decade I have had quite a close relationship with the school. It is now a very good place of learning with excellent facilities and somewhere I would love to attend if I could be young again. There have been some major changes since I attended, one of the most important of which saw a move from a boys' only school with girls being admitted for the first time. Secondly it no longer takes in borders and thirdly Saturday morning school has been done away with. So, things have certainly changed and very much for the better. We shouldn't always hold onto the idea that the "old days" were the best. A few years ago, I was honoured by being named ON of The Year for my work in the community. ON stands for Old Norvicensian which is a term used for former pupils of the school. Today it feels like a delightful place to be. Sadly, that wasn't the case in the early to mid-1960s, although I never disliked it completely and now look back on those days with a mixture of amusement and confusion.

In this chapter I'm going to talk about how the school was in the mid to late sixties which turned out to be a period of incredible change as it was dragged out of the Victorian era into the modern. As I've said my descriptions bear no resemblance to how the school is today, but this is an honest description of my life seen obviously from my own point of view. I am sure there are many former pupils around who enjoyed and thrived at the school in those days.

I must address the subject of bullying here and say that at no time in my school life from the age of five to 18 was I subjected to any bullying. Certainly, I cannot remember a single incident at the Norwich School. So, my time there was largely happy, although I did struggle and that was mainly due to my character at the time – something I will now describe in greater detail.

The teachers were ancient, and I mean ancient. I know for an 11-year-old anyone over 20 is ancient. But these teachers were ancient and most were well past the natural age of retirement. On a recent visit to the school chapel, I viewed a commemorative stone to one of the teachers. Using some simple maths, I worked out that he was in his late sixties when he taught us. And there were many others who were equally senior or even older. They all had nicknames – some of which were amusing, some of which made no sense at all and some of which were quite cruel.

The Headmaster Andrew Stephenson was known as Tinny. I always assumed that this was a derogatory nickname but have since found out that there was nothing sinister about it. It referred to the war years when Stephenson operated in a classroom with a tin roof which made an awful noise when it rained. The only female teacher at the school was his wife who, not surprisingly, was known as Ma Tinny! This was just wife of Tinny and had nothing to do with an alcoholic drink.

Stephenson ruled the school through fear. He was not a nice man – or that was my view. I know others felt otherwise but he was very much a disciplinarian and at times this became overpowering. I'm not sure whether boys were genuinely afraid of him or not. I wouldn't say I was afraid, but I did my best not to come onto his radar.

Each morning, I caught the bus from a stop just a few yards from my home and got off three miles later in Tombland. This is an area of Norwich close to the city centre that has no connection with tombs or graves. The term Tomb in this case refers to an open space or marketplace. This area was renowned in the Middle Ages for its markets and as a meeting place. Just a few yards from the bus stop was Norwich Cathedral and Norwich Cathedral Close. Places that I now love and have a great affinity with but which I probably took for granted in those days.

The school is literally at the side of the cathedral. If you walk towards that historic building and look to your left, you can't miss it. You will see the playground.

In my first year at the school, I caught either the number 84 or number 86 bus. Then there was a change. My parents sold the shop to Dixons next door and we moved to a bungalow just round the corner but on a different bus route. I don't think there was ever any discussion about keeping the shop in the family or handing it down to me as their only son. I certainly wouldn't have wanted it anyway. But back to the changes the move made to my life. Now I walked to Windsor Road to catch the 85 or 87 bus. We were at the end of the line for that service. The bus would go a short distance down Windsor Road and then back into a side road and come back to the stop.

There was a significant difference and that revolved around money. If you lived over three miles from the school, you were given a free bus pass from Norfolk County Council. If you lived less than three miles you didn't and had to pay for tickets out of your own pocket. Distances were checked from a direct line or as the proverbial crow flies.

Our shop was just under three miles, so we got no financial relief. But our new home was just over three miles and so I got a free pass. The irony was that I often caught the previous buses home if they came first. I could use my pass and only had a short walk from there.

I had mixed feelings about leaving the shop. It had been the hub of my life and made me what I would like to think to be a reasonably sociable person through regularly speaking to people whilst my mother served. I assume we were open on Saturdays but really can't remember. We were certainly closed on Sundays.

On the other hand, we were moving to a brand-new bungalow with central heating etc and so that was quite exciting. I remember going with my parents to look at a number of properties before deciding on one about 400 yards away from the shop which was near completion. I favoured one close to the local recreation ground which had nothing to do with the property but everything to do with the fact that it was opposite the place that I spent a great deal of my life playing football, cricket, tennis or just running around. It was also where the local library was. So, in essence it encapsulated two of my great loves that I retain to this day – literature and sport.

Dixons bought our shop for a song. I well remember them asking my father how much he wanted for it but they said that there might be a delay as they would have to get the money from the bank (things were very simplistic for an 11 year old). When my father named a price, they took out a cheque book and wrote him a cheque there and then which just proved that he should have asked them to make an offer and then upped it. Buying our shop was the only way Dixons could expand as on the other side of their business, was a road. I suspect my parents were just happy to cover the cost of the new bungalow with no mortgage needed. A figure of £12,000 springs to mind although that may be very wide of the mark.

The new bungalow was down a rough road which was part of the main Middleton's Lane but unmade up. It stayed that way as long as I lived there although the last time I passed I saw it had been tarmacked. Living in the bungalow didn't change my life very much. I got a different bus on a slightly different route as I've said but it was about the same distance from the playing field as the shop and I regularly still rode my bike around. I had a couple of friends living close by who got the same bus, so we would meet up in the mornings. One obvious difference was I no longer had to climb stairs to go to the bathroom or bed and we had central heating.

One place that held a big attraction for me at that time was the Firs Stadium and this is where I picked up my love of the sport of speedway. I can still smell the shale and the bikes as they roared round the corners of the track. The bikes had no brakes. I was introduced to Norwich Speedway by my cousin's boyfriend who was also called Peter. I believe his surname was Coffin (a name you are unlikely to forget). Every other Saturday (we never went to the stockcar racing which was held when Norwich were riding away) he picked me up and we walked to the Firs. It was a 10-minute walk from the shop but a five-minute walk from the new bungalow.

There was something magical about speedway and it was my first sporting love – coming before the days when I got interested in football and went regularly to watch Norwich City at Carrow Road. I can't explain what it was or what it is about speedway that captivated me so much. Perhaps it was being with Peter with whom I struck up a genuine friendship. Perhaps it was the excitement of the sport or perhaps it was just the feeling that I was part of something and had somewhere special to go on a Saturday night every two weeks during the summer months. It did appeal to my love of maths as in the centre of the match programme you kept a record of each race and each rider's score along with the running match score. I have bought a number of these programmes over the years and each has scores filled in which adds to their attraction.

The Norwich riders became my idols – none more so than the Swedish pairing of Ove Fundin and Ollie Nygren. Speedway was big in Sweden. No speedway was very big in Sweden. So many of the top Swedish riders came over here to race. It wasn't until I read Ove Fundin's autobiography that I realised that his week often involved riding for Norwich on one day and then jetting off to Sweden or somewhere else on the Continent to ride for another team before returning to Norwich. I remember at a very early age being asked by somebody what I wanted to do when I grew up. "I want to be a Norwich City footballer in the winter and a Norwich speedway rider in the summer," I immediately replied not realising that the idea was ridiculous because firstly it was logistically impossible and secondly, I hadn't the skill or ability to achieve either. In fact, I have never been on a motorbike and have never had any wish to do so.

Many years ago, Ove Fundin was made a Freeman of the City of Norwich. He is still remembered fondly in Norwich and Norfolk. Our large department store Jarrolds, which always has the best selection of local books including I must say one that I have written, often holds author events where authors sign copies of their books (again I must boast that I have done one of these). Often this brings a queue inside the shop (not in my case I have to add). When Ove Fundin turned up to sign his autobiography the queue snaked through the shop, through the door and around the block. That's how popular he was and is. At the time of writing, he has just celebrated his 91st birthday.

The thing about Fundin was that he was simply the best – streets ahead of other riders and that brought him five world championships. He was so good that they even devised a system to try to stop him winning races. To be fair they tried to stop other top riders from other clubs from winning as well.

The ridiculous idea they introduced was a front and back marker system. The top rider in each team would start as a backmarker, behind everyone else. I believe this would be 10 yards. Most of the rest of the team would start at the tapes and inexperienced riders would start 10 yards in front. This was an attempt to make the sport fair for all, but it just made it more chaotic. Fundin was so good that often he caught the other riders up by the first bend anyhow. Thankfully the sport eventually stopped this nonsense and sanity returned.

I couldn't understand why my cousin ditched Peter as a boyfriend, but it might have been because he preferred to spend Saturday nights with me at the speedway than with her, bearing in mind the fact that she had no interest in speedway or any other sport for that matter.

I did go a couple more times with him when he got a new girlfriend, but my speedway came to an end when they sold the stadium for housing in 1964. I put a curse on the properties built on my lovely Firs but it has never worked and the houses built are still standing even if the architecture is a tad strange to say the least.

Many years after the closure of the Firs I got to know Bill Smith who had two claims to fame. Firstly, he was the head driving test examiner in the country and secondly, he was the announcer at The Firs. Bill told me that by the time the place was sold it was falling to bits and becoming dangerous. There was a good chance that had it not been sold it would have been condemned. We lived two doors away from Bill's son Steve who later went on to have an illustrious career in Academia which resulted in him being knighted for his service to education. He became Sir Professor Doctor Steve Smith. I contacted him shortly after his knighthood and asked how we should address him.

"Steve will do nicely," he replied.

But back to Peter's new girlfriend. I didn't like her. That assessment was completely due to my Saturday night mates night out being ruined by this new person.

"She's fat," I told my mother.

"She's not fat she just has a big bust," came the reply.

I had no idea what she was talking about, but I suppose we were talking Mrs Culley territory here.

I never saw Peter again, but I will always remember him for his speedway and his Bubble Car where the front lifted up and three people sat side by side with one of them obviously driving. It made me feel very travel sick and I'm sure it never got past the 40-mph speed. I cannot remember where we went in the Bubble Car, but I still remember it to this day especially when we are driving through Lincolnshire and see a sign indicating the Bubble Car Museum. I must make a visit someday if it is still there. I just remember the whole of the front of the car lifting up. The engine must have been in the back. Actually, dredging up my memories we may have gone to Pretty Corner near Sheringham on the North Norfolk Coast in that Bubble Car. Similarly, I remember that my uncle had a caravan somewhere or other and one day we went to a large park at Guist where they had a caravan rally – more memories.

I have a feeling that Peter's life went bad as I seem to remember a newspaper report many years ago stating that he had been sent to prison for burglary.

But I must get back to school and Andrew Stephenson as I seem to have left him somewhere which is precisely what I wanted to do with him. I had no respect for this man who tried to rule by fear. When he walked across the playground on his way to lunch in the refectory all ball games had to stop, and everyone had to stand still. When he walked into a classroom, we all had to stand up (in fact this was the same with all the teachers who walked around in their robes and mortar boards). I think you are getting the idea that this school was a rather antiquated place. Mind you many years later when I started working for Norfolk Police, we were expected to stand up when a senior officer walked into the room. I'm not sure as a civilian employee that I ever did. It certainly wasn't the kind of thing I would be prepared to do. I respect people for what they are and not for their status or rank.

The Head was very handy with a slipper or a cane. I never suffered at his hands but was once called a ragamuffin along with a couple of other boys for being late for one of his lessons. The problem was his English lesson came immediately after PE. In the summer PE was on the school field which was at the other end of the Cathedral Close and a good five-minute walk to the main school. Often the PE teacher wouldn't allow enough time for us to get showered and walk/run back to the school. If you were last into the showers, you had virtually no chance of making it. On this occasion we were panicking because we knew that the wrath of Tinny could be awful. So, to get away with being called ragamuffins was probably a light admonishment. Thankfully it's the kind of thing that wouldn't be tolerated today and it's the kind of thing that shouldn't have been tolerated then either.

When we had the Head for a lesson, we used to take it in turns to act as lookouts. There would be all kinds of mayhem in the classroom, but two boys would be stationed to see when the Head left his office. The furthest one would wave to the nearest and then run round the back of the building and into the back entrance of the classroom. The nearer lookout would run into the classroom with shouts of:

"He's coming."

As a result, there was complete silence in the classroom when Stephenson walked in. And that's all I remember about him which probably means that his lessons were pretty awful, particularly as he was teaching my favourite subject – English. I certainly cannot remember having lookouts for any of the other teachers. It did teach me something I have always believed and that's simply that you earn respect from the kind of person you are and not through discipline or ridiculous rules.

Close to the main playground was a series of noticeboards covering pretty much every aspect of school life. Some of these were good, some not so good. A glimpse of the left-hand board could send a feeling of panic creeping up one's spine. This was the one with the heading "The Following Must Report to the Office."

Names and forms were posted. So, you might see Morgan T Lower Fifth or in my case it might be Steward P O 4X. If your name was there you had to stand in a queue outside the office which was split into two. The first part was a room occupied by the Head's secretary – another gorgon in her own right. That room led to the Head's study and that was a place you just didn't want to go into.

If you were lucky, you were just wanted by the secretary over a trivial matter – maybe a letter home on some inconsequential subject. If you were unlucky, you would be told to see the Head. In you would go to collapse under his withering look. I will say no more than that.

The rest of the boards were much more pleasant. They included sports teams and school clubs. Every Tuesday and Thursday I had to remember to pack all my sports equipment. For rugby this meant a white rugby shirt and another which had red and black stripes. Checking on the board would tell you which pitch you were playing on, who was in your team and which shirt to wear. I think the teams were picked at random.

I disliked PE which was rather strange for somebody who loved playing sport and whose life has revolved around it both in an amateur and a professional capacity. Above all I hated circuit training because I was no good at it.

We had the large circuit and the small circuit. These would be in the indoor gym. They alternated on a weekly basis. The large circuit included many items of torture such as climbing ropes, leaping over horses (the dead kind and not the living), climbing bars and much more. You spent an allotted time on each piece of apparatus before a whistle was blown and you moved onto the next.

Even worse was the small circuit. This consisted of boys being divided into teams. On the whistle you hurtled round the gym vaulting over a bar and jumping over benches. Each team was timed with the time of the first and last to finish being added together. It was all pretty pointless. The problem was I was incredibly slow to get over the vaulting beam. Others jumped straight over. I had to jump halfway, hang on the beam and then jump over the other side. It was slow and ponderous progress. I always came last. When they took the beam away and just got us to use our running skills over the benches, I would often finish first. This didn't escape the notice of the PE teacher who tried to teach me how to get over the beam faster. He was wasting his time. I have always been absolutely useless at climbing over things. Assault style courses have never been for me.

In one particular year I did suffer from psychological problems that surrounded Monday mornings. Every Monday without fail I felt ill on getting to school. This feeling of being sick would last until morning break when it would usually disappear as if by magic. I would have to self-analyse myself to explain that one. It only happened for one year and I always felt better around the same time. Add to that the fact that I wasn't unhappy at school in any way and it becomes quite a conundrum. I often made mental plans to leave at breaktime and get the bus home, but I never did as the feeling always disappeared. Many years ago, during my working life I used to develop what I referred to as sick headaches on Monday nights. There was never any reason for this. I didn't dislike my job at the time. The only thing I could think of was it was the first day back at work after a two-day break at the weekend. In those days I had what has been referred to as an ESSO job – Every Saturday and Sunday off.

The teachers at the Norwich School could be very cruel. Classrooms were in blocks and in our block in the third year (this is very confusing because the third year was actually the first year for all those new to the school. The first two years were at what was called the Lower School which co-incided with my last two years at junior school) there were three classrooms on the ground floor and another three on the top floor. The décor of these buildings and classrooms was very dark with lots of black and heavy wooden panels.

I was in Form 3X or IIIX as it was always written. My classroom was on the right as you went through the doors. There was a one-way system in operation – in one door and out another. On this occasion when I was very new to the school, I slightly lost my bearings (something I have done all my life) and wandered into the classroom on the left where a lesson was already underway with the Rev Bowden (always known as Billy Bowden) in charge. This would suggest that it was a Religious Instruction or RI class.

But the Rev Bowden showed no signs of being a Christian by taking the opportunity to ridicule me in front of his class of older boys.

"Sorry sir I think I'm in the wrong class," I stammered.

"Nonsense boy come here. So, what's your name?"

I stammered out my name. He then made me stand at the front of the class while he pointed out my failings and had a good laugh at my expense.

Boy, was I glad to get out of that classroom and to the safety of my own. This is just one of the small things that I remember vividly. It was a relatively small incident, but I remember it 60 years later. I now know it to be a form of bullying but at the time it just seemed to be a natural part of school life and one that had to be endured.

I must mention names here. It was a culture shock. At junior school we were always called by our first names. At the Norwich School it was surnames all the way. All the way that is until you got into the sixth form when some teachers would go back to using your first name.

I mentioned before that many of the teachers had nicknames. We had an Oeufy because it is alleged, he had a hatred of eggs. Apparently, he had a hatred of rhubarb as well. We never found out why, but it was known for bits of lunch rhubarb crumble to be spread over the walls of a classroom where it was known he would be teaching. How pathetically childish I hear you say. But we were children after all.

This teacher was very old. It was rumoured that he had suffered shell shock during the war. He had what are known as petite mals or small fits. This usually took the form of him stopping in mid-sentence and staring into space for a minute or so and then continuing the sentence as if nothing had happened. Now I spoke of the cruelty of teachers, but pupils could be pretty cruel as well. During these seizures all hell would break lose with kids throwing stuff around and shouting.

This master was extremely easy to wind up. He taught Geography and would often give us tests. I remember one day the question was about the native fruit of somewhere or other. When it came to the answers he said.

"The answer to number five is oranges."

To which a bright spark replied

"I've put lemons sir is that okay?"

"No oranges is the answer."

To which another bright spark said:

"I've got Grapefruit sir is that ok."

"No the answer is Oranges."

"I've got tulips sir is that ok?"

At which point the beleaguered master lost his temper.

On another occasion there was a knock on the classroom door and in came three sixth formers carrying a full-size canoe.

"Thought you might like to see what we made in woodwork sir," they said.

"very good, very good," he replied.

They left and 15 minutes later they came into the same classroom and went through the same spiel. Oeufy didn't cotton on until the third time they tried it when he started shouting whilst the rest of us tried not to burst out laughing.

There was always the possibility of changing or dropping subjects. Early on I realised I would never be any good at learning German and so switched to English Literature which quickly became one of my favourite subjects.

I could also never take to Geography which I think was due more to the appalling teaching than the subject. Oeufy taught Geography. He taught Geography very badly. I can't remember a single thing he taught me on that subject.

When my mother and father went for a parents' evening, he told them to "buy him a book on tall ships" which had absolutely nothing to do with anything. When I dropped Geography, I still had to go to the classes but was allowed to read a book, do homework or a few other things as long as I sat at the back and kept quiet. Come report time we were all surprised to see that under Geography was a comment about how much I had improved in the subject during the year – that's despite the fact that I had given it up. I put this down to the fact that Oeufy must have been bordering on the edge of senility. Having said that you might be surprised to hear that I'm now involved in organising and running dementia groups. But I guess that's how we change through the years.

Pupils were so good at finding a teacher's breaking point and playing on it. Thankfully there were a number of teachers who were so good and so respected that no-one would dream of trying to wind them up.

Two of these were English teachers and both were Peters. They were best mates. One was 6ft 7in and the other 5ft 5in but they were both hugely respected – one because he was a thoroughly nice person and the other because he was a strict disciplinarian but knew his subject inside out. It is because of Peter Clayton that I love the poetry of W B Yeats and the metaphysical poets, love the novel Wuthering Heights, love the novels of Charles Dickens and much more. He made his subject come alive and boys knew they couldn't mess with him. Sadly he died a couple of years ago but lived into his nineties.

Peter Macintosh was the tall one and was a very kind man whom everyone loved. I have a feeling that he stood in an election as a Liberal Party candidate but didn't get elected.

A third English master, however, was fair game as he had a rather destructive temper. On one occasion three boys tied a load of collapsible desks together with school scarves, leaving one end loose at the front.

The teacher saw that something was going on and demanded to know what. He then made the mistake of pulling the scarf at the front with the obvious result that desks began to topple like dominoes. We sat there as desks toppled all around.

"I don't think you should have done that sir," one boy shouted.

The teacher threatened to send the entire class to the Head, then threatened to put everyone in detention and then just dismissed the class whilst he got his composure back. This same teacher lost his cool on a school trip to the historic Grimes Graves in Norfolk's Breckland.

The entire coach started singing:

"Where will we be in 100 years from now" to the tune of the Funeral March. Once again, we saw a teacher lose it.

Of course, I played no part in any of these wind ups (actually it's true I didn't but I can't say that I didn't enjoy the results of many of them).

Eventually we reached the point where Andrew Stephenson retired. It had long been known that his mind was with the Maddermarket Theatre in Norwich rather than with Norwich School and I'm sure there weren't that many sad to see him go particularly when Stuart Andrews came through the door like a breath of fresh air.

Stuart was young and a modernist, although it was difficult for him to immediately cast off the antiquated rules that existed. One of the first things he said was that he would change any rule that any boy suggested should be changed providing he agreed with it and they could show that it was pointless.

So out went belts on raincoats, caps for sixth formers (always looked ridiculous), the ban on playing football in the playground (under Stephenson this was virtually a hanging offence which is why we invented the game of heading which involved heading a tennis ball but never kicking it. Heading wasn't strictly football whilst kicking positively was). Out also went standing still in the playground when the Head went to lunch. Out went a load of other pointless rules although some like hair not being below collar length and sideburns not lower than the middle of the ear remained and of course no beards for those of us who could grow them. Which reminds me that I can't remember when my voice broke or when I had my first shave. Isn't it strange how major points in your life are forgotten whereas small inconsequential matters are remembered?

School lunches – oh dear how bad were they? The horrible stew in which, on more than one occasion, we found wasps, and those meat pies which tasted of cardboard. That horrible semolina with half a spoonful of jam to make it a bit more palatable. We sat in order on long tables with a member of staff at the head of the table. On occasions boys were asked to help serve the gruel (sorry dinner). On these occasions somebody would get the food for those serving. As a consequence, when they got to their meal, they would not only find it cold but would also find a whole saltcellar tipped into it.

There was certainly nothing Oliver Twist about these meals – nobody would ever ask for more, although the roasts were good but seemed to be served infrequently. Even now I can taste and smell this food simply by thinking about it.

But back to bad teaching. There was one master who thought that the way to teach history was to write notes on a blackboard, get us to copy them down in a notebook, take them home, learn them parrot fashion and then start the next history lesson with a test.

And that takes me to tests and the dreaded "three weekly orders" which became a regular part of life at the school. You received a mark in each subject over a three-week period. This could be for homework, for classwork or for tests. At the end of each three-week period the marks were added up and you were given a position in the class.

Now this was a perfect illustration of how I lost my way in the early years at the school. I started in the top maths group based I guess on my 11 plus marks. But then I came up against ridiculous subjects like Algebra,

Geometry, Trigonometry and any number of other unfathomable things. Nobody told me about those.

At junior school we had just done addition and subtraction with a sprinkling of division and multiplication and times tables. I was ace at times tables as I've already said. I'm delighted to say that my grandson has picked up the same ability and prides himself on it. We regularly have competitions to see who is the fastest and on the way into Norwich is an electronic board which tells you how many places there are in the city car parks. We both try to add up the places available in total which is ok if the traffic has come to a halt but is a bit difficult if you are travelling at 30 mph and also trying to drive the car. I still manage to do it, although there's no way of knowing whether I'm correct or not. I do the same thing in churches when I always add up the hymn board in the hope that the total will have three or four digits that are all the same. To date this has never happened, but I did get 1121 as an answer once which, you will agree, was pretty close.

The geometry left me so cold that I think I failed O level maths three times. That's because I no longer saw the point of any of it whilst mental maths at least makes it easy to add up darts or snooker scores!

I have already talked about adding up various thing – I seem to have an obsession for doing this.

Many years ago, we went as a family to Canada and was in Vancouver, staying in a hotel. Our boys were old enough to be left alone in the room but not for a huge amount of time. One evening we left them watching television and went out on a date night to a local restaurant.

We had a nice meal but when it came to paying, we were told that they couldn't give us a bill because the computer had gone wrong so they couldn't tell us how much we owed. I quickly looked at the menu and added up what we had and told them. But they seemed incredulous that somebody could do that without the use of a computer. In the end we just gave them the appropriate amount, told them we had two boys who we needed to get back to and left them the address of the hotel and room number if they found out it was any more when the computer sprang back into action. We knew they wouldn't find any discrepancy.

I have mentioned two of my favourite teachers – both English teachers. There are two more who I must also mention – one for having the patience of Job and the other for fostering my love of music.

Bernard Burrell was a true one off. An organist at Norwich Cathedral he was just a lovely lovely man and he managed to foster a love of music in me. On Wednesdays we had a double period of music and he said he would listen to our music if we wanted to take LPs in as long as we listened to his. But what he made us do was think about what we were listening to and discuss it.

I remember "Whiter Shade of Pale" by Procol Harum being played and then the wonderful rock opera "Tommy" by The Who. I remember Bernard listening intently and then asking us why we liked the music. I remember him asking why the vocalist in Procol Harum sang with an American accent. Until then I had just loved the record and didn't realise that Gary Brooker sang in an American accent. I still think this was unintentional on his part and just his natural voice, but it was something Bernard picked up on. He then told us that "Whiter Shade of Pale" was based on a piece by Bach. Nobody had told him that he just worked it out for himself. And sure enough the band later admitted that they had been inspired by Bach.

After listening to our music, Bernard played us Dvorak, Smetana, Beethoven, Mahler and much more. I love all four to this day. I can remember having a reel-to-reel tape machine and deciding that I was going to buy some music for it and I couldn't decide whether to get The Supremes Greatest Hits or Beethoven's First Symphony which we had been studying. I actually bought neither.

Pop and rock music were beginning to become a major part of my life. Every morning from the time I started Norwich School we had an assembly in Norwich Cathedral. This would have lasted only a few minutes (probably about 20) but it marked the start of each day. I don't remember much about these assemblies, but I do remember the sixth form when we were allowed to put together our own short services in the school chapel instead of going into the Cathedral.

I didn't get to go to too many of these as I became a prefect which meant I had to be in the Cathedral to ensure none of the younger pupils were messing around. If they were we had the ability to give lines of even a detention. Lines were called impositions and there was one particular one that went round and round and made all the prefects feel as if they were being very clever. I can remember it to this day.

"Persistent perversity provokes the patient pedagogue to participate in particularly painful punishment." I doubt very much that we knew what perversity was or what a pedagogue was but there was an awful lot of "p"s in it.

This got banned when a parent made a complaint about it being totally inappropriate and so we returned to "I must not talk in Cathedral! Assemblies."

One service I did remember in the school chapel involved listening to an American band by the name of Chicago. I think they may have started life as the Chicago Transit Authority. The two tracks played were "24 or 6 to 4" and "Question 67 and 68". I failed to see any religious content in either and, when the person whose name was Malcolm Phillips was questioned about what religious relevance the pieces had, he simply said with a straight face.

"None I just like the music."

The other teacher I remember with huge fondness was Alec Humphrey who lived well into his 90s. Alec was a very kind man who knew that, when it came to art, I was a complete no-hoper. I couldn't draw anything and most of the time he drew things for me and I just coloured them in. I always came bottom or second from bottom in art but it wasn't for lack of enthusiasm on my part. I remember one year our art lesson was the last two periods of Saturday morning. The art room was above a very historic gate leading to the Cathedral Close and on Friday nights at home I daydreamed about climbing the stairs to the art room because I enjoyed being there so much and also because those periods were the gateway to the weekend, although with Saturday morning school our weekends were greatly truncated.

One incident at school combined English and Art in a way that made me angry at the injustice of it all. I've always been intolerant of injustice in all its forms as was evidenced by what happened to me at junior school when I was wrongly accused of things I hadn't done. And here was another example. I was good at English and poor at art. So in the three weekly order my marks for English would be high and my marks for art low. They would balance each other out. That's until the day that Tall Peter decided that our ENGLISH homework should be to draw a scene from The Legend of Robin Hood. This just wasn't fair. I couldn't draw and this wasn't English homework. We were never asked for art homework to write an essay which I would have been good at.

Now I have mentioned that my grandmother had a lodger named Ken and so this must have been a Wednesday as that was the day I caught the bus to meet my mother at my grandmas. I told Ken about how I thought it to be unfair. His reply was "I can draw a bit. Let me do the homework." So I did and he produced a lovely piece of art which I submitted.

I was very pleased when the books came back and I had been given 18 out of 20. Pleased that is until Tall Peter said he had been so impressed by the pieces of art that he had shown the best to the art teacher. All those scoring more than 15 had been passed on to Mr Humphries who would immediately twig that I hadn't drawn the piece.

The only thing I could do was to come clean. So I went up to Tall Peter and confessed that somebody else had done my homework but I added that I thought it unfair to set drawing as English homework. He just smiled. "We knew you hadn't done the work but I'm keeping your mark of 18 for showing initiative and yes you are right it wasn't a piece of English homework." I told you the guy was a wonderful teacher.

Sometimes teachers acted completely out of character. There was an incident involving another pretty ancient teacher who used to delight in calling assemblies in the rather cramped gymnasium.

So there was no surprise when one was called on a specific day. He had us all lined-up in forms waiting for some devastating announcement. In he marched with gown flowing after him.

"April Fool," he said, simply turning round and walking out again.

We all trooped out again, most of us not finding it remotely amusing,

But back to Tall Peter. I once had an argument with him. Well really it was a reverse argument. He had decided to print a book of poetry written by pupils. I used to have a copy but it is long lost which is a shame. I don't know how or why he got hold of one of my poems, but it was a truly awful piece of writing. I called it "The Little Yellow God" and it's so bad that it makes me cringe when I read it. But in the interests of being honest and open I will reproduce it here and I really won't be offended if you say "My goodness (or something a little stronger) that is truly awful."

The poem was probably inspired by some classical nonsense, and I do detect a likeness in some of the words to a song written by David Bowie called "Wide Eyed Boy From Free Cloud." Due to copyright rules, I cannot quote that here but the words are easily found on the Internet.

So when Tall Peter told me he was including it in the anthology I tried to protest.

"But Sir it's awful" I said.

"I think it's pretty good," he replied.

"Sir it's absolute s—t." I always had a way with words.

"Well I'm going to include it because I like it."

And so he did. Perhaps at that time I was unsure about my writing. Come to think of it I probably still am.

You can make up your own mind because ladies and gentlemen, boys and girls I give you "The Yellow God."

His coming was threatened, But none took heed
The world would soon know.
The Yellow God came down one day,
Alighted on the silvery earth,
Pronouncing people out of date,
Banishing all and sundry.
When up in spite he dashed through
Towards the clouds of celestial strife
He touched up the heathen spirit
With a gay tra-lee.
A sportive touch did dwindle away
As lovers sang on a Birchfield Bank.
Aligning homeward, fleeting free.
With whistling touch of platted hair,
He reached the doors of Kingdom's home
Determined on retrospective announcements.
He lighted on a toadstool green
Intent on impish deeds
Of daring defiance against the human race.
The jockey was the first to fall, his horse it did not warrant
The canoe man lost his paddle quick, a victim of the torrent.
The babes were wild, the children chilled
While Demion switched to trade.
Wild Demion, lusting for life
To misery aft-enthralling.
But once came down with a showering thrust
The bolt of Cremaithius' trade
And smote our God upon the breast
And caused his heart to fade.
No more to danger the lives of us
He returned from whence he came.

I wrote lots of poetry during my time at the Norwich School – 99% of it is unadulterated rubbish. In fact there's only one poem I have written that gives me any satisfaction and that's called "London" and was written many years after I had left school and had a family and children of my own and you can read that later on in this epistle.

I wrote lots of poetry in the style of W. B Yeats and John Donne when I should have been writing more original pieces. I even called one poem "A Poem in the Style of Leda and the Swan by William Butler Yeats Celebrating One Who Should be Admired." Yes I was ripping off the classics.

So let's return to music. My music appreciation was developing at the Norwich School thanks in no small part to the delightful Bernard Burrell. Another aside here. A few years ago, I signed up to be involved in the administration of local and general elections. I was accepted and, to date, have officiated at five sets of local elections and one general election. One of the people who I handed a ballot paper to was Colin Goodchild who was Bernard Burrell's predecessor.

"You taught me music at the Norwich School," I told him.

"Did I," he replied. "What's your name?"

I gave him my name and it meant nothing to him. I didn't expect it to as I was pretty quiet at school and I doubt whether any of the teachers would remember me, although sadly very few of them if any are still alive.

A couple of years ago I met Shorter Peter the English teacher who was still very much alive but sadly has since died as I've said. This was at a school reunion dinner and shortly after I had written a piece for the school old boys' magazine on teachers that had inspired me. I mentioned five by name – Shorter Peter (Peter Clayton), Tall Peter (Peter Macintosh), music teacher (Bernard Burrell), art teacher (Alec Humphrey) and Head Teacher after Andrew Stephenson (Stuart Andrews). Shorter Peter had read my article and was determined to seek me out after being told that I would be there. Incidentally he had the nickname of Duffy Clayton. I never found out why. Tall Peter was not surprisingly just known as Mac, Bernard Burrell was equally not surprisingly known as Bernie and Alex Humphries and the Head just didn't seem to have nicknames.

Peter Clayton came up to me and gave me the longest handshake I have ever had and he was in tears. That to me is the power of the written word and it's a power that I am so thankful to have in some small way. People seem to like what I write and for that I am eternally grateful.

He grasped my hand firmly (this was before lockdown stopped any kind of physical contact apart from with one designated person).

"It was such a lovely piece that you wrote," he said. "Mac was my best friend and I miss him so much, but your article brought him back to life. I can't thank you enough."

"It was a pleasure. Every word was truly meant," I replied. The handshake went on so long that I almost missed my first course.

"I'm sorry but I don't remember you at school," he said. C'est la vie.

I have always stood up for what I call the "Quiet Ones." Our world seems to be absolutely chock full of arrogance and people spouting about how good they are. I guess that's called self-promotion. But there are those who are really skilled at something but very quiet about their achievements and don't push themselves forward. I'm always looking out for these people.

Being quiet hampered me at school in sport on a couple of occasions that stick in my memory even today.

In the sixth form we were at last allowed to play football (soccer). As I mentioned when a new head came to the school, he said he would reverse any rule he felt was pointless or inappropriate. So a number of us went to him and asked why we couldn't play football rather than rugby. The previous head loved rugby and hated football as I have already mentioned by his banning the round ball game in the playground. We had the backing of a recent addition to the teaching staff Howard Thomas who was a Welshman and a football fan (yes the two can occasionally go together).

We were told that providing Mr Thomas could find a pitch for us to play on there was no reason that boys in the sixth form shouldn't play football. We then asked if we could have a school team and the answer was the same: if Mr Thomas could sort out fixtures against other schools that would be fine.

So Mr Thomas got to work. He agreed with CNS Old Boys Football Club that we could use their pitch at Britannia Barracks on Tuesdays and Thursdays. He also sorted out a couple of fixtures against other schools. CNS Old Boys was a very famous amateur Norfolk football club with a long and distinguished history. Sadly, they went out of existence many years ago. Britannia Barracks was an interesting place to play football. It was within comfortable walking distance of the school changing rooms known as The Stables because they had previously housed horses and often smelled as if they still did.

I would say running distance, but we changed in the Stables and then walked in our football boots for the 10 minutes to take us to Britannia Barracks. Running in football studs would have been a touch dangerous. I have no idea why we didn't wear shoes and change into our boots on the pitch. We just didn't.

Britannia Barracks is in an area of Norwich known as Mousehold and from opposite the football pitches you could get a wonderful view of the city. We never stopped to admire the view though as we were too keen to get on with our game. The pitch was also very close to Norwich Prison as well but the name Britannia Barracks became important in my research many decades later as the place where many men signed up to serve in both the First and Second World Wars. Some walked tens of miles to sign up there.

But back to football. Howard Thomas divided all those who wanted to play into two groups. The main group were the more gifted players and made up a full 11-a-side game on the main pitch. Those who were left shall we say were not quite so good but were enthusiastic players like my mate Paul who couldn't kick a football to save his life but still loved the game.

From the 22 players on the main pitch, Howard Thomas picked 11 to represent the school and I was lucky enough to be included. He loved my style of play because I always gave 100%, mainly because I loved the game so much and was so relieved that at last I could play it and not rugby which I was beginning to hate. In later life I made my peace with the sport of rugby and today enjoy watching it.

I always played in the same position – on the right wing and in those days, it meant wearing the number seven shirt, although I don't remember having numbers on our shirts. I modelled my play on a Norwich City winger called Ken Foggo who was my footballing idol. In fact at school, I was often called Kenny because of this. Ken Foggo was a direct winger with a tremendous shot and, probably more importantly, was pretty much the same height and weight as me. As far as I was concerned my job was to get the ball, motor down the right wing and centre it for onrushing forwards. If I put the ball into a good area in the penalty box that was my job done and it was the job of teammates to get on the end of it. I also took corners.

I also liked scoring goals by cutting in from the wing, latching onto through balls and beating the goalkeepers in one-on-one situations. I prided myself that I scored many more than I missed.

It was a couple of days before our first school match against Thorpe St Andrew's School. I was taken aside by Howard Thomas.

"I want you to play in midfield," he said.

"But I'm a right winger," I replied.

"We need your energy in midfield," and then he said something to me that is one of the nicest compliments I have ever had.

"You are our Alan Ball."

Well how could I say no? Alan Ball was known for his non-stop running and was an integral part of the England 1966 World Cup winning team. I have a DVD of the final against West Germany and, when I watched it, I realised just how good Alan Ball was in that match. He was everywhere. Now just a couple of years after the cup final I was being likened to one of the nation's key players.

So I played in midfield. I buzzed around, chased everything and scored four goals in an 8-0 win. At the end of the game Howard Thomas came up to me.

"Told you you could play midfield," he smirked.

"Can I go back to playing on the wing" was my only response.

So back at Britannia Barracks the following week I went back to playing on the right wing. I remember Howard Thomas deliberately fouling me on a couple of occasions. On one occasion I was clear through when he came from the side and wiped me out. As he was refereeing as well as playing, he waved play on. I took it as his way of saying I was a decent player who had to be stopped.

"That's what they do to Alan Ball," he said afterwards.

So if I was so successful why did I suffer huge disappointment for being quiet? Well a few months later Howard Thomas announced that he was leaving the school. I guess he was only there for a couple of years.

There was no other teacher interested enough to take our football. So it was given over to a prefect who had the nickname of Bunty. He was rather overweight and not made like a footballer. He picked the teams and as he didn't know me and wasn't interested in what had been achieved the previous year, I found myself playing on the second pitch with the kids who had problems kicking the ball.

I put up with this for a couple of weeks and then, backed up by my friends, told him what I thought about the situation which was a risky thing to do with a prefect. Had I been much younger it probably would have been a detention at the least.

I think it was quite reluctantly that he put me back onto the main pitch. I smirked when I saw he was on the opposite side to me and waited until he had the ball and went in with a two footed over the top tackle designed to injure him. Luckily it didn't but I think he got the idea about how I felt. I can't even remember what happened after that, but I guess I continued to play on the main field. That's the only time in the few years that I played football that I went out deliberately to injure someone. I soon gave up playing the game as I turned to reporting it and then coaching it. You can read much more about my life of sport in the second volume of a trilogy of books that I am putting together,

The same thing happened to me in tennis and again it was because I never put myself forward or made a lot of noise. I have mentioned that I played tennis for the school at both junior and senior level. I mentioned a teacher by the name of Colin Goodchild earlier. Well, he was a keen tennis player and organised tennis at the school.

Actually, it wasn't at the school. In those days there were no school tennis courts, illustrating how poor the facilities were. We had to get a bus to Angel Road School courts which were a couple of miles away. I think we had to go ready changed.

We had teaching from Norfolk coach Brian Blincoe who sadly died many years ago after suffering from Motor Neurone Disease. Brian was a decent coach and picked a few of us out for special Norfolk County training on Saturdays. This training was quite intense, and I believe I played for Norfolk Under-16s at one point. I remember my parents buying me the top racket of the day. This was of course a wooden racket and one used by professionals. I still have it. The strings are broken but it is a reminder of my tennis past. Many years ago, when I was playing tennis at Cromer and the racket was hanging up in a local sports shop ready to be restrung, a Pakistan Davis Cup player offered to buy it from me. I turned his offer down and now of course it's no use to anyone except as a museum piece. But enough about rackets.

Very often myself and my doubles partner David Kingsley (whom I have to say I let down on a number of occasions as doubles wasn't really my game and I wasn't that good at it. Now I prefer doubles to singles but at the age of 70+ that's probably reasonable) would play against Colin Goodchild and Brian Blincoe.

One day Brian took me aside and said "I want to have a game of singles with you."

"Wow," I thought.

Now Brian was one of two major Norfolk coaches (Frank Ong being the other) and probably nationally ranked and can you believe it I beat him 6-4. But there were no wild celebrations because he soon brought me down to earth.

"You have just beaten yourself," he said.

I must have looked confused.

"I've been playing how you play and you managed to adapt your game to beat yourself. You found a way of changing your game to win," he said.

It was an interesting lesson that taught me that at times you can be your own worst enemy and I'm sure that is a theme that will run throughout this book as it progresses. I got the same kind of vibe many years later when I studied for a diploma in sports psychology. When it comes to sport very often it's all in the mind.

So I happily partnered David K in representing the school at senior level. I can't really remember any of the school matches apart from one at Langley School where the memory has nothing to do with the score or how we played but from the fact that a number of black children were employed as ball boys. That's the one and only time in my life that I have played tennis where balls have been thrown to me. Sadly, it was probably an example of racism and colonialism, but I was too young at the time to be concerned about that.

So here I was being accepted as one of the best six tennis players in the school (the school team featured three pairs of players always playing doubles and never singles). Then what happened? You have probably guessed after what I wrote about football. Brian Blincoe stopped coaching us (maybe he cost too much to employ) and Colin Goodchild left the school and the new man in charge of tenuis didn't know who I was or how well I could play. So I was put with the group who could scarcely hit a ball and stupidly never stood up for myself but started going AWOL on tennis days. Again, this wasn't sorted until I was asked why I wasn't turning up for games and told them. A quiet boy had once again been overlooked.

To me pushing oneself forward was akin to boasting and this is something I still feel, although at times you have to get involved with that kind of thing. I prefer to think that actions speak louder than words but all too often that doesn't work.

And of course, the problem is I'm now writing a book all about me and telling you all the things I have done in my life. I hope you don't think it's boastful.

The tennis situation had a strange effect on me. I gave the game up and didn't play again until a few years later when I joined Cromer Tennis Club and fell in love with the game all over again and enjoyed some very amusing incidents. But you'll have to wait awhile before I describe the day I played with a national entertainer, the day I partnered someone who insisted on singing hymns and the day I beat my flatmate because he was put off playing by a lack of underclothes.

I have moved quite some way from talking about music which I intended doing. So here goes. I have mentioned that at my old house we had a wind-up gramophone with some 78 discs by Little Richard. I played these to annoy my grandmother but didn't really like the shouting and hollering of Small Dick (sorry about that).

I don't remember a great deal of music from the 1950s, although I have now grown to like it. Neither do I really remember the advent of the Mersey Sound, the first wave of Brit Pop, or the advent of the Beatles. To me it all just happened, and I was more into Anthony Newley than anything serious. But gradually my taste in music began to change at the Norwich School but it took some time.

In the school holidays I began to listen to the Pirate Radio stations including Radio Caroline (my favourite) and Radio London. They were new, they were exciting, and they were anarchic. And I would always listen to Alan Fluff Freeman doing his Sunday chart countdown of the top 30. It was one of the highlights of the week and probably heralded the end of the weekend but at least gave us two hours of enjoyment before bed and the thought of returning to school on the following day.

I had a number of good friends at school, many of whom I played football or cricket with at the weekends and during school holidays and that meant often biking some distance to their local parks. I have already mentioned my mate, Paul. His mum, a lovely lady called Eileen whom I always referred to as Mrs Smith until she started sending us Christmas cards long after I had left school and signing them Eileen, invited me to stay there one weekend and that led to me staying there on a fairly regular basis.

I think she felt I was a good influence on her son as I often wore shirts and ties and he didn't. One Christmas I became even more popular as I bought Paul a tie which he wore. It just happened to be a Norwich City tie and both of us were very keen supporters of the Canaries, so he was happy to wear a tie with a Canary on it, This was in the days before my first real attempts at becoming a fashion guru by wearing a black shirt with a white tie which I thought was incredibly trendy and now think must have looked horrible with my, at the time, long hair. Since that day I have cast off any pretensions to being savvy when it comes to fashion.

Recreation Road became a regular haunt of mine. Mrs Smith made the best lemon meringue pies with meringue that was crisp and melted in your mouth. The rest of her cooking was none too shabby either, so I enjoyed my time there.

We went to the park to kick a ball around, played board games such as Wembley and Escalado, the latter of which is a strange horse racing game where a track is stretched across a table and a handle turned which makes a wave on the track which forces the horses forwards until one passes a finish line. The course includes a number of raised yellow dots which can either knock the horses back or make them fall over. It doesn't sound much but it was a lot of fun. We used to bet matchsticks!

Paul's home was where I watched the 1966 World Cup Final with England winning 4-2 against West Germany. Those were the days of the Cold War, with Germany divided into East and West, West Germany was probably the best team in the World (I still claim England's triumph was partly prompted by the fact they were at home rather than anything else although they did have some world class players) whereas East Germany were strictly also rans.

Above all myself and Paul listened to music. He had what was known as a sampler album entitled "Bumpers." It had a pair of plimsoles on the cover. It also had what I would refer to as "strange music" on its two vinyl LPs. Music that I now love. Paul was into this strange kind of music, years ahead of me. Mrs Smith liked me because I was into The Batchelors who were an Irish boy band full of wholesome haircuts and suits. They sang ballads like "I Believe" and they were the kind of guys you would love your daughter to bring home. Not that we ever had a daughter.

What Paul was listening to was music by strange hippy type people who were beginning to set trends that I would later embrace.

Bumpers had pieces of music by Traffic, Bronco, Spooky Tooth, Quintessence, Mott the Hoople, Jethro Tull, Jimmy Cliff, Blodwyn Pig, Dave Mason, John and Beverley Martin, King Crimson. If, Free, Nick Drake, Fairport Convention, Cat Stevens, Renaissance, Fotheringay and a few more.

Many of these are the bands that began to colour my youth. I still listen a lot to Renaissance, King Crimson and the tragic Nick Drake was a forerunner of so many of the singer-songwriters of today.

Paul also had an LP entitled "Zero She Flies" by a guy called Al Stewart. He played this a lot. I hated it. All Stewart had what I thought was a feminine and wimpish voice. His songs were dull and he waffled on and on. Guess what: Today I love Al Stewart, "Zero She Flies" is one of my favourite albums and on my bucket list is to see Al Stewart in concert. I did see him many years ago in St Andrew's Hall in Norwich which is a hugely historic building. Stewart's introductions to his songs lasted longer than the songs themselves but it was still a delightful evening.

At school, people's musical tastes were changing. Many were into what was called Underground music. This was just a general title for some of the best rock music ever. I began to appreciate the likes of Chicago which I have already mentioned. Then there were glorious bands like Deep Purple, Black Sabbath and above all Jethro Tull.

Somebody along the line must have asked Stuart Andrews whether six formers could have their own space where they could relax, perhaps do homework but where they could drink coffee and maybe purchase some snacks. He must have thought about it and said yes and so the crypt of the school chapel was turned into a sixth form club. There must have been a committee to run this and I even think I might have been on this and it must have had some funding because very quickly old sofas and armchairs began to arrive along with a bar for the serving of coffee and a football machine which soon became very popular.

This was a great place to go during lunch break, on days when games were called off, early in the mornings before assembly or after school when you just wanted somewhere to hang out with mates rather than going straight home. This crypt brought me my everlasting memory of the happiness I had at the school in the sixth form. The old teachers had been pensioned off and everything was more vibrant, and we have Stuart Andrews to thank for that. It was a place I wanted to be and I was studying English, Economics and History at A level. Ok economics now leaves me feeling flat but the other two have become an integral part in my life. Without English I could never have become a journalist and fallen in love with writing. Without history I could never have become involved with many of the groups I have enjoyed being part of (more of this later).

I remember the smell of the sixth form club. I remember the layout of the chairs. I remember the record player that was always on. I remember the smell of the free coffee but above all I remember the Saturday night social events which soon became legendary and I'm sure will be remembered by anyone in the sixth form at the school at that time but probably remembered with horror by anyone who walked past towards the Cathedral on a social club night and heard loud rock music. For me this is where I started to grow up.

So let me set the scene. You are walking through the Erpingham Gate (so called after Sir Thomas Erpingham) and in front of you about 150 yards is the main entrance to Norwich Cathedral. On your left is the school chapel and down some steps is the crypt that today is an art studio but which in the late 1960s was the sixth form club. Look to your right and there is a largish stretch of grass which is part of the Cathedral Close. At one end of this grassed area and closest to the Cathedral is a statue of Norfolk hero Horatio Nelson. At the other end is a statue of Wellington.

Somebody (probably the committee) asked the Head if we could have Saturday evening socials in the sixth form club. He said yes as long as there was no alcohol served.

"How about cider", somebody asked?

Now for some reason the Head said that cider would be ok. So you can imagine what happened next. The roughest, strongest scrumpy cider was purchased for sale at the Saturday socials. Added to this the White Lion pub (now renamed the Whig and Pen because it is close to the law courts) was just a couple of minutes' walk away and somewhere we often congregated before socials because landlord Arthur didn't check ages although quite a few of us were over 18 at this point and of legal drinking age.

So, after a couple of limbering up drinks at the White Lion, it was back to the club. But it wasn't just us. We were allowed to bring girlfriends along, so you can imagine what happened when boy meets girl and rough cider is involved. We also had access to one corridor with loos and also to the school library. I expect the Head thought we might like to do a bit of homework or research during the evening. Research probably was done but not into Nelson or Wellington.

I still laugh when I think about those evenings. Norwich Cathedral Close is a wonderfully tranquil place. Norwich Cathedral is a wonderfully tranquil place. Imagine that tranquillity being shattered on a Saturday evening in the late 1960s with "Paranoid" by Black Sabbath and "Black Knight" by Deep Purple being blasted out at top volume into the night air.

Then there was all that land. And I must say, and I'm not proud of this, that most of us didn't walk along the corridor to the loo. No we peed up against Nelson or, if we fancied a short walk, we peed up against Wellington.

Often we would go down to the school field and it wasn't to get a better view of the Cathedral. I will just leave it at that. Let's just say I have always had a love of Pull's Ferry at the bottom of the close. After all it's a very historic place.

On one occasion after a particularly heavy scrumpy session one of my mates turned up at home very late looking very dishevelled and very wet as it had been raining. It appeared he had fallen in a gutter and gone to sleep on a pavement.

His mum phoned the school on the following Monday morning and I believe spoke to the Head who seemed incredulous that one of his pupils could end up in such a state.

"He was extremely drunk," said the mum.

"Well that wouldn't have happened at the school," replied the Head.

"But he said he was drinking cider at the club," she said.

"Yes he probably was," said the Head.

Apparently, the Head hadn't seen a connection between alcohol and cider!

I mentioned taking girlfriends to the socials but haven't mentioned boyfriends. I have no memory of any of my fellow pupils being openly gay. In those days I doubt whether they would admit it anyway. So it was very much a girl and boy thing. We were encouraged to go out with girls from Norwich Girls High School. When I say encouraged, I cannot remember what form this encouragement took but we were always aware that going out with a Norwich High Girl was good and going out with anyone else wasn't.

I never went out with a girl from Norwich High School but I did go out for a couple of years with one from Notre Dame – the convent school. I have no idea what was wrong with Notre Dame and there probably wasn't anything tangible. A friend of mine was going out with a girl from Notre Dame and she had a friend who expressed an interest in as they say in the old days of "stepping out with me."

We started by meeting up at the school's cinema club where we watched films whilst sitting on very hard and uncomfortable tables. I can't remember what films we saw now. But after that we would go out to various places on Saturday evenings. I would get the bus into the centre of Norwich and my father would pick me up. It was my first steady girlfriend. Although I had been friends with other girls for short periods without anything really developing.

We were very close, but eventually I got what might be described as "dumped" which didn't worry me too much as it was shortly before I left school and went to journalism college where a whole new chapter was ready to open up for me. I believe my girlfriend, who came from a very well-known and well off Norwich family whom I never met, went on to marry someone with the same surname as myself. She is one of those people I would love to meet again. She was a few years younger than me.

I can't remember getting my A level results. They weren't spectacular but at least I passed all three to add to my six O' Levels. I assume I had left the school by the time they arrived which meant sweating on my future career. Those were the days, however, when it was said that all school leavers could virtually be assured of a job with the Norwich Union Insurance Group if they wanted one. I definitely did not.

Sometime during my two years in the sixth form I had applied to what was then Eastern Counties Newspapers for one of their six annual places on what was known as their training scheme. If I was successful, I would be sent on a nine-month journalism course to Harlow Technical College in Essex.

I had a couple of interviews and was accepted on condition that I passed my three A' levels. You can imagine the relief when I received that letter to say English pass, Economics pass, History pass. Incidentally I passed History A level despite failing History O level. This has happened to me twice in my life. Later I was to pass shorthand at 120 words per minute, having failed at 100 words per minute. I rather like doing things the wrong way round. My A level grades weren't great but all I needed was three passes.

I have no idea what I would have done had I not achieved those three passes. I had put all my eggs in one basket. Early on in my time at school I considered trying to be a teacher myself, but the written word always won out.

To his credit, Stuart Andrews was fully supportive of my decision to go to journalism college. I wasn't alone in trying to take this path as a friend also decided to go for it. He didn't stay in journalism but changed career and went into law and ended up becoming a High Court judge.

Boys from the Norwich School were expected to go to university and preferably either Oxford or Cambridge. My grades were nowhere near good enough to go to either, but I didn't want to anyway. At the annual prizegiving the Head mentioned where youngsters were going which might suggest that we got our results before leaving. He mentioned names and universities and then said me and another Peter were going to journalism college and we were the first two boys to ever decide on this path. I have no idea whether that was true, but I have to believe what he said.

I remember my last day at Norwich School, saying goodbye to teachers that we respected and ignoring those we didn't. There was a lot of handshaking and proverbial back slapping and good wishes for the future, before I got onto my bus to travel home from school for the last time. I was out of the educational system or so I thought before realising that in less than two months I would be back in it again but this time not as a schoolboy.

End of Chapter Note: I came across Stuart Andrews once more when I was a young reporter in Norwich. He was a member of Norwich Rotary Club and I was sent by the editor to cover a talk by international football referee Norman Burtenshaw. Now this was a very pleasant task. Not only was I going to listen to somebody talking about football, but I was getting a free meal as well.

I walked into the hall which I seem to remember was probably the Royal Hotel in Norwich (now long gone). I was met by a smiling Stuart Andrews.

"Hello Peter good to see you again. You must sit with me."

"Thank you Sir," I replied.

"Oh for goodness sake drop the Sir. My name's Stuart."

I still found it difficult to call him by his first name during the meal.

Not so long-ago Stuart Andrews was interviewed for the magazine for old boys of the school. He is still alive now in his 90s and living I believe in the Bristol area. In that interview he was asked if there was anything that particularly stood out as a memory of his time at the school.

He failed to mention the sixth form socials for some reason, but he said the thing he remembered most was the trial of Richard III which was written and enacted by one of the year groups he taught.

That year group was the one I was in. I was picked by Stuart to lead the prosecution case against the King. The premise was that he had survived the Battle of Bosworth Field but had been put on trial for murder and the imprisonment of the princes in the tower.

The King was found guilty (not surprisingly) and sentenced to death. We then had to write an essay on some aspect of Richard III. I wrote an essay in which Richard III had survived the battle and the trial and how this affected England over the following one hundred years. He loved it and gave me an A+ for originality. It was incredible that over 50 years later he would pick this out as the highlight of his years at the school, but it's something I also remember with great affection.

As a result of that work, I was made a school prefect which meant I ditched the red and blue tie and had to wear a fully blue one with fleur de lys on it.

Stuart (and I'm allowed to call him that now) also had a keen sense of humour which he would often deliver with a sardonic grin that I can picture as I'm writing this. I remember in the sixth form having to have time off school after contracting mumps. It was painful and the only thing I could eat for a couple of weeks was chicken soup. I haven't been able to face chicken soup since that time. The smell is enough to put me off. Similarly, I have never touched rum and blackcurrant since getting horribly drunk on it in Spain. Again, I can smell and taste that sweet and sickly substance as I write this.

But back to mumps. On my report Stuart wrote at the bottom something along the following lines:

"Peter has enjoyed a very good term and I wish him well in his future endeavours, but 18-year-olds just shouldn't get mumps."

My parents were quite angry when they read this until I explained it was a typical comment by the Head and made in jest. To me it said that he liked me, and he felt he could make such a comment. On another occasion he apologised to me for making me study Chaucer. I didn't understand why he apologised until he explained that it had wrecked my spelling as I was writing many words in old Chaucerian English. Come to think of it I probably still do.

Yes I owe Stuart Andrews a lot. I remember him vividly and like to think that he at least shaped some of my future. On a visit to the school a few years ago I visited the sixth form coffee bar which is now well away from the chapel crypt. In a room close by were portraits or photographs of the school's head teachers. Stuart Andrews' pose was exactly as I remembered him.

As for Norman Burtenshaw. I reported on his talk to the Rotary Club, particularly missing out his joke which went something like this:

"When I was refereeing in Japan I was told by the local people that after making love or having sex you have to take a shower. I was the cleanest man in Tokyo."

Isn't it strange how you remember small things like that?

Little was I to know that Norman Burtenshaw would later play quite a major part in our buying our first property. Norman died in 2024 when well into his 90s. But I'm getting ahead of myself. First, I must describe the following nine months and what was probably the happiest year of my life for any number of reasons but first a final footnote to this chapter.

This one is about how I failed to leave much of a mark on the Norwich School and came to light when I was doing some research in Kirby Hall Library, the home of the Norfolk Family History Society and I found some bound copies of the Norwich School magazine which covered some of my time at the school. Under a tennis report for the season, it stated "P.O Steward also played!" Perhaps that's what I should have called this memoire – "P.O Steward Also Played." But I think on balance I will stick to "A Charmed Life."

CHAPTER FIVE – OFF TO COLLEGE 1970

I often claim that my nine months at journalism college were threequarters of the best year of my life as I will explain.

I call it a year as there was excitement at the build-up and then excitement at the end when it was announced where I was going to start work. So, let's call it a year and if you have an argument with that well you can refer to it as nine months or the gestation period roughly for a human being.

That summer break must have been a slow moving and long one as I couldn't wait to leave home. That doesn't mean that I disliked being at home, but I just wanted to get on with the next part of my life and that existed over 80 miles away at Harlow in Essex.

I had a car; I was one of the few people at college to have a car. My paternal grandparents bought me a second-hand mini. I grew eventually to love it but at first it scared me, if you can be scared of a car. The problem was I wasn't and still am not a natural driver. Unlike some people I don't enjoy driving and I find driving in traffic very stressful despite having driven in many different countries.

I think my grandparents must have bought me a car to mark the passing of my driving test, although I seem to remember having it earlier when I believe my father would go out with me, probably under sufferance. A bit like when I was learning to ride a bike and he ran behind me as I pedalled up the road and suddenly realised, he was no longer there, and I was still on the machine. It never crossed my mind that being a smoker and not playing any sport, he would soon have run out of puff anyway. As far as the car was concerned, I always thought there was considerable danger involved in going out with a novice driver who could make a mistake at any time. My driving instructor – a Mr Bond – had a dual control car which meant if I made a complete mess of things, he could slam the brakes on or grab the steering wheel. Thankfully he never had to.

He taught me to treat every other road user as "an idiot." When somebody did something wrong on one of our lessons he would say "Ye Gods and Little Fishes". Ever since I have treated every other road user as an idiot, having to think both for myself and for them. Sometimes I fear, however, that it is me that is the idiot.

I failed my first test, although I can't remember exactly why. But I passed second time. I remember being too nervous to go out on my own and the car sat outside our home for about three days before I realised I really did have to go for it. So, I drove about three miles up the road, turned round and came back to recover and stop shaking. It seems ridiculous to me that I once had this response to an activity I no longer think twice about doing.

Things must have got better after that as I remember driving back and forth to college. Initially I didn't take the car with me. So fast forward to my first day at college which quite set the tone for the coming weeks and months.

I was given a lift by the other Peter's parents. I think we ate in a restaurant somewhere before going to the college for the first time. That afternoon was spent being driven around Harlow New Town (it was still referred to as a new town despite being in existence for over a quarter of a century). The drive around was for two reasons. Firstly, it showed us the town and secondly we were then all individually dropped off where we would be staying for the next nine months.

After that drive round, two of our number went home and never returned. I have no idea how they could make up their mind so quickly that they wanted out. Perhaps it's because I didn't think along those lines. I was too enthusiastic about what was ahead and the possibilities of being away from home were so intriguing. I later experienced this inability to come to terms with the future again when we took our eldest son to his new flat in Eastbourne ahead of him starting a degree course at Brighton University (Eastbourne Campus). His friend came with us to start the same course, lasted a few days and returned home. Our son stayed the course if you will pardon the pun and still lives on the South Coast and probably always will.

But this is my story and so back to my introduction to college life. A number of the students, and there were probably about 30 of us from various parts of the country, were dropped off at the YMCA or was it the YWCA – not that it made much difference whether it was the Young Men's or Young Women's Christian Association it was always referred to as the Y. These people had their own room and more or less looked after themselves. I'm not sure how they were chosen for the Y as I don't think we were asked beforehand what kind of accommodation we wanted. It was all probably pot luck.

And so, we went on our tour with more and more people being dropped off. We finally got to a road called The Maples and my name and that of another guy from Norwich was called out and there we were at 123 The Maples to be met by a very tall and glamorous young lady and two very young children.

Some of our number found themselves living with elderly people. We found ourselves living with a young family and was that a culture shock for an only child from Norfolk?

I think the owner Sonia was either 30 or in her early thirties – in other words little more than 10 years older than myself. Her children – a boy and a girl – were four and six. Suddenly I was thrust into a family situation and the kind of situation I had never encountered before, and I absolutely loved it and thrived within it.

I regularly rang home to talk to my mother and she thought I was homesick. I wasn't in the slightest and made myself go home every two or three weeks when I would rather have stayed in Harlow. My return home usually co-incided with Norwich City home games.

I think the nine months could be divided into the educational and the social. The educational meant studying British Constitution, journalism, journalism law, shorthand, politics and much more in the classroom. The social side – well I will get to that shortly.

The following day after the drop off was our first at college. The group was divided into two classes in two separate classrooms and we sat in a square with tables in front of us. It was a little like being back at school, but the difference was we were free to leave at any time, but nobody did because this was our future.

Financially I was relatively well off. I received a grant from Norfolk County Council. These were the days when they paid you to go to college and not the other way round. In addition, I was given a salary of an equal amount by my sponsors and employers Eastern Counties Newspapers. Half of my income covered my lodgings and outgoings, and the other half was for fun. In addition, every day all six of us sponsored by ECN received rolled up copies of the Eastern Daily Press and Eastern Evening News newspapers. We rarely read them. Sometimes we had a fight with them though. I suspect that at this time we weren't all that interested in what was happening back in Norfolk – apart from for me the fortunes of Norwich City of course.

On the first day we went round the room to introduce ourselves and say where we came from. I sat on the far side of the classroom next to a guy called Paul Sutherland who sadly died a few months before I started writing this. Paul was slightly weird – being obsessed with the music of Pink Floyd. At one point he put a stereo unit in a wardrobe and locked himself in to listen to Floyd. Being in close proximity to the speakers meant he felt closer to the band. I assume he took the clothes out of the wardrobe before going in himself otherwise the sound would have been rather mushy. He used to insist on reading the sleeve notes from Floyd albums to anyone who would vaguely listen to him. Before he died, I was in touch with Paul and pointed these things out.

"Yes I was a bit of a prat wasn't I," he said. He later became a well respected journalist and an authority on matters astronomical.

As we went round the table, I gave my name and said I came from Norwich and then we came to Bob.

"So what's your name" our tutor, who I believe was called Cherry and who was permanently pursued by one of the other lecturers, asked?

"Me," came the reply.

"Yes, but what's your name?"

"Me" came the reply.

This went on for a short while until he probably decided that the joke had gone far enough.

"My name's Bob Mee and I'm from Leicester."

That was the day I met Bob. For some reason we became firm friends. I have no idea why, although we did both like football. Bob could be very caustic, but he had a wonderful sense of humour. Over the years we have sporadically kept in touch and in 2022 met up in Norwich when he came to the city to support West Bromwich Albion in a game against Norwich City. For me Bob's friendship has been an important part of my life and I cannot tell you why. Sometimes certain people are just really special. Bob was really special. Perhaps it's because we shared what was a very important part of my life and memories that are now firmly inside me.

I still look upon him as a friend despite the day that he really took the Michael out of me. Every Wednesday we were given the morning off to go to Harlow Sports Centre to play football or, if you didn't like football or sport, you could do something else, like stay in bed and sleep. On this particular morning there had been a lot of rain and so the football pitch was unplayable.

We were told that we could go into the sports centre and play an indoor game.

"Do you play table tennis? Bob asked me.

"Yes, a little bit," I replied trying to put a horrible evening in East Grinsted out of my thoughts when I had gone to visit some distant relatives and been told to join their boys in a garage where they were playing table tennis only to find they didn't want me there and only let me play one very short game.

"Can you show me how to play and teach me the rules?" Bob asked.

"Ok," I replied explaining how you served, how many points constituted a game (21 in those days. Now I think it's 11), how to hold the bat etc etc. I dropped short of explaining how to put spin on the ball thinking that would be a bit advanced for his first try at the sport.

I suggested we just hit the ball back and forth until he got the idea of the game. I decided just to gently hit the ball to him. So off we went. I hit the ball to him and he hit it off the table on the side. I hit another and he hit it so hard it hit the back wall. This continued for a short while.

"Can we try a game?" he enquired.

"I'm not sure that's a good idea until you can get the ball on the table," I replied, trying to be kind as I always try to be kind.

"Let's just have a go anyway," he said.

I served the first ball slowly and flat to him and back it thundered past me. This time Bob had hit it onto the table. The second went the same way.

"You've been pulling my plonker. You can play table tennis," I said.

"Yes, sorry I'm a Leicestershire county player," he replied.

We did play a couple of sets. I think he won 21-4, 21-2 or something like that. I didn't ask him for lessons though and I can't say I was angry. In fact, for some reason, I found it amusing. Bob has apologised for that over the years and when we met up in 2022, he apologised again and used the same words as Paul Sutherland.

"In those days I was a bit of a prat." I didn't disagree.

After that we went to pubs together, went to football matches together, but we never played table tennis again, primarily because I've never been that good at it.

After our introductions we all got to know one another by undertaking regular pub crawls and meeting up in the centre of the town in the evenings. The problem there for me was I lived the best part of two miles away from the college. That wasn't a problem once I had brought my car back with me. In those days the central car parks in Harlow were free and parking was easy. This has long stopped being the case.

A walk to college took about 45 minutes, so I often took the car although on occasions, when we were walking, one of the lecturers stopped and gave us a lift. On a couple of occasions when we were wandering home late after a night out the police stopped and when we told them we were journalism students they gave us a lift home.

Our lecturers were an interesting bunch. There was Ted Ware who was very much a disciplinarian and tried to teach me shorthand. I say tried because learning shorthand was akin to learning a foreign language for me. I did manage to learn a kind of shorthand and still use it today, but I had a problem with it as I found out one day.

Pitman shorthand outlines differ according to whether they are placed above the line, on the line or below the line. Once you start using shorthand the position doesn't matter much because you know what the word is according to the sentence it is in and its general sense. But when you are learning you are expected to get things right (or should that be write) and there were tests to ensure you did.

On one test I had a couple of outlines marked as wrong when I was sure they were correct. I took it up with Ted Ware and, after a discussion, we came to the conclusion we were both correct. He was correct because I had put the outlines on the wrong part of the line, but I was correct because the vowel sounds of a Norfolk man are not the vowel sounds of people from other parts of the United Kingdom. For instance, in those days, I used to pronounce roof (ruff). Actually I probably still do.

Other lecturers included the very tall and willowy Wilf Graham who had previously been a drugs officer in the Metropolitan Police. Wilf was a great guy who might have taught law or might have taught British Constitution, I cannot remember exactly which, but I think it was the latter.

We had Wilf for the last period on a Friday afternoon. He was aware that the people from Norwich had the furthest to go if they wanted to go home for the weekend. Virtually every week he would say.

"If the Norfolk people would like to go to the toilet and then accidentally forget where the classroom is and find themselves at the exit instead, nothing will be said."

We often did lose our way deliberately and take an early dart, even if we were staying in Harlow for the weekend.

Then there was a politics lecturer that we named Red Mole. I cannot remember what his real name was. We thought he might well be a communist, hence the Red part but he also stared at us from behind a large moustache and through a pair of very thick bottle glasses which made him look like a near sighted mole (or should that be a far sighted mole?).

Then there was Joe Barrett who probably deserves a chapter on his own, but I will keep it relatively short. Joe Barrett was a big guy. Joe Barrett was a big loud Scottish guy who had worked on numerous national newspapers – some of which weren't necessarily wholesome.

He immediately told us that we needed to be "operators". At first, I thought he meant we needed to go to medical school, but he was actually talking about a brand of journalism. This was so far away from the brand of journalism I was interested in. I always like to look at the true meaning of words and to me a journalist was/is somebody who keeps a journal. In other words, somebody who records what is happening or taking place. Being an operator meant an aggressive style of journalism that I didn't want any part in but which I got involved with later in my career – and I hated every minute of that as you will find out.

Joe Barrett had a bad back and had an annoying habit of opening the door and putting his hands on the top and then bending his back. Don't think it worked because the next day his back ached just as much, and of course true operators are far too hard to go to the doctors. Ironically one of the other journalist lecturers was also called Joe Barrett and certainly two Joe Barrett's were never better than one. Our Joe Barrett apparently had a large family and he would often mix his post as a journalism lecturer with an overnight stint as a sub editor on a national tabloid. He needed the money. I found this out not so long ago when I re-established contact with another student who I looked up to. This guy was a real operator and the coolest kid on the block. He copped off with a fellow student on the first day of our course. I recently told him how cool he had been.

"You were the cool one because you had a car," he told me. I don't think anyone has ever called me cool before or after that. When it comes to coolness, well I'm not really there although I was once told that I have bedroom eyes. I wasn't sure at the time just what this meant as I felt that most of the time they were a touch bloodshot! But back to Joe Barrett.

Our Joe Barrett went on and on and on about the importance of a good contacts book. Of course, today contacts are put into a mobile phone and little black books have become redundant in the same way as Filofaxes have. My how the world has changed.

These contact books were meant to be full of names, addresses and telephone numbers of essential contacts like the Prime Minister, the President of the United States of America and George Best. Of course, none of us would ever need those numbers but it was always good to have them just in case.

Winding up Joe Barrett wasn't a good idea either. We got to the point in the course where we had to undertake what are known as Vox Pops. This meant simply going out into the town centre and asking members of the public for their views on a given subject and then returning to college and writing a story from it. All well and good. That is until Joe Barrett asked us to give him a subject we could tackle. It was all part of his idea of democracy, letting us choose the subject. Unfortunately, somebody shouted out primarily as a joke, "How about birth control?"

And so we were sent out into the middle of The High (that's the name given to the town centre) to ask people about what methods of birth control they used! Thankfully I came across my landlady and her friends and so explained what was going on and they gave us some comments. After that we didn't mess with Joe. We could of course have made the comments up.

Joe would like to have messed with Cherry though and he made no secret about it. I think both were married and Cherry certainly wasn't interested in any way. It became quite embarrassing (Joe's behaviour that is).

The head journalism lecturer was Bill Hicks who had previously been sports editor at the Daily Express. He was a regular guy whom we liked. He knew Norfolk well and had a flat on Cromer seafront and we visited him there after leaving college. I still think of Bill every time I pass that block of flats and many years ago, we even considered buying one – but that wish only lasted for a very short time.

Three other lecturers I remember with a decent amount of affection were Brian Downey, Ted Mawdsley (he of the lifts to college) and Frank (I've forgotten his surname it may have been Warner and it may have been Warren, although I'm very aware that the latter is the name of a boxing promoter) who spoke with a distinctive Bristolian accent, probably because he came from Bristol. I'm sure some time after this book is published that I will wake up in the middle of a night and remember his name.

We had one very weird weekend when about 10 of us stayed at Brian Downey's flat. He used to hold what he called T Groups which were strangely early seventies self-assessment thingies where everyone was taught to be a team and trust each other. He had people standing in a circle and one person would stand in the middle and turn round a few times and then fall backwards safe in the knowledge that he trusted his or her teammates to catch him or her.

We did point out that it wasn't a matter of trust but one of strength. However much you trusted each other you couldn't expect an eight stone girl to catch a 14 stone boy.

We all spent the weekend talking about ourselves at Brian's and drinking lots of beer or it could have been wine. I think I may have slept in the bath. Although it did sound weird you must remember that this was just after the swinging sixties and just into the sensationally open seventies. Essentially it was fun but there were a few concerning moments but nothing that we couldn't handle..

They may have been sensational, but they were troubled times. We had the four-day week, strikes galore and lots of unrest (a bit like our current times as I write this shortly after COVID lockdown). It made things interesting and enjoyable in a strange way. Many of us would congregate in a pub that had lights and when those lights went out, we would move to another pub. We did that until we realised that drinking beer by candlelight was quite enjoyable.

I don't remember Harlow being a particularly violent place, although I know it now has quite a few social problems. We had the protection of the local Hell's Angels' chapter, and it all came about following a party at 123 The Maples. My landlady was very broad minded and was happy for us to have parties if she was away, providing we cleared up any mess and paid for any breakages. I think we might have asked the neighbours round to negate any problems with noise etc. I'm sure none of them ever came.

One of our fellow pupils was a Hell's Angel and self-confessed football hooligan in the days when football hooliganism was rife. This guy came from Ipswich, which is in Suffolk, the next county to Norfolk. There has always been a rivalry between the two counties and not necessarily a healthy one. This guy was an Ipswich Town supporter, and I was/am a Norwich City fan and this was in the days when things could get quite violent.

We were on friendly terms, but he was quick to point out that if he ever saw me at a football match all friendship would go out the window. This was the equivalent of a threat. Thankfully we never did meet at a football match. And yet again I have been in touch with him quite recently and you can probably guess what his response was:

"Yes, I was a bit of a prat in those days."

Wouldn't it save time if we could admit to being "a bit of a prat" when we were younger and not wait until decades later to obtain this realisation?

This guy turned up at our Saturday evening party with the leader of the local Hell's Angels' chapter. Not surprisingly they pitched up on a motorbike. The head of the Hell's Angels turned out to be a Canadian woman. She spent the evening talking to everyone and at the end said how refreshing it had been to spend the evening with intelligent people as opposed I guess to spending it with unintelligent and at times brutal Hell's Angels. I'm sure there were some intelligent Angels.

Before she left, she gave us all a phone number.

"If you are ever in any trouble in Harlow, just find a phone and give this number a ring and I'll get the boys out to help you."

As far as I know nobody ever had any use for that number.

But my Hell's Angel journalism mate is now like everyone else elderly and no longer a Hell's Angel.

So that's three people from the course who subsequently admitted that they were prats. So was I a prat as well?

Not according to Bob when I asked him that question:

"No, you were one of the few people who were normal." I have never been quite sure what that meant and whether being called normal is a compliment or not, but I'll take it. There is of course a term "Normal for Norfolk" which is a rather derogatory label which means anything but normal.

You could say I flew with life at college. I loved every minute although towards the end I know most of us were becoming tired of lessons and just wanted to get on with the world of work, after all we had all come straight from school where it was lesson after lesson after lesson. I think the social skills I learnt at college and the experiences I had were far more important than the lectures. I read a lot, I drank a lot (a lot for me that is), I partied a fair amount and I made some good friends, some of whom I am still in touch with over half a century on. We had a reunion a few years ago which I attended. Another was scheduled for 2022 but went ahead without me when we got stuck in a tailback from a serious accident on the A11 which meant we couldn't get to Harlow. Other reunions are already on the cards.

I loved being a part of a family and there was a never-ending number of lodgers who booked in. I think we practically had the upstairs part of the house. There was the middle-aged Irish guy from Manchester who was so homesick we had to almost guide him through his stay there. There was Ted and Wally and I know not from where they came and where they went back to or what they did. But they were only there for a short time. They were in their mid-20s which I thought to be very old at the time.

Then there was Marcia whom I went out with for a while and I'm ashamed to say that when she left, I didn't say goodbye – something I have always regretted as it wasn't very friendly, and I presume I felt I had something more important to do. I often wondered if I had said goodbye properly whether we would have kept in touch. I did try to contact her after we had left to apologise but got no response.

And there was Veronica who worked on lighting at Harlow Playhouse and whom I was very jealous of because she met David Bowie, although she did say he was "really up himself." Veronica had an Hungarian boyfriend whom she wanted me to meet, but the only time he came to the house for the evening, I was in bed feeling crap with a bug of some kind or it may have been a headache which I used to get in those days and I just couldn't drive him back into the centre as she wanted me to do.

One evening there were a couple of us in the lounge when Veronica came down to show us her new blouse and ask what we thought of it. I think we almost choked on our coffee as it was completely see-through, and she didn't have a bra on. Well, these were the enlightened years of the early 1970s. She was extremely well endowed as they say and I was never sure whether she was asking for our opinion of the blouse or something else.

"What do you think of the blouse. I bought it today," she said.

Do you know I can't remember our response. I think we just asked her if she wanted a cup of coffee. I don't even remember what the blouse was like. At least I didn't accuse her of being fat like a previous female I have already mentioned.

Our landlady was very generous and often took us out to the local Chinese restaurant where I insisted on eating English – anything with chips. Looking back what a waste that was. Today I love Chinese food but in those days, I was still suffering from my father's taste in food which was totally basic. No salad, no sauce of any kind, no vinegar, gravy without onions and nothing that might be tasty and interesting. That was how I was brought up. My mother was never allowed to cook anything with spices or herbs. Mind you I adored her late-night fritters which she would make around 9 pm and which consisted of big wedges of potato dunked in batter and then fried and served with salt and vinegar. It makes my mouth water just thinking of them. It was a bit like getting scraps from the local fish and chip shop which was just down the road. They were crispy, crunchy and lovely with vinegar and salt but probably dripping full of cooking oil and very fattening and unhealthy, particularly if eaten late in the evening and just before bed time.

On a couple of occasions our landlady asked us to stay away from the house until 11 pm. She gave us money for a meal, and we went out straight from college, had something to eat, went to see a film and then had a couple of pints. We soon realised that this might have something to do with benefits and visits from tax inspectors. The next day it would be back to usual. Mind you I don't know how she fitted everything in. She was a single parent, had a full-time job as a teacher, looked after and cooked and washed for any number of lodgers and still seemed to have time for a social life, although she did get stressed and quite short tempered with the children at times. Later in life I was able to appreciate how demanding and difficult young children can be.

I remember a few films from those days. There was "Clockwork Orange" and "The Devils" both of which were quite shocking in their own way and then there was "The French Connection" with Gene Hackman, "Straw Dogs" which was a violence fest with Dustin Hoffman and Susan George and the much mushier "Love Story" – the music for which I still play on the piano to this day.

Music played a big part in my year at college. One of the guys on our course, Steve Clarke, was in charge of booking bands and I saw America, Medicine Head and many more including an awful group called Hieronymous Bosch (named after the artist) and another one called Cochise (named after an Apache chief). To be fair to Steve, I don't think he was responsible for the last two of these.

But one concert at Harlow Technical College changed my music taste for ever. Steve told me he was putting on a band one Saturday night named Barclay James Harvest and would I go along. Originally, I had planned to go home but he emphasised how good this band was. So, I changed my plans and went along.

I knew there were a couple of support acts, so I got there nice and early. The first band came on and they were terrible. Then I thought BJH would come on but no it was another support band, and they were terrible. The next band must be BJH. I had no idea what they looked like or what kind of music they played. On came a band and they were terrible. I thought about giving up and going home, but I soon became glad that I didn't.

Mel Pritchard (drums), Les Holroyd (bass guitar), John Lees (lead guitar) and Stuart "Woolly" Wolstenholme (keyboards) were Barclay James Harvest and they were magnificent. They have been my favourite group ever since in spite of the fact that they split into two. Sadly, Wolstenholme committed suicide many years ago. They played what could be termed symphonic progressive rock. At that time, they had released two albums (LPs) and the next day when the local record shop was open, which would have been the Monday, I went out and bought those two albums (Barclay

James Harvest and Once Again). The latter is my favourite album of all time and "Mockingbird" from that album is my favourite track ever. I have seen them numerous times since but the magic of that first concert has never been surpassed. Thanks to the internet I have actually been able to date it. It was at Harlow Technical College and on November 13th, 1971.

I also went to see David Bowie at Harlow Playhouse – the day that Veronica met him. It was one of his first gigs as the character Ziggy Stardust and we got Bowie on his own with a guitar and piano in the first half and then with the band The Spiders From Mars after the break. This was without doubt my favourite rock concert of all time and I don't think it will ever be matched because it was in the years when music could amaze, and rock music seemed to be in its infancy, both fresh and vibrant.

I listened to a lot of music that year and still hold it as my favourite year ever. I had a Dansette player on which we played the discs. My landlady particularly liked Richard Harris' Love Album which I suspected she played regularly when we weren't there. I was a kind of closet Richard Harris fan (and I am talking about the Irish actor here). There was another guy on our course who loved Harris as a singer. I think we kept it as a little secret between us. It wasn't something you brought out into the open. I still love his interpretations of the songs of Jimmy Webb – probably my favourite living composer (other than Paul McCartney of course).

Memories are strange things in many ways. My favourite Harris track is his version of MacArthur Park. I can prove what an anorak I am by stating that I have over 100 versions of MacArthur Park. I vividly remember MacArthur Park being played on the radio whilst I was helping my mother with the washing up in our kitchen a few years previous. One piece of trivia here. Harris sang MacArthur's Park adding an s to the title. The composer Jimmy Webb never tried to change this. Apparently, you didn't mess with Mr Harris. The duo often went on benders where they lost whole days, probably as a result of drink and drugs. I always helped my mum to wash up. She did the washing and I dried but I can say without much fear of contradiction that when it comes to writing I haven't dried up since.

Towards the end of my days at college there were exams. These were what I might call silly exams because we were given the questions. Well actually we weren't given the specific questions that would be asked but a number from which they would be picked. So as long as you prepared an answer to every possible question you couldn't fail – and I didn't although we did tend to study late at night whilst sitting on the toilet. No, we weren't nervous it was just that every other room in the house was used as a bedroom and so the loo was the only one available without disturbing others. That's how many lodgers there were in a relatively small house. As

I write this, I can still remember the lovely warm smell of that house. I actually had dreams of living there again long after I had left. That's how much I enjoyed being there.

The only thing that dragged me homewards in those days was going to watch Norwich City as I've already mentioned. The 1970/71 season was a pivotal one for the club and saw it win promotion to the top tier of the English League for the first time in its history. That was Division One in the days long before the Premiership. I went to London to see Norwich play on a number of occasions, notably at the Den for the game against Millwall which ended in a considerable amount of crowd trouble that I thankfully avoided but I still remember the impassioned plea by the guy on the PA system for people to stop fighting and "destroying our great club." The club he was referring to was obviously Millwall and not Norwich. Even today Millwall fans still have a chant along the lines of "We are Millwall, super Millwall, nobody likes us but we don't care."

I was also at Orient the night that Norwich made sure of promotion with a 2-1 win. There were big celebrations that night. Unfortunately, I had to miss the away game at Watford that followed due to a ridiculous college trip which consisted of travelling somewhere on British Rail, staying the night somewhere and then writing about the trip. I suppose it was supposed to be a bit of creative writing although I'm sure there wasn't much creative about what we submitted. I seem to remember the organisers of that trip made a complaint about our behaviour, but I can't for the life of me remember us doing anything that could be considered bad in any way.

As part of the course, we had to write an essay or dissertation to use the posh name on a subject of our choice. I thought about doing something on the Samaritans – a charity I was very supportive of and one that would play quite a part in my life years later as I will explain. I probably should have done this but instead I chose the topic "Norwich City – A Religion and a Way of Life." You might feel that this was slightly blasphemous, equating religion with football, but it wasn't. I interviewed three main people – the Bishop of King's Lynn, the manager of Norwich City and an international referee. Two of these were gentlemen and one was difficult.

I stayed at home after a weekend visit to complete two of the interviews. Firstly, I met the wonderful Aubrey Aitkin. Aubrey was a man of God but also a man of football. He was a committed Christian and a committed Norwich City fan and would often bring football into his sermons as Bishop of King's Lynn. I later came across a Methodist Minister by the name of Jack Burton who had a similar passion for Norwich and also drove buses as his main employment. He also talked football in his sermons. He died quite recently. Then I met Ron Saunders, manager of Norwich City. He was renowned as a hard man. I was a very young and raw reporter and was quite overawed. I have no idea what questions I asked but I do remember his short and almost staccato replies which were issued with the famous square and jutting chin pointed firmly in my direction. But at least he was kind enough to give me some of his time.

My third interview was with an English referee whom I chose because he lived in Harlow and he was very welcoming and friendly and the tea cups soon came out. It took me a long time to remember his name but as I sit and write this, I recall it was Arthur Dimond. His name was very apt as he was certainly A Diamond in more ways than one. I have used a bit of journalistic licence there as his surname missed out an A. Again, I cannot remember what questions I put to him. My essay was completely manufactured and of little or no interest. I remember it was criticised and, as I've said, I probably should have chosen the Samaritans.

The subject was a pretty poor one – the idea that for many people football is more important than religion but the two can go hand in hand. I have no idea what happened to that dubious piece of literature. I suspect it ended up in a waste bin somewhere, which was probably the best place for it. On reflection I can't help but think of a parallel comment when John Lennon once said that the Beatles were more popular than Jesus which, at the time of the comment, they were.

Before the end of my year at college I received a letter from my employers telling me that, after finishing my college course, I would be joining the staff of the Lowestoft Journal newspaper in Suffolk. I was delighted to find that friend and fellow-course pupil John Andrews would be working in the Eastern Daily Press office at Lowestoft which would be in the same building in London Road North.

I even forgave John for dragging me into London to a theatre to see Stomu Yamashta and the Red Buddha Theatre Company – something that he thought was wonderful and something that had me utterly bored for two hours, thus proving that we all have different views on the same thing.

As I've already said, I passed all the necessary exams and hoped that these would be the last I would ever have to take but then I realised that to obtain my National Council for the Training of Journalists' Proficiency Certificate, I would have to sit some more and then there were those dreaded shorthand examinations. But I mustn't get ahead of myself, but rather talk about my first real job in Lowestoft in Suffolk as I said farewell to Harlow.

END OF CHAPTER NOTES: There is irony in the fact that while I was at college over 80 miles away from my home, my future wife was studying back in Norwich at the University of East Anglia and living in accommodation at Fifer's Lane which was under a mile from my family home.

Ironically too, we weren't destined to meet in Norfolk but in Russia of all places, but more about that in a coming chapter.

Possibly the most famous person to have undertaken a journalism course at Harlow College is musician Mark Knopfler, the leader of multimillion selling band Dire Straits. Knopfler was there in 1967 and the story goes that senior lecturer Bill Hicks told him to put less emphasis on playing the guitar and more emphasis on his studies. Bill is supposed to have said to him "you'll never make a career out of playing guitar." There are of course lots of similar stories featuring similar rock legends and so it's difficult to know whether this was true or not. Apparently, newspaper editor and so-called personality Piers Morgan also went to Harlow Tech to study journalism a number of years later. But we will gloss over that as I detest the man.

Another amusing incident from those college days featured the two young children of our landlady and her complicated love life. She was divorced and was going out with two men at the same time. Both were called John. One was married and we really didn't like him because he was very arrogant and could be quite insulting. The other John was unmarried and a nice guy. We often told our landlady that there was a future with one of the Johns but not the other. I have no idea whether she listened to us or what happened to them all after we left college, although I have taken steps to trace them on numerous occasions without any success. Incidentally my landlady had a few conversations with my mother. They seemed to get on well although I'm sure everyone liked my mother. In the words I have already used, she was a Diamond.

But back to the story. My Landlady referred to her boyfriends as John One and John Two when she was speaking to the children who were obviously aware of both. John One was the married one and John Two was the single one. One teatime the telephone rang. The little girl answered it and shouted to her mum.

"Mummy it's John"

"Which John" shouted back the landlady?

To which the little girl took hold of the receiver again and said "Is it John One or John Two?"

I think that night John Two, who was on the other end of the phone, realised he wasn't alone in the John stakes. I think after that the landlady received an ultimatum along the lines of either it's him or me. As I've said I never did find out how it all ended.

PART THREE – OUT TO WORK AND MORE
CHAPTER SIX - LOWESTOFT

Many years ago, I wrote a very silly novel which I just called "The Seaside Novel," mainly because I couldn't think of a better title. At the time of the publication of this book, this novel was unpublished.

It was about a young reporter in a seaside town and was actually based on my time working in Lowestoft and was very similar to a book by Monica Dickens entitled "Your Turn to Make the Tea."

There must have been many similarities between Dickens' book and mine because I found myself making the tea on quite a regular basis. That was because of the editor whose name was Cecil Arger but whom I referred to in my book by the name of Shad Greene. One day I'm hoping to get that book published.

Mr Arger didn't engender respect amongst some of his colleagues on the Lowestoft Journal because he never spoke to most of us. What he did was point at you through the window of his office whilst holding up a teapot. This of course meant he wanted a cup of tea. We seemed to take it in turns to chuck a couple of teabags in said teapot and deliver it along with a cup into his office where, if you were lucky, you got a grunt as a token of thanks.

The only time he spoke to me during my time working there was one day when I gave him a lift home as his car was in the garage. I cannot remember whether he said anything meaningful, but I suspect not.

It was different elsewhere in the office thankfully. The Chief Reporter and Assistant Editor who I believe subsequently became editor was George Smallman (who I previously mentioned as sharing a birthday with me although I didn't find this out until many years later). George was a cockney geezer and a lovely man who was so supportive of his young reporters. He used to have great delight in sending us out to lunchtime jobs which he referred to as "boozy dos" because he knew we would come back half cut and then he could make a joke about it and wind us up as we protested our sobriety.

George was very extrovert as well and very much a part of the community rather than being "An Operator." This was exactly what I wanted. Unfortunately, it wasn't possible for me to really become part of the community at Lowestoft as I was there too short a time and it was too big a place, but I did learn plenty from George and the sub editor- a Welshman with long sideburns by the name of Glynne Gwilliam. Many Saturday afternoons were spent reporting on Lowestoft Town Football Club at their home ground at Crown Meadow.

Glynne could be spikey and some just didn't get on with him. I got on with him like a house on fire as we shared a love of football and shared the coverage of Lowestoft Town. I often travelled to away games with Lowestoft, and I covered them for the Norfolk based Pink Un football paper whilst Glynne covered them for the Suffolk equivalent The Green Un. Lowestoft was in Suffolk but looked more towards Norwich in Norfolk than Ipswich in Suffolk. You might not be surprised to find that one of those papers was printed on pink paper and the other on green.

I was also given the remit of covering the arts in Lowestoft which didn't mean anything highbrow and usually involved the summer show at one of the piers. Lowestoft is the most easterly place in the UK. Ness Point has that distinction and Sparrow's Nest is both a park and a theatre. At the other end of town was the Pier Theatre. I went on a fairly regular basis to both during my time in Lowestoft. I believe there's also a Seagull Theatre in the town but am not sure whether that existed when I worked there.

I remember that summer show at the Pier Theatre, the year I worked there. I met some fascinating people like Tommy Bruce who had a gravelly voice and had a big hit with "Ain't Misbehavin." Then there was Kim Cordell, a very large lady with a belter of a voice. On Sundays there would be a variety show with magician Gerald Morter who went under the name of Geraldini.

Tommy Bruce was a delight to interview in his dressing room, always happy for a chat and talking about having his barnet cut, meaning his hair. I also met Lance Percival who was quite famous at the time and must have been appearing in a show somewhere in town.

"Could I have a chat about your career?" I inquired.

"Are you a football fan," he replied.

"Yes."

"Who do you support?"

"Norwich City," I replied.

"I support Chelsea. Let's go and have a couple of pints."

And so we did. I'm not sure what would have happened had I said that I wasn't interested in football.

During my time in Lowestoft, I had lodgings in St Margaret's Road along with John Andrews. We had access to the downstairs kitchen and rooms upstairs. The house was owned by an elderly lady called Christine who was ever so slightly mad and drank a lot. We tried to keep out of her way. She was a friend of George Smallman's and spent most of her time and probably most of her or our money at the bar of the Conservative Club.

Opposite the house and just to the left was St Margaret's Church. I never visited it during my time in the town. Many years later my research has shown that I have quite a number of ancestors buried there.

We used to cook our own meals in the kitchen. My pancakes became legendary – not for their quality but for their stodgy thickness. But enough of my culinary skills. Let's get back to journalism.

I learned a lot from George and Glynne including a need to always check facts. One day I wrote a story that involved a local church and a local vicar. With a sub editor in the office all copy (stories) went through him. He would write headlines, correct text and then design pages and send them to the headquarters of Eastern Counties Newspapers in Norwich where the pages would be made up. Later in my career I became a sub editor myself and learned those skills, skills I still use today in my voluntary work and indeed in the writing of this book..

On this particular day, Glynne queried the spelling of the name of the vicar and asked me to walk down to the church to check what I had written with the name on the noticeboard. It was 15 minutes' walk away and 15 minutes' walk back. I had got it wrong. It's a d and not a t I told Glynne.

"Yes I know," he replied.

He knew I had got things wrong but made me take a lengthy walk to check. After that I always checked names and still do. Of course in those days there was no such thing as the internet to check anything.

Although my silly novel about the life of a young reporter in a seaside town is light-hearted it does contain a number of true stories like the young female reporter who was after a story from someone who didn't want to talk to her. She ran after him down the High Street. He disappeared down the men's toilet. She stood at the top shouting questions at him and then reported that he had no comment to make. He must have stayed down the toilet for some time as she was quite persistent.

The same reporter was sent on a day out with Lowestoft Lifeboat on one of their exercises. Unfortunately, she quickly got seasick and spent much of the trip slumped in the wheelhouse and was very glad to get back on dry land. Two days later George asked her where her feature on the lifeboats was.

She replied that she hadn't written one because she had been too ill and hadn't seen what was going on.

"But that's the story," said George.

And that taught me to look beyond the obvious – another lesson that has kept me in good stead through many years. On that trip the reporter told her story through her own experiences and made it obvious what the lifeboat crew went through every time they launched. I later learned that this kind of thing was the essence of creative writing, a course that became famous at the University of East Anglia. I never took that course but did appreciate what it was all about. I particularly remember the words of lecturer Malcolm Bradbury. It was something along the lines of.

You can report a cricket match by giving the score, telling everyone who scored the runs and took the wickets and who won the match. But that's not creative writing. Creative writing is explaining that the umpire had to take a break because he suffered sunstroke or that the wicketkeeper collided with a fielder due to the greasy nature of the pitch. In other words, build up some kind of atmosphere.

It was at Lowestoft that I first became involved with the Samaritans organisation. I have already mentioned how my college dissertation was on football but probably should have been on the Samaritans. So, while in Lowestoft I decided to do a full feature on the local branch. They were very happy for me to do so, and I met their director and some volunteers at their headquarters which were just down the road from the newspaper office.

The result was a feature in the Lowestoft Journal, shortly after which I was contacted by the Samaritans who asked permission to reproduce the article for local and possibly national publicity. Of course I was chuffed to little meatballs to say yes. They turned the article into a four-page brochure. I never forgot that and a few years later I became a Samaritan volunteer myself. But I'm getting ahead of myself again.

At college we were told to keep a scrapbook of our work. I never did and now I regret it as it would be good to look back on the articles I wrote in those days. I am hoping that eventually newspapers will all be digitised, and I can download some of the stories and relive those days.

Two stories I worked on during my time in Lowestoft stand out in my memory. I believe the first may be the first newspaper story I ever wrote which is probably why I remember it. It was a simple enough piece but one that has stayed in my mind. It revolved around a problem in a series of Lowestoft streets that were narrow but had cars parked on both sides. This made it impossible for the refuse lorries to get down and the drivers were refusing to pick up the rubbish due to this. I can't remember how the problem was solved but I doubt that cars were banned from parking there.

The other story that gave me a lot of satisfaction came when I just happened to be working late in the office one night. The phone rang. I didn't have to pick it up but decided to just in case it was a call for myself from someone who knew I was in the office.

It was from a couple who had been staying on a houseboat which had sprung a leak and was sinking. As a result, a whole family were made homeless and one of the daughters was sick. I went to meet them at Oulton Broad, took them back to the office to give them a warm drink and then contacted social services and the medical services before finding them somewhere to stay for the night. A couple of days later they phoned to say they had found a new home.

That is a very simplistic version of what happened as it was over 50 years ago, but I did get a good story from that for the newspaper, and it was also the first of many social-based stories that I would write. I do remember how unhelpful the local doctors were on that one, basically saying that they couldn't or wouldn't help.

Quite a few of the reporters returned to the office in the evening, but it had nothing to do with work. We had devised a football game using a small ball and creating leagues and cup matches. This could get quite violent as one of the reporters was a big guy. He must have been around 6ft 4in and 20 stone and could really belt the ball. As a result, one of his shots knocked the clock off the wall and it smashed. I'm not sure whether he owned up or not, but I don't think anyone was going to argue with him. I think George Smallman knew exactly what was going on but wasn't about to ruin our fun.

This senior reporter wrote a regular quite hard-hitting column in the newspaper. Because of its content it had to be passed by the editor who of course was more interested in pointing to one of us with his teapot than reading newspaper stuff. The reporter was the only person other than Glynne who had permission to write and design his own page. I believe the column was called Rover.

The editor never made a comment so Big Tone, for it was he, decided to put together a spoof page full of naked women and risqué stories just to see whether the editor automatically passed it as he thought would be the case.

He left it on the editor's desk and waited for its return. It didn't come back. Then there was a tap on the glass and a finger pointed at Big Tone without a teapot being held up. The editor had read the column and wasn't particularly amused, which just proved that pulling the wool over his eyes wasn't quite as easy as we had suspected.

It was whilst at Lowestoft that I began to seriously collect LPs and that was thanks to a second-hand record shop just up the road. I got to know the owner, told him who I was interested in, and he would put LPs aside for me when they came in. I spent quite a few lunchbreaks in his shop.

They say that you should always know who your neighbours are. That certainly wasn't the case in Lowestoft. I heard that a veteran local footballer was shortly going to make his 1000th appearance for the same team – I believe it may have been Oulton Broad. That was some going. I asked the club for his phone number and gave him a ring, explaining who I was.

"So could I come round and have a chat? I enquired.

"Certainly, but I'm at work all day so can it be one evening?"

"Yes that's no problem where do you live?

"I'm in St Margaret's Road." He said.

"Oh that's a co-incidence so am I. What number are you?"

Now in my defence St Margaret's Road was over a mile long.

"I'm at number 209," he said.

Cue sharp intake of breath. He was my next-door neighbour. I didn't charge mileage for getting to that job.

Another memory of my time at Lowestoft was going to watch powerboat racing on Oulton Broad on Thursday evenings, often after we had shorthand lessons. Us young reporters still had to have lessons and our counterparts from the Eastern Counties Newspaper's Yarmouth office came over to Lowestoft for that. So afterwards we either went to the powerboat racing or over to Yarmouth for ten pin bowling which was usually followed by a pint or two (if not driving) in the Cliff Hotel in Gorleston. That's the same hotel that I used to go to with my parents and where I first heard that electric guitar riff by The Kinks on "You've Really Got Me." Again, the miniscule things you remember.

Just going back a bit as a young boy, I also went to a pub on the side of a river at Stokesby which is between Norwich and Great Yarmouth. I believe my parents knew the owners. I once wrote a short story about a murder at this pub. It was in the style of Francis Durbridge whose work I loved watching on television as the plots always had so many twists and turns. My mystery featured the murder of somebody at the pub with seemingly no motive. It's long been lost which is probably just as well, but I still remember the wonder with which I viewed Durbridge's pieces on television. I also connect that pub at Stokesby with Frank Sinatra's "Strangers in the Night". Strange how I associate places with music. It must have been played on their jukebox whilst I was there.

There was a strange co-incidence about the visits to Gorleston. My contemporary Andy Knowles, who was the same age as us but didn't go to Harlow College but joined the newspaper group later, was renting a flat with two others in the town. One was a young person who worked locally, and the other was an older man whom he referred to as Geordie. One day I popped round the flat to pick Andy up and there was Geordie who was none other than Ken – he of the lodger of my grandmother and saviour of my artistic English homework. I'm not sure who was the more astonished – him or me.

Back to the powerboat racing. On a couple of occasions, we met the world famous (well world famous in that sport anyway) Tom Percival who came from a renowned Norfolk boatbuilding family. Tom was later tragically killed in a powerboat crash abroad. The racing was both fast, furious and dangerous.

Lowestoft itself was full of characters. The pub we frequented was full of slightly strange people like the guy with a peg leg who everyone knew as Peg Leg Smith and the prostitute who was of a certain age. My favourite was the parrot which had been taught to swear.

The locals knew all about this foul-mouthed bird and took very little notice of it. But you can imagine how astonished strangers or holidaymakers were when they opened the door.

"F—k Off" said the parrot.

They often wondered where the words had come from.

Then there was the local drunk who had a broad Scottish accent and was known as Bluebird because he had a bluebird tattooed on his forehead. He regularly appeared in court on various charges. One of our jobs, and a job particularly for young reporters, was to cover magistrates' court which was on the same road as the back entrance to our newspaper office. So, it took less than a minute to get there. I remember the police prosecutor was an Inspector Russell Balls who later became a Superintendent. I always thought it an amusing name and wondered if his middle name was Of as in Russell Of Balls!

I remember one day Inspector Balls was prosecuting Bluebird who, as usual, was claiming his innocence, despite being identified by a witness.

"It weren't me sir," he said.

"I wasn't there sir. If I wasn't there sir how could I possibly be identified as being there sir?" he added in a kind of logical way.

"Perhaps it's because you have a distinctive bluebird tattooed on your forehead and the person who reported you said that the person we were looking for had a distinctive bluebird on his forehead. Now how many people in Lowestoft do you think fit that description," added Inspector Balls.

"You mean having a bluebird tattoo?"

"Exactly."

It always ended with Bluebird owning up and saying.

"Ok it's a fair cop!"

I knew that my time at Lowestoft was coming to an end. It was the custom of the company at that time to move junior reporters around to give them experience of working in different places. Notice always came in the same format.

The editorial director called you up to head office in Norwich and used the same words.

"We think you have got everything you can out of being in (name of place) and it's time to move on."

It usually meant they were moving us as chess pieces around their board.

I was told that I would be moving to work on the Eastern Evening (now the Norwich Evening) News in Norwich. That meant moving back to live at home, but it turned out that I wasn't there all that long anyway, but long enough to experience a little of what it was like to work at the hub of the organisation and somewhere I would return to later in my career.

I have already mentioned my love of local football which was fostered during my time at Lowestoft. I did make a big mistake with one of my comments, however. Playing for Lowestoft at that time were two young people – one by the name of Stephen Wright and the other by the name of Richard Money. For me Wright was much the better player, but it was Money who was offered a professional contract with Scunthorpe. Off I went to have a chat with him and his parents. I believe he lived in Oulton Broad. I asked very insightful questions like.

"How excited are you at the thought of becoming a professional footballer?"

I wrote the feature up and it duly appeared in the Lowestoft Journal. I remember saying to Glynne Gwilliam: "Richard just isn't that good. He'll never make it as a professional."

I was wrong. Stephen Wright never made it, probably due to a lifestyle not conducive to being a footballer. A few years ago, he read one of my blogs which said what I have implied here. Apparently, he agreed 100% with me and in his words had "screwed up" his chances.

But back to Richard Money. He played 279 games for Scunthorpe in two different spells followed by 106 for Fulham, followed by 14 for Liverpool, 44 for Luton, 17 for Portsmouth. That meant he played 465 professional games and scored eight goals. He then went on to manage or coach 10 different clubs both in the UK and abroad. So, Mr Money, whose nickname was Dicky Dosh for obvious reasons, made more than just a good living out of football. Who knew? Certainly not I.

It might be of passing interest to describe journalistic procedures at this time, maybe just as a piece of print history. Remember we were in the very early 1970s.

We worked on our own typewriters. I used my small greeny/blue one that had been a present from my parents. We typed our story on small pieces of paper which were offcuts and usually had adverts on the other side. We would give each story a one-word title and then number each page. The first page would have a word and the number 1 ½. The slip with the heading on would become number 1. Subsequent pages would be numbered sequentially as in 2, 3, 4 etc.

At the bottom of each page would be typed or written the word more to indicate there were subsequent sheets. The final sheet would have the word ends to indicate it was the end of the story. Stories would then be passed on to the sub editor who would mark up type sizes that he wanted them set in along with other instructions and headings and sub headings etc. Beside our desk we kept a metal spike which was set in a wooden base and on this we would keep press releases, our own notes and anything that we might need to refer to in coming days. Every few weeks we would clean out these spikes, getting rid of the older information.

Once the sub editor had marked up the copy (stories) and designed the pages they were collected on a daily basis by a company van who also delivered copies of the daily papers for sale in the front office. The drivers of these vans delivered the copy to head office in Norwich where it would be set in type. In those days it may well have been in heavy metal slugs that were made of metal and loaded into pages which were called galleys. Later things became much more mechanised, and type was set in bromides which was little more than typed columns of paper with sticky backs. These would be pasted onto page templates and then photographed for printing.

CHAPTER SEVEN - NORWICH

I can't say the thought of moving back home filled me with a great amount of joy, but I only looked upon it as a temporary measure. I loaded up my car and moved back to Hellesdon. By this time, I had swapped my mini for a larger Fiat.

Each day I drove or caught the bus into the office. At that time Eastern Counties Newspapers owned a very large building close to the centre of the city. This building had two huge golden ball sculptures at the front. I worked in what was known as the Eastern Evening News Box which was a small closed off compartment in the main reporters' room, although it didn't have a door so was partially open.

There were six of us in this box, so it was quite cosy. It consisted of specialist feature writers, the women's page editor and a couple of desks for a local gossip style column that I would end up contributing to very shortly.

I started by being part of the features team which was quite pleasant. My job was simply to set-up features, go out and undertake interviews and sort out jobs for the paper's photographers. I did this for a short while before moving desks to become part of the two-man Whiffler's City team.

At the time, and some older readers who live in Norfolk may remember this, the Evening News included a daily column entitled Whiffler's City which as I have said was like a gossip column without the gossip. It was just a pleasant section of the newspaper featuring local people and writing it was very easy, very pleasant and very undemanding.

That was for two reasons. I have already talked about a couple of my bosses and it's fair to say that over my working years I have had very good bosses, good bosses, less than good bosses and appalling bosses and I will mention some of them in the coming pages.

My boss on the Whiffler column was Neville Miller – one of nature's gentlemen. Everyone loved Neville apart from the chief sub editor who seemed to dislike him and that was a comment on the chief sub editor rather than Neville.

This chief sub editor seemed to make it his duty to make Neville's life a misery. In addition, he didn't like me much either, although we did tolerate each other. This man was the epitome of Joe Barrett's newspaper operator. He was tall and gangly and wore a waistcoat – a throwback to the days of earlier journalism although he didn't go as far as wearing a visor with the word Press on it. He was a chain smoker and heavy drinker

– neither of which I have ever been. I remember attending a course one day being led by him. I think it was on new technology being introduced into the industry. He spoke with a piece of chalk in one hand and a lighted fag in the other. At one point he got rather mixed up and put the chalk in his mouth and tried to write on a blackboard with the lighted cigarette. Somehow it summed him up. Those of course were the days when smoking was allowed in public places. Smoking was also allowed in offices and often there would be a thick fog of smoke drifting around. How things have changed and certainly, in this respect, for the better. I am sure that my lungs were clogged over the years from ingesting other people's smoke. People of a certain age will remember a night at the pub ended with your eyes watering and clothes smelling from other people's smoke. Smoking used to be allowed on the top deck of buses as well and these had low ceilings, so the smoke just rebounded. Looking back as a life-long non-smoker I can now see how unhealthy this all was.

But back to Neville. As well as being the official Whiffler he was also the art critic for the Evening News covering music, plays and the arts in general. I became assistant Whiffler, and it was one of the easiest jobs I ever had simply because the column was so popular that people came into the office asking to speak to us.

They brought us stories about themselves, about their families and about life in general and we wrote it up along with pieces on local history. It was nice stories about nice people and that word nice has always taken me back to my days at junior school where Mr London would call you out front if you used the word nice. He would then twist your ear which could be vaguely painful and certainly wouldn't be allowed today. But Whiffler's City was nice stories about nice people and would never rock any boats.

It was all so easy that each day we would produce a set number of stories for the next day's paper. Often the number of pieces we wrote would exceed what we needed, so we just popped some of them in a drawer to give us a start for the following day.

I don't remember Neville Miller ever raising his voice or being nasty with anyone. He was hugely respected on the arts scene and was a fan of amateur drama, often appearing himself in plays at the Maddermarket Theatre in Norwich (the place beloved many years earlier by Headmaster Andrew Stephenson). But there was a world of difference in the characters of Mr Stephenson and Mr Miller.

Neville was one of those people who made everyone feel important and, when he talked to them, they felt that they were the only person in the world, and he was listening to their every word. That was because he probably was listening to their every word.

Many years later when we had our own children, we asked Neville to be their Godfather and he graciously accepted.

The editor of the Evening News at the time was a Northerner by the name of Bob Walker – another lovely man who I believe was rarely seen without a pipe in his mouth (back to smoking again). His boss was Maurice Beales – an old school editor who you either got on with or didn't. In other words, another man who either liked or disliked you. Thankfully he seemed to like me, although I did give him cause for concern by videoing him when he had imbibed slightly too much at our office Christmas lunch. I think he had been surprised and delighted to have been asked along. I took video footage of him walking rather unsteadily across the road in the Tombland area of Norwich. When he viewed the footage he had a good laugh, thus proving that he did have a sense of humour.

One day the phone rang on my desk. I picked it up and in a cheery voice said, "who's calling the Golden Shot?" to which a very deep voice replied "Name's Beales."

"Oh s—t" I thought. This wasn't good. It was generally known that Maurice Beales didn't tolerate what he viewed as nonsense, but I always seemed to be on good terms with him and he took that phone call in good part and once again did show that he wasn't as stern as he looked with his very small and very dark moustache and swarthy complexion.

One day fate took a hand with my career. Another young female reporter was struggling with her life in general and asked to come back to work in Norwich. I was picked to replace her. I wasn't given the option of saying no, but I wouldn't have anyway as the thought of going to work beside the sea again pleased me no end and I was soon packing my bags and going off to Cromer in North Norfolk. Thus began a life-long love affair with Cromer and the whole of North Norfolk.

There now followed the best years in my working life – firstly at Cromer for a little under two years and then back to Suffolk to work in Beccles for the best part of three.

My time in Norwich had been short but interesting.

CHAPTER EIGHT - CROMER

I loved Cromer and still do. I loved living there, loved the job, loved the people and for the first time felt part of a community. In fact, it was the community spirit in Cromer that probably unknowingly set me up for undertaking voluntary work many years later.

The office was in Bond Street which was pretty much in the middle of town. For the first time in my career, I would be working for two newspapers. At Lowestoft I was employed exclusively on the weekly newspaper with the daily having its own staff. At Norwich I only worked for the Eastern Evening News and not the morning one. In Cromer I would work for both the North Norfolk News weekly paper and the Eastern Daily Press daily paper.

My first job was to find somewhere to live and I'm not sure how it came about but I ended up renting a flat in Corner Street which was literally a stone's throw from the historic Cromer Pier and the beach. I expect I had placed an advert in the local newspaper looking for somewhere to live. We were given free adverts to do this. Living in Cromer you might think I went for long walks along the beach in winter and sat on the beach in the summer. Not so. I can't remember ever going onto the beach apart from going to a very quiet stretch and hitting golf balls into the cliff – which bearing in mind the rate that the cliffs around that area were crumbling was not a good idea. It didn't improve my golf either.

On more than one occasion I went to see people whose homes were about to drop into the sea. This is something that continues to happen today, particularly around the Hemsby area.

The North Norfolk News covered a very wide area of North Norfolk including the towns of Aylsham, Holt, Sheringham and North Walsham. I loved North Norfolk then and I love North Norfolk now. There is nothing better on a bright spring day than walking parts of the Norfolk coastal path – with a short stretch between Morston and Blakeney my favourite. There are vast expanses of open marshland and beautiful sunrises and sunsets. I have travelled all over the world, but North Norfolk continues to attract me like a magnet. You will hear later how I went to live in North Norfolk many years after working there even if this was through having a second home which I guess wouldn't have made us very popular.

I had a flatmate for a short while at Cromer but he never seemed to be there and soon moved on and so I was allowed to advertise for a replacement and had a number of people wanting to share the flat at 7 Corner Street. Firstly, a teacher came along but, after viewing the property, decided against staying there. Later I came across him again when I worked for the Police. He had left teaching, became a police officer and was a sergeant.

Two other people came along and seemed to be ideal as flatmates. And that's how I shared a flat for the next year or so with Clive Whitaker (always with one t) and John Scott. Clive was from Morecambe in Lancashire and John from Northampton. Clive was an entertainments' officer with North Norfolk District Council, helping with the annual summer show and events in North Norfolk in general. John travelled to Norwich every day to work but just wanted to live by the sea. He later got the job as manager of the local wine shop and so lived and worked in Cromer.

There was only two bedrooms in the flat but for some reason there was a third bed in the lounge but none of us wanted to eat and sleep in the same room, so Clive and I ended up taking the biggest bedroom with a bed up each corner and John had the smaller room all on his own. He always slept with his window open, even in the winter when it was snowing and the temperature at Cromer was officially classed as "bracing" whilst many would refer to it as "Brass Monkey weather". In other words, it was cold. One night John woke up to a layer of snow on his carpet. That's how cold it was.

Much of my life at Cromer revolved around sport. Flatmate John, who was almost 10 years older than me and Clive, seemed to be good at virtually every sport. I believe he may have represented Northamptonshire at rugby as a youth. He was a county standard tennis, table tennis, squash and badminton player. In fact, the only sport he was absolutely no good at was golf. We tried to analyse this and came to the conclusion it was because it involved a ball that was stationary, and he could only play sport where the ball was moving or coming at him.

Together we joined Cromer Tennis Club which had one of the best sets of grass courts in the county and probably one of the best in the country. In the summer we must have played four or five times a week and the cost was very small. I worked it out once and it came out as something like 0.1p for every set played. The tennis club was a very good social space as well. Each Sunday they had potluck doubles where members, guests and holidaymakers were paired up at random so you never knew who you would partner.

Around that time there was a variety act known as the Brothers Lees. They were very popular following appearances on the BBC show "The Generation Game." They came from North Norfolk and one Sunday one of the trio turned up and I got pulled out of the hat to partner him. It was very difficult playing as he kept doing impressions of Tommy Cooper and many others. On another occasion I partnered the local rector Derek Osborne – another wonderful man. He insisted on singing hymns during the game. At one point I mishit a serve and the ball slammed into the back of his head. I was wondering whether that was God's way of telling him to stop singing. I was full of apologies, but Derek just rubbed the back of his head and carried on singing and telling us how wonderful it was to be alive. Sadly, Derek died a short while ago. I have no idea what happened to the Brothers Lees and I suspect, like the Walker Brothers, that they weren't real brothers anyway.

My friend and flatmate John was a very good player as I've already said. We often played singles against each other, but I think I only beat him about three times and one of those was when he felt unwell. It took me ages to work out that some games he played right-handed and others he played left handed. He was ambidextrous.

But one Sunday for the potluck doubles, John was decidedly off colour. I can't remember who I was partnering on this occasion, but John was playing with a young lady who I seem to remember was called Charlotte Windows (I have no idea how or why these names come back to me). I have to say here that John was a full-blooded male if you understand what I mean. He used to go to wife swapping parties but, being unmarried, always took someone else's wife!

On this occasion, John's serves kept going into the net. His game was very wild, and I think myself and my partner won. Afterwards, as we were enjoying a drink in the Red Lion (a regular occurrence), I asked John if he was well as his game had been very under par.

"Yep, I'm fine but I couldn't serve as my very attractive partner wasn't wearing knickers and kept bending over at the net," said John.

Often us three flatmates would shop together. This was usually in one of the local supermarkets. Clive was very money conscious often working out which the cheapest tin of beans was. So, one day myself and John decided to wind him up. This was after John had been appointed manager of the wine shop.

On this day he came home grasping a bottle of red wine (remember I was in on this joke) and announced that he had been given 50% off this special bottle of vintage wine. He said we could split the remaining cost three ways.

Clive immediately asked how much that would be.

John mentioned a figure that was approximately equivalent to a week's rent.

Clive spluttered but couldn't say anything as myself and John agreed that it was a bargain.

I think Clive eventually suggested that John should have checked with him before committing to buy the bottle.

We did come clean and told him it was a bog-standard bottle of relatively cheap wine. You could see the relief spread across his face as he pretended he knew that all along.

Clive often shopped at the northern end of the town at an independent shop run by Syd Wild. I often accompanied him there. Syd was a fellow Lancastrian which is probably why he and Clive got on so well. Added to that Syd was a very cheery and friendly man. Years later I heard the terrible news that Syd had been murdered during a robbery that obviously went wrong.

Move forward many years and I had a lengthy chat on the phone with the detective who caught the murderers (I believe two men were involved). Maurice Morson had a photographic memory of the case and how they had caught the perpetrators. They have served their sentences and are back living in the area, he told me. That was rather chilling. Maurice had initiated contact with me through a mutual friend after I had written about the murder in one of my daily blogs. Maurice wrote a number of crime and Norfolk based books and died shortly before I finished this book.

There was another amusing story from my days in Cromer. The newspaper office was divided into two. The front part with access from the main road consisted of the front office where people could buy newspapers, place adverts and come in to see reporters with stories etc and just behind that was the reporters' room with an office for the chief reporter.

Through the back there was a passage with a back door and then two more rooms across this passage. One was the toilet; another was the photographic dark room. The two parts of the office could be locked independently.

Each evening at 5 pm the front door would be locked so anyone still working would leave via the backdoor. It was the job of the last person to leave to ensure everything was safely locked as we all had a set of keys.

Now the chief reporter during my time there is what is generally known as a fuss bag. He was a perfectly nice guy, but he fussed over what was being written. We placed all our copy (stories) during the day in a wire basket. At the end of the day all the stories were put in a large envelope and either picked up by the van delivering newspapers or taken down to the bus station where a bus driver would take them to Norwich Bus Station where they would be picked up. It seemed a very laborious process but one that seemed to work, very few stories got lost. Today this would be an incredibly antiquated system and one that could never take place today with all the technology we have.

The chief reporter would regularly stare at something in the basket and use the immortal words "what's this?" It became a standing joke when what he was staring at was something like a re-written Women's Institute's report.

A day came when I was last in the office (or so I thought). The front office was locked up and it was probably about 5.30 pm. It was the middle of winter and a particularly cold day. I had stayed on to finish a story. So, I locked the door to the photographic room/toilet and locked the door to the reporters' room and left via the back door which was kept unlocked.

Home, I marched. I left the car outside the flat whenever I could, particularly in summer when it was virtually impossible to get back into a parking space once you had left it. I was keen to get into the warm. My flatmates were already there. We had tea and settled down to what probably would be an evening of television.

About an hour later there was a knock at the door. Once inside the door of the flat you were faced by a flight of stairs leading to the lounge on the left, the kitchen in the middle and the toilet/bathroom on the right.

One of my flatmates offered to go down to see who was at the door. A few minutes later he returned with the chief reporter trailing after him. The chief reporter had no coat and was standing in his shirt sleeves.

"Isn't it a bit cold to be out in this weather without a coat. Do you want a coffee?" I asked.

"I'll give you coffee you little bugger," he replied. It was something like that but might have been a bit stronger. In fact, I knew it was much stronger.

When I locked both doors, I didn't double check that somebody wasn't left somewhere inside. I had checked the reporters' room but not the toilet. The chief reporter had been in the loo and of course I had locked him in. His keys were back in his coat which was in the other side. He had been locked in the back-room toilet and it had taken him a long time to squeeze through a window and out into the street. He had then hurried to the flat to pick up my keys to go back to get his coat.

"I'll drive you round, that's the least I can do particularly as you don't have a coat," I said, hoping this would lighten his mood – it didn't.

"At least have a cup of coffee," I replied.

He accepted this offer. Then things got worse. He took the coffee and lowered himself towards an armchair just as I said the words.

"Don't sit in that chair."

I got as far as "Don't" as he sat down in the chair and fell straight through and onto the floor, spilling coffee all over his shirt."

It was a broken armchair that we hadn't got repaired. Of course, we knew that and didn't use it. The chief reporter didn't. It took me a long time and a new shirt to get back in his good books. Not sure I ever did.

Number seven Corner Street was not surprisingly next to Number nine. Number nine was the home of Julie and Richard Davies. Richard was a local fisherman and coxswain of Cromer Lifeboat. More than that he was a very brave man who sadly died many years ago from a brain tumour. Richard boiled the crabs (that's crabs as in shellfish by the way) round the back of our properties and Julie dressed them for their shop in Garden Street which was just around the corner.

Richard was the latest in a long line of coxswains of the lifeboat. The most famous of these was the legendary Henry Blogg who for many years lived in a cottage opposite. I believe this cottage was called Primrose Cottage when we lived there. It's now been re-named Henry Blogg Cottage. Henry Blogg is a great hero of mine. Also, a fisherman, he hired out deckchairs on Cromer beach when he wasn't busy saving lives at sea – and he saved a lot in the days before motorised lifeboats. There is a bust of Henry overlooking the sea front at Cromer.

Of course, Richard knew I worked on the newspaper and so was always happy to talk about lifeboat call outs. The problem was he thought I should know about a call out as it happened. So, at 3 am when I was fast asleep and the lifeboat alarm went off, he just had time to ring our bell and hammer on the door before racing off to the boatshed. On more than one occasion I staggered bleary eyed out of bed to open the door and see him disappearing round the corner. I soon got used to ignoring any early morning door knocks. "Tell me about it when you get back," I said on more than one occasion.

One Christmas, Richard was given a keyboard or something similar. He was desperately trying to play Silent Night but kept getting the wrong note at the same place every time. One night I was having a good old soak in the bath which must have been next to his lounge. The same bloody note wrong time after time after time. I got up, got dressed and knocked on his door.

"Would you like me to show you which note it is," I said. And so I did.

Often, we would open the door to the flat in the morning to find two or three crabs there. I didn't like crab and indeed might be allergic to it, so I usually took mine home to my parents.

One New Year's Eve we had a party at our place, inviting all the local people along including miserable Gordon from Primrose Cottage who never seemed to be anything but miserable, hence his nickname. On this night Gordon came knocking at the door. We didn't know it was Gordon because he was dressed as a chicken which must have taken some pluck!

A few years ago, we went to a food fair at Cromer and Julie Davies was showing people how to dress a crab. We went to have a chat and I explained how I had once lived next door, Julie didn't remember me until I reminded her of the day Richard lost a note and the day miserable Gordon came to the door dressed as a chicken. Then she remembered me. The important thing is I remembered her and Richard. More people in my life story.

It was while I was working and living in Cromer that the me of the future started to emerge. I became a member of groups. I had never been what I would call a joiner. Growing up I hadn't attended cubs or scouts, had avoided going on school trips, never been abroad or gone to youth clubs or anything like that and never had any wish to do so.

At Cromer I joined the tennis club as I have already mentioned. There I helped with tennis week which brought some of the best players in the country to Cromer for a tournament. I helped serve in the set-up bar which was in a marquee. We had some famous (well famous at the time) visitors. I remember serving Ian Wallace who was quite a well-known singer at the time with a very deep voice..

I also played table tennis for a team at Roughton which was a village about three miles outside Cromer. We played in the Cromer League. I think our team was in the bottom division and we didn't win too many matches as we had some very young players and basically because I pretty well lost all my games. I did have a big scalp in the league handicap knockout competition when I beat the number one seed and unbeaten in the league Eric Craske. I have no idea whether he was related to Craske's the shop in Norwich of the Christmas sausages and long queues.

I didn't beat Mr Craske because of my table tennis ability but because of a handicap system which game me a 17-point start over a 21-point set. All I did was try to smash the ball back and it worked. So, in reality to win a set, Eric had to score 21 and I had to score just four. Playing that match, I remember seeing the ghost of that game against Bob Mee in Harlow. I must have been knocked out in the next round as I don't remember anything more about that competition. I probably didn't have a 17-point start.

Over the years I have had a mental bucket list of things I wanted to do and achieve. I add to this as and when. Three things on the bucket list were to run a marathon (see later in this story), have a book published (and here you have it in your hand or on your electronic device and it's actually my second published book after the non-fiction "Hell in Paradise.") and to appear in a play.

So here I was back in the early 1970s joining Sheringham Players. You will already have read about this at the beginning of this epistle. I believe there were two drama groups in the area – the North Norfolk Players being the other. Looking back, I probably joined the wrong group. Sheringham Players were looking for members – I suspect their attitude may have put people off joining.

How to describe Sheringham Players. They were rather posh. The main organisers were a posh couple from Sheringham who lived in a rather large house in the posh area of Sheringham and Sheringham can be very posh when it wants to be, or it certainly could be in those days.

I have already talked about the play I was part of. It was my first stage performance since I played Dick Whittington at Kinsale Avenue School at the age of 10.

There was one incident that had me in stitches. We did rehearsals sitting on a bed.

One day the person at the top end of the bed got up and I fell off the bottom end as a result of their movement. I lay crumpled on the floor laughing my head off in a fit of giggles. The director didn't bother to ask if I was ok but had a go at me because "I wasn't taking things seriously." They may have been correct.

A slight aside here – I have also got into trouble over the years for not taking country dancing seriously but that's another story for another day.

As I've already said that was my first and last time on stage other than in the school production..

Every year Cromer and Sheringham both had carnival weeks. We watched the Cromer carnival from our newspaper office but when it came to the Sheringham one, well we took part. We took part in a wheelbarrow race that I'm sure wouldn't be allowed today thanks to Health and Safety and all that sort of thing. This was a straight race down Sheringham's main street with people lining the route. I doubt that any risk assessment had been carried out.

I seem to remember that we were all dressed as gnomes or pixies or elves. I think we entered two teams. I was in the wheelbarrow and was being pushed along by Malcolm Robertson who later became quite a high-profile reporter on Anglia TV. Malcolm spoke with a Scottish accent and was a proud Scotsman apart from one important point that he kept quiet – he was born in West Runton which is between Cromer and Sheringham.

Anyway, halfway down the course Malcolm lost control of our barrow and tipped me into the crowd. Thankfully nobody was hurt although our pride took a battering. I think after that the race was discontinued in following years.

Whilst at Cromer, the Red Lion was our usual drinking place, mainly after playing tennis or squash or table tennis. The landlord at the time was a former police officer whose name I believe was David. So, there were quite a few lock-ins for regulars, and we were never troubled by the local cops. Sometimes it was the early hours of the morning before I got home although I never drank that much. It was more the social side of being in the Red Lion that was important.

There was one very amusing incident involving drink that gave me a tough time deciding how to report something. I was watching and reporting on a Cromer Town football match. The goalkeeper was having a nightmare. Three shots went through his legs, and he was quite obviously drunk. So drunk that he let in eight goals before the team took him off and played the rest of the game with 10 men as they didn't have a substitute.

Whilst in North Norfolk I mainly reported on Sheringham's Football Team – one of the top Norfolk local clubs. I also remember an annual tournament held for charity and involving most of the local teams. This was often won by Corpusty who were notorious for bringing a different dimension to football – violence. They seemed to have a number of players who were related to each other. Brought a whole different meaning to the words The Family.

*   *   *

Something happened whilst I was working at Cromer that would change my life forever and I'm not talking about work here. Fate took a hand.

Along with two other reporters I had shown an interest in going on what was billed as a British Council Exchange visit to the USSR. I don't think there was much of an exchange to this. As far as I know no Russian youngsters ever came to the UK. They probably wouldn't have been allowed to be exposed to western ways.

We knew that there were three trips during the year and so applied for all three of us to go on the same trip, but it didn't work out that way and I almost pulled out when I found out that the other two were on the first trip, but I had been assigned to the third (or it may have been the other way round). I really didn't want to go on a trip by myself but, after a lot of thought, decided to go as I really did want to go to the USSR having studied its history at A' level.

Now it's a matter of conjecture as to whether I met my future wife in London or in Russia. Technically we may have said hello at the West London Air Terminal where the party met up. I had stayed in an hotel in London the night before.

We always tell people that we met in Moscow, however, and that may have been true because that is definitely where we started to get to know one another..

We visited Moscow, Leningrad (then called Leningrad rather than St Petersburg) and Tallinn in Estonia. It was a time when the USSR was beginning to break up. The atmosphere in Estonia was very different to that in Moscow. The local people wanted independence and wouldn't talk to our interpreter because they thought he was Russian. When they found out he was English they couldn't have been more pleasant. In Tallinn I met some fellow journalists who were advocating independence. Leningrad was beautiful even if a day at the Hermitage Art Museum was a little bit tiring. Moscow on the other hand was rather frightening. We were shown round the Park of Olympic Achievement which was absolutely dripping with gold, power and wealth. A few blocks away people were living in what could only be described as shanty town squalor.

The food in Moscow was terrible. We often had to travel for breakfast. The food would be put out at a given time and, if we were late due to traffic conditions, it would just go cold and eggs would congeal. There was also a lot of cabbage soup. But I did like Borscht which was beetroot soup and very red in colour.

I remember a horrible overnight train journey from Moscow to Leningrad which was only eclipsed for its awfulness by an overnight journey in Vietnam many years later. I also remember communal showers (men and women were thankfully separated) which were overseen by rather rotund and quite elderly women who were very scary.

I shared a room with two other guys, and we got on very well. I remember our first night in Moscow and how dry we were, desperate for a drink but there was no bar in the hotel, and we didn't dare to go out onto the street where there seemed to be hundreds of people in uniform, many of whom had guns. On the train ride we found out that most of these were young men our own age who had been conscripted into the Russian army. That night we could only dream about a pint of cold Guinness.

There was a lot of nodding between us and them on the train. They spoke very little English, and I mean very little and we spoke no Russian. But they did know English football and so a chat would go along the lines of:

Them: "Bobby Charlton good yah."

Us: "Yah Bobby Charlton good."

Them: "Bobby Moore good yah."

Us: "Bobby Moore good yah.

And so we pretty much went through every member of the English football team all of whom were "good yah."

We tried our best to come up with some Russian footballers but the best I could do was:

"Lev Yashin good yah."

They gave me a strange look.

In Moscow we were taken to see what was described as "a typical Russian family."

Strangely in a time when people were queuing up for the basics of life due to serious shortages, we enjoyed chocolate cake, beer and much more. Obviously, this typical Russian family had been carefully chosen and supplied with the kind of goodies we might expect from a British tea party. I don't think it fooled anybody in our party. Did they want us to think that we were just like them or was there a more sinister reason?

The family were particularly friendly towards me and towards the end said it was because I looked like their son who was serving in the army. They brought out a photograph to prove their point. The guy had a nose, two eyes and two ears and a mouth but apart from that I couldn't see much likeness. Perhaps they wanted to adopt me, but I think I preferred living in Cromer to Moscow.

Here I have to bring up the subject of vodka. Russians like vodka. Russians like vodka a lot. Russians drink vodka. Russians drink a lot of vodka. We had vodka in our hotel. Presumably it had been given to us. Being a fairly friendly person and sharing a room with a couple of fairly friendly people, we got to know a lot of people on the trip and became friends with quite a few. It was a nice, tightly knit band of brothers and sisters. We particularly made friends with two young ladies who came from an industrial town in West Yorkshire. One of them had a degree from the University of East Anglia and had lived in Norwich for three years (you know where this is going). She had also worked in the library of the Yorkshire Post newspaper and so had worked closely with journalists.

One night the five of us were together in a room and there was a lot of vodka going around. I really didn't like the taste and so one of these young ladies drank my share of the vodka. Many years later a similar thing happened in Switzerland when we had a load of what was called Heidi wine and I managed to get rid of it to that same girl because I disliked it. By that time, we had been married for quite some time.

I remember on that Russian trip being part of a wind up that backfired. Our group leader was called Liz and was very vivacious and lively. One night we rang her room from ours and when she answered played some Russian dialogue from a radio. She panicked and reported it to the hotel authorities as she had no idea where the call came from. I'm not sure whether we owned up or just kept quiet about it. It did illustrate how things in the USSR weren't quite right then in the same way as things in Russia definitely aren't right now (and that will probably get this book banned over there).

We used to get the local buses in Moscow. It was all quiet and peaceful until the bus came and then it really was the survival of the fittest as we were elbowed aside by elderly women who came from behind us. I called these women Little and Lethals as they were short in height but very rotund and powerful and they would use anything they could to knock us out of the way. We soon learned the ropes and barged them out of the way when the surge forward happened.

That certain person I have mentioned had her passport, money and other documents stolen on public transport. That all ended up with a visit to the British Consulate for an emergency passport out of the country and that entailed filling in many and assorted forms. She also had to sign a document to say that her papers and passport were lost and not stolen – presumably because there were no thieves or lawbreakers in Russia and there was also no crime!

As a result of the loss, we had a whip round and contributed an amount each (I forget how much although it may have been £10). This is a sum I have never had repaid. I should have put it in our pre-nuptial agreement, although we never had one.

The holiday to Russia lasted a couple of weeks and then I returned to my job in Cromer feeling slightly flat after such an enjoyable experience. Now we have a difference of opinion what happened next. I say that Anne wrote to me, and she says I wrote to her. She was training to be a careers' officer at the time and had a coming secondment in North Walsham and wanted to visit me in Cromer which she duly did.

We went to a local pub and got on well and as they say the rest is history. We got married in July 1976 in Yorkshire, but before that I was on the move again.

It was during my time at Cromer that I took my last ever exams (but not my last pieces of learning as I will explain later). I was tired and fed up with exams which had become very stressful, but there was just one more set to pass. I failed 100 words per minute shorthand but passed 120 which is slightly illogical. I almost begged to be put in for 120 wpm and was told that I had no chance of passing if I couldn't pass 100. But I got my way and proved that it wasn't impossible. Earlier I had done the same thing by passing A level history despite failing O' level. I often wonder what it would be like to re-take history exams now that I love the subject as an interest and hobby and not as something I had to do.

I also passed the National Council of Training for Journalist final exams which officially made me what was known as a senior reporter. It was a load off my mind. Before taking the exams (and I remember little about them or even details of where I sat them) I went on a week's refresher course to Portsmouth College.

I think there were two or three of us doing the same thing, but we had lodgings in different parts of the city. On the way down we were feeling rather peckish and so stopped at a service station and had a full meal before continuing on our way. I dropped the others off. This was in the days long before Sat Nav but I guess we had decent directions. I then found my lodgings which would be my home for the week.

It was with a very pleasant elderly lady who told me that I was the first lodger she had and so she was very keen to impress.

"If you'd like to settle in your room and then come down again, I've cooked a roast dinner which I hope will be ok for you. I take it you are hungry," she said.

Of course, I somehow forced the food down and pretended that indeed I was hungry. The food was good but sometime when you have the time and inclination try eating two full meals straight off within about an hour of each other. It isn't easy. A few years later they had an episode of the excellent comedy series The Vicar of Dibley where the vicar eats numerous Christmas dinners one after the other pretending that she hasn't already eaten any as she is afraid of hurting people's feelings. This was exactly what I did, although, thankfully, my dinners only numbered two.

CHAPTER NINE - BECCLES

I got the call up to Norwich to see the editor in chief and I knew what that meant. It meant I was being told that I had got everything I could out of Cromer, and it was time to move on. But just where would I be going this time? I certainly would be sad to leave Cromer. I felt I still had much to do there, but leaving wasn't up to me.

It was like getting an envelope with the words "and the winner is" written on it. I was off back to Suffolk to Beccles – a place I would call home for three years during which time I would get married and buy our first home. It also gave me the chance to say that I lived in Norfolk but worked in Suffolk and went across the border every morning and late afternoon. Another important point, I was promoted to second in charge of the office.

I didn't know much about Beccles. But it soon felt like home and that was in no little measure due to my new boss Tony Clarke. Of all the bosses I have had, Tony was the best of the best. He was just great fun.

You know the saying that when the cat's away the mice will play. Well, if Tony was a cat the mice wanted him there to play. The office was more fun when the boss was there than when he was away although I did enjoy the added responsibility of being in charge of the paper when he was on holiday. From day one, Tony was a delight to work with and I looked forward to going into the office every single morning. There have been two occasions when I have moved from a job, not because I disliked it but because I felt that if I didn't make the effort to go, I would be there for the rest of my working life. One of these was when I was at Beccles and the other was when I eventually left the world of newspapers to join Norfolk Police. My decision to leave Beccles was because the same jobs were coming round for the third or fourth time and I decided it had to be then or never to move. Today the newspaper world is very very different, but I'm getting ahead of myself.

I reluctantly left Cromer but there was no reluctance in taking up the new challenge. It was back into lodgings for a while, staying with an elderly lady who had this strange woolly dog that only had three legs. I think it was a Bedingfield Terrier or some such breed. Looking at the quality of this woman's food I think we might have eaten the other leg at some point. This was a large house in Upper Grange Road which was about 10 minutes' walk to the office. I often drove as there was a car park at the office under an arch leading from and to the main road through Beccles which was known as Blyburgate.

I shared the lodgings with a young PE teacher by the name of Henry. We spent most evenings listening to music on the radio and trying to be the first to guess the name of a song as it came on. We also played a lot of Scrabble and overall, I think I lost more games than I won.

We largely listened to a Radio Caroline reboot station. I had always loved the Pirate Radio stations and you can read more about this later on. I remember there were two main DJs on in the evenings although their names escape me. They were always prattling on about "loving awareness" although we never really found out exactly what this was. One of them also used the phrase "spontaneity is a happening" although we never quite understood what that meant either. The younger one was always going on about what a character the older one was but to us they were just pretty boring. I suspect they might have been high on some illegal substance or other as they broadcast.

I wasn't all that happy in the lodgings and one day a reporter, who was working in the office, told me there was a room going at the house where she was staying which went down to the River Waveney and it was mine if I wanted it. So, I moved about a mile away and this was as different as chalk and cheese. Again, it was 10 minutes to the office but in a completely different direction and very close to the picturesque Beccles Quay. There was a pub on the Quay called the Loaves and Fishes, obviously some Biblical context there. Closing times for pubs in Suffolk was 10.30 pm but over the border in Gillingham which was in Norfolk it was 11 pm. So, if you wanted to continue drinking you just wandered a couple of hundred yards across the River Waveney to the Gillingham Swan. Of course I don't remember doing that!

My landlords George and Betty were a strange couple. I don't mean strange in a weird sort of way but just that they were very much contrasting characters. George was laid back and very quiet. He too was a journalist – now retired. He had been a newsreader on one of the BBC channels and often told the story of the day he mangled up the name of a government minister in a live news bulletin.

He should have said Sir Stafford Cripps but instead said Sir Stifford Crapps. I don't think he had ever lived that down. On the other hand, Betty was ever so slightly mad and very extrovert but very friendly and welcoming – a great character. She loved parties and loved staying up late. In fact, it was almost a return to the scenario I had back in Harlow but with somebody who was decades older than my young landlady in Essex.

This Beccles house was sizeable and indeed did lead down to the River Waveney. There were numerous lodgers whilst I was there including a couple of Swedish Au Pairs who were still learning English.

The food was good and plentiful and after one particularly gargantuan meal one of the Au Pairs said:

"I am how you say in English fed up."

We had to explain the difference between full up and fed up.

On more than one occasion I was hauled from my bed by Betty. On one day I had retired for a much-needed sleep but there was a party going on downstairs and Betty decided that I needed to be part of it. So having only been in bed for under an hour and just drifting off to sleep I was forced to get up again and drink beer (well that's my side of the story anyway).

I lived in four places whilst working in Beccles. When we got married, we put our names down to live in the flat which was attached to the office. We had to wait for some other people to leave and that took some time, but we eventually got in. The downstairs had a smallish lounge with an open plan kitchen and upstairs there were two largish bedrooms. Living there helped us to save money as we paid a relatively low rent which included lighting, heating and all the other charges. It was a good way of saving money.

I remember having a joke with Tony one winter. There was heavy overnight snow which was very deep, and the roads were icy. I knew Tony was in the office as he lived within easy walking distance and so I rang his number,

"Sorry won't be able to get in today as we are snowed in," I said.

"OK not a problem," he replied.

I put the phone down and it rang almost immediately.

"Hang on you're in the flat and there's a connecting door between the bedroom and the office," said Tony.

"Oh yes," I replied trying to stifle a laugh.

We didn't stay in the flat all that long but negotiated a mortgage to buy a bungalow in Kirby Cane or Ellingham depending on how you looked at it. The signpost on one side of the road said Kirby Cane while the signpost on the other side said Ellingham. Our postal address was Kirby Cane, as was our telephone number.

We were in the days when mortgages were hard to come by – the Building Societies weren't lending too much money and getting a loan could take many months and much form filling. But we had a trump card and it came in the shape of International Football Referee and the cleanest man in Tokyo, Norman Burtenshaw.

But back to the flat. One day Anne's family came down for a visit. That meant sister-in-law Joan, brother-in-law Peter and their children – Rosemary, Janet, Kathryn and Martyn. We were all in the flat enjoying an ice cream after a lengthy walk around the town and the common. The car park at the flat was on a slope and we watched in horror as Peter's car took off of its own accord and slipped slowly towards the entrance which led onto the main road.

Luckily, or unluckily depending on how you look at things, the car didn't go through the entrance but slid gracefully into my vehicle doing a fair amount of damage as we looked on in horror! Just one of those silly incidents that I still remember all these years later.

I have already mentioned my wish to be integrated into local communities, something that began at Cromer but which developed further at Beccles.

My boss was chairman of Beccles Football Club and encouraged me to join the committee which I did. I also played a couple of games for the club but by this time I realised that my playing days were over. To be fair they never really started. I remember playing a few games for a firm of solicitors in Norwich and whilst at Cromer signed for a local club, played about 10 minutes in a home match and ended up in A and E at Cromer Hospital to have my shin stitched up after it got gashed in a tackle. I was limping for quite some time with that one and fellow reporter Malcolm Robertson, who played for the same team, told everyone in the office that I had broken my leg and would be off work for weeks. You can imagine their surprise when I limped into the office. When I was fit again I was looking to play for this team once more but I never got picked again.

At Beccles, I raised my first amount of money for charity, although it wasn't technically a charity. I wrote and delivered a sports quiz for a contest between Loddon, Beccles and Bungay Football Clubs. I can't remember who won, although I suspect it may have been Loddon, but the money went to Beccles FC.

There was an incident in a Beccles football match that raised a laugh, although it could have been a serious one. A Beccles supporter went onto the pitch and threatened the referee. The threat came from an old guy in his eighties, and he raised his walking stick at the ref. The league decided not to take any action against the club on the grounds that the referee thought the incident was funny.

So back to our first bungalow. Living next to the office was all well and good but it meant I was always on call. The telephone was linked to the office so I could be there enjoying a beer and watching the television in the evening and the phone would ring with somebody wanting to place an advert for his lost goldfish or something like that. It was also all too easy to go back to the office in the evening to do some more work. And one of the problems at Beccles is lovely Tony couldn't say no to any invitation to attend a parish council meeting or go to an event and most of these took place in the evenings. At one point I think I worked 17 evenings in a row which just wasn't good for work-life balance. It did mean no need to go into the office the following day until around 10 am but I always felt once you were out of bed you might as well go into work.

We decided to move out of the office flat. I can't remember how many properties we looked at, but we were very keen on a bungalow in Nursey Close in Kirby Cane. It backed onto a large rectory which had horses in it. This had a certain attraction.

As I've already said, mortgages were difficult to come by. Norman Burtenshaw was at this time manager of the Gateway Building Society in the town. He sponsored a football competition in the Beccles and Bungay Journal, and I did the work for this. So once a month myself and Norman would go out to present a brand-new match ball to a club who were our "club of the month." It wasn't a great prize and that's probably why we referred to it as a brand-new match ball rather than just a match ball.

Norman managed to get us a mortgage in 12 days flat. He was forever pointing out how fast this had been and we were certainly glad that he had used his influence to fast track us. Anne seemed to be less than impressed which I think was a source of confusion to him. So, we moved into a three bedroom bungalow in Norfolk.

Most days I cycled to work because we had an office car if I needed to go out during the day. This often meant driving to Lowestoft to cover planning meetings. There were other evening appointments that I regularly kept such as covering Holton and Worlingham Parish Councils. Holton is next to Halesworth in Suffolk whilst Worlingham is next to Beccles. When I attended my first meeting of Worlingham Parish Council after my wedding, two councillors waited for me at the door and helped me to my seat. An amusing incident I remember all these years later. They were rather suggesting that now I was married it made me something of an old man (perhaps they knew something that I didn't).

The essence of being a good reporter in a small town is to get to know key people. In other words, in the words of Joe Barrett from many years previous – to build up a good contacts' book. It did make things easy as we would know exactly who to contact for comments on specific matters. The Mayor of Beccles during part of my time working there was a lovely lady by the name of Pauline Wooden. There was nothing wooden about Pauline apart from her name. She was a great friend of the newspaper and had free run of the office. If she came in during the day to see one of us, she would just be allowed to go up the stairs to the reporters' room unannounced.

The office closed at 5 pm and that's an important part of this next anecdote. Each day at 5 pm the two office girls locked up and shouted upstairs "we're off now." We all had keys to the office as the only way out was through the front door apart from into the flat which was a living space.

One day it was very very hot and we had no air conditioning, just a couple of electric fans. There were three of us in the office – all male. Tony had been suffering with the heat and, thinking all female people had left the office, decided to strip off, taking everything off apart from a pair of briefs. Imagine his surprise when the Mayor walked up the stairs. The office girls had let her in before locking the door knowing that we would let her out.

There was a sharp intake of breath from the boss.

"Don't worry I've seen it all before," the Mayor said as Tony tried desperately to put on sufficient clothes to make himself decent.

Tony had a great saying that we always loved.

"If a job is worth doing it's worth putting off until tomorrow. Let's go and have a drink."

Going to have a drink usually meant beer at either the King's Head in the marketplace or the Waveney House Hotel on the banks of the river. There were few things more pleasant on summer days than sitting outside the Waveney, watching the boats go by. There was also a Lido outdoor swimming pool and it's still there. Always good for a dip, although I don't actually remember going there as, at the time, I couldn't swim and that's another story for later in this book.

One day Tony had been to the Waveney on a reporting job and came back a bit the worse for wear. He came up the stairs, threw his hat at the hatstand, missed but didn't bother to pick it up off the floor and announced he was going home. I was living in the flat at the time. Midway through the evening the phone rang. It was Tony's wife Pat.

"Do you know where Tony is? She asked.

"No he left the office about three hours ago and said he was going home," I replied.

She was obviously quite worried as they lived about half a mile from the office.

She rang up later in the evening to say she had found him asleep sitting on the outside loo.

An evening at Tony and Pat's featured a lot of laughter and a lot of alcohol. Tony dispensed brandy in a tumbler. I don't think anyone had ever told him that you just had a small shot in a brandy glass.

Now I don't want you to think that everything with this boss revolved around drink. Tony could be very serious on occasions, and I think that occasion was probably 23rd February 1976. Other than that, it was pretty much laughter and fun all the way. He did get angry, however, when he saw the previous chief reporter, who had retired but still sent in stories, interviewing somebody in the road outside the office. I think Tony thought this was now his territory.

When he wasn't entertaining us in the office, Tony gave talks in and on Norfolk dialect. He was a member of a group of newspapermen known as The Press Gang who went round Norfolk and Suffolk entertaining people with stories. I believe Tony had also written a couple of books in Norfolk dialect under the name of Boy Jimma.

He was also known for playing the odd practical joke. The following wasn't a joke, but it led to pay back time from me.

We were newly married and so kind-hearted Tony would often ask us to do Saturday evening jobs where food was involved. Most newlyweds struggle for money and we were no different, particularly as we were saving for a deposit on the bungalow. So, he asked us to cover an evening dinner-dance that the newspaper had been invited to. It was being organised by the Waveney branch of the Conservative Party. They made us welcome. No it was better than that – they made us very welcome. The local MP at the time was Jim Pryor who was also a government minister. We found ourselves sitting next to Mr Pryor and his wife on the top table.

As the starters were being served, I glanced at the menu. I was the main speaker. This was something that must have slipped Tony's mind. I probably swore a bit. Actually, I probably swore a lot. I jotted some notes down on the menu and managed to waffle for about 20 minutes and then propose the toast to the ladies. I think I just about got away with it although I have no idea what I spoke about. It could have been along the lines of the things you have been reading about in this chapter. I needed to get my own back on the boss, and it didn't take too long for me to find the opportunity.

One day I was in the office when the local WI secretary rang to speak to Tony who was on a day off. I took the call.

"We were wondering if Tony would be the speaker at our annual dinner at the King's Head," she said.

I took details of the date and time and told them I would ask him the next day. I asked what the dress code was for the evening, and they said dinner jackets. They also told me that they wanted him to talk about life on a local newspaper.

The next day I told Tony about the call, gave him the date and time and told him they wanted him to wear his smock, tell his Norfolk Tales and take his dog with him. I had better explain that Tony gave these talks wearing an old smock, a hat and a cane. He took his very clever pet with him and Sam did various tricks.

Tony duly turned up at the appointed time dressed completely wrongly and with the wrong speech prepared. It had been payback time. And guess what he said the following Monday in the office.

"You owe me a few pints."

I think he went home and did a quick change or, knowing him, just toughed it out.

I have mentioned earlier in my section about Lowestoft that I had a pint with celebrity Lance Percival who wanted to talk about football rather than his career – which was ok with me. At Beccles I came across a similar situation, but this was much more unpleasant.

The landlord of the Buck Public House at Flixton contacted us to say that Cy Grant was staying there and would I like to go over to do an interview for the newspaper. The Buck was a well-known pub in the Waveney Valley that was previously owned by Alan Breeze who older readers will remember as a celebrity singer with the Billy Cotton Band Show on television and radio. There was always a clever sign on the main road which said "Don't Pass The Buck".

Alan Breeze was long gone and there was a new landlord. I popped along assuming Mr Grant had been told I would be going to see and interview him. Cy Grant was another celebrity who was big in the 1960s and 1970s. He used to sing calypsos on BBC television.

He turned out to be virtually impossible to interview – only wanting to talk about philosophy and not about his career. I tried to keep my end up as they say but took no notes and didn't bother to do a report for the newspaper. Today I would have turned all that into a story in itself, remembering the lifeboat episode at Lowestoft. The owner rang up a couple of weeks later to ask why a piece hadn't appeared in the newspaper. All he was interested in was some free publicity.

I have mentioned that the trick of working in a small community is to know who to talk to on any subject. Sometimes people were compromised by being involved in more than one organisation that weren't necessarily mutually compatible. Such was the case with local solicitor Ted Gilbert who was also a member of Beccles Town Council.

On Wednesday he defended a yob in court who had smashed up an area of the town, making a point of explaining that the yob wasn't a bad lad at heart. The following day at a council meeting he spoke about cleaning the town up and "driving these people out."

Many years later I found out that this kind of double standards is quite common. I was a spokesman for the police and regularly went on television to say things that on a personal level I didn't agree with but on a professional level had to promote. Of course, politicians do it all the time.

We also liked to wind up our photographer who worked all over the county and came to Beccles once or twice a week. We would put together a job list for him and he would often complain that he didn't have enough time to drive between jobs as well as covering them. We often accompanied him on these jobs.

On one particular day we gave him an impossible list sending him in all directions and leaving very little time to think let along take pictures. What we didn't tell him was that most of the jobs were fictitious. He looked at the list and went absolutely mad. That is until we pointed out the date – April 1st.

On Thursdays, after the week's paper had been completed, we often retired to the Shadingfield Fox for lunch. This was quite close to the Flixton Buck which we did indeed often pass without going in. At the Fox we would play darts and try not to drink too much. It was the relief of getting another decent newspaper out.

Towards the end of my time at Beccles I was on the twinning committee which was planning to twin with the Little Currant - a small town in France close to Paris called Petit Courant. I never saw the twinning through as, by the time it was in place, I had moved 150 miles away for a chapter in my life that I would rather forget but which I must address here. I still have a signed copy of the twinning brochure, however, with a note from the Mayor Pauline Wooden thanking me for all that I had done in support of the town of Beccles.

As I have already said I left Beccles as I feared getting in a rut and being stuck there. It was perhaps just a touch too cosy, and I was reporting on jobs for the third or fourth time – the annual carnival, summer fetes and much more. On one occasion I sat through a Beccles Road Safety Committee meeting which took 20 minutes discussing how many jellybeans should be put in a jar for a "guess how many jelly beans in the jar" contest. At that point I probably realised it was time to move onto something a bit less parochial and a touch more challenging.

I had applied for a football writer's job in Portsmouth but didn't get an interview. There was another twist as well in the fact that Beccles Rotary Club were offering to sponsor me for a scholarship to work and live in an English-speaking country abroad. I often wonder what would have happened if I had followed this through. I could now be living and working in Australia or the USA or South Africa. My sons and grandchildren would have dual nationalities and my sons would in all probability be married to different women. Isn't it strange how we make life choices and they aren't always the best ones? Although ultimately mine did work out.

At this time, I subscribed to a magazine entitled UK Press Gazette. Virtually the only reason for doing this was because it listed jobs in journalism and public relations. I don't know why a particular job attracted me, but it was for a reporter in charge of the Nottingham office of Raymond's News Agency which had its head office in Derby and also had an offshoot office in Norwich.

So off I trotted to Nottingham for a job interview. Again, I don't remember much about it, but I did get the job. From what I later found out I suspect that I was the only applicant. In other words, it was my job to lose and I didn't lose it. In addition, the salary was higher than that I received at Beccles. Unfortunately, my move to the Midlands really didn't work out.

CHAPTER TEN – THE MIDLANDS

I didn't suit the Midlands and the Midlands didn't suit me. Strangely at the same time as I moved, so did other colleagues. John Andrews and Andy Knowles both moved to live in Derbyshire and shared a flat in the Derbyshire Hills. Another good ole Norfolk boy Keith Skipper dipped his toes into working in the Midlands and, like me, found it not to his liking and soon returned to his native Norfolk where he has ever since enjoyed himself as a local luminary writing tens of books about the county and becoming a quintessential Norfolk gentleman.

We put our bungalow up for sale and I moved to Nottingham. Anne stayed back in Norfolk. At weekends I returned to Beccles and, during the week, looked for a new home. She came with me to Nottingham on a number of occasions and we eventually found a house by the side of a canal in Long Eaton which meant once again that I would be living in one county (Derbyshire) and working in another (Nottinghamshire).

From the start of working in Nottingham I realised it wasn't the job for me. I disliked the work and soon came to understand it was completely the wrong choice of job. The reason is I had moved to Joe Barrett Land where operators worked and not people who wanted to reflect and report on their communities. I had no problem with living in Long Eaton as it was quite a pleasant town. It was purely the job and the fact I was homesick for Beccles. I find it strange that today, having lived in the same village of Hethersett for longer than I care to remember, I feel no great affinity for Beccles and feel much closer to Cromer of all the other places I have lived.

Before buying the house, I lived for a while with the photographer with whom I worked and his wife. Bob and Liz Mason looked after me well, but these were hard months for me. I was relatively newly married, living in lodgings again and doing a job I didn't like and for which I was spectacularly unsuited.

So, what was wrong with the job? I have spoken before about a journalist being a keeper of journals and a recorder of life and times. Well in Nottingham I was anything but this. The headquarters of Raymond's News agency was in Derby where the majority of staff worked. My job was simply to send them information of things happening in Nottingham, usually taken almost direct from the evening newspaper. In other words, a lot of what I did was copying other people's work. The news agency was paid according to how many stories it could sell to the national press and the seedier the better. This was a land of sensationalism and kiss and tell journalism.

There was very little writing involved as I was just needed to relay the facts and comments and they would be turned into a story in Derbyshire that fitted the style of the newspaper the agency was selling to. Writing for the tabloid Sun was very different to writing for the Times.

It was very much a dog-eat-dog situation that I never came to terms with. The office I worked in was part of a block in a large house and overlooked Nottingham Playhouse. Each day I would drive first from the lodgings and later from Long Eaton and park my car on side roads. There was nowhere to park other than side roads. The only other possibility was to pay for a car park which would certainly eat heavily into my wages. My salary was a little more than I received with Eastern Counties Newspapers but not by much and I certainly couldn't afford to continually pay for car parking. So every couple of hours throughout the day I had to move my car to another road and sometimes that meant driving around trying to find a space and that was costly in petrol.

The carpet in the office was threadbare and the whole place had a rundown feel to it. It wasn't a pleasant place to work. I can't remember whether I had visited the office when I had my interview in Derby but if I didn't it was a big mistake. I guess I was just so keen to move on with my life that I took the first job offered without thinking about it. That might have been reflected in the fact as I have said that I was the only candidate for the job.

One day there was a knock on the office door. I opened it to find a Police Officer standing there. He tried to give me a court summons, but it was for the previous reporter who had clocked up masses of parking fines for leaving his car on timed roads and not moving it every few hours. It took some convincing to prove I wasn't the person they were looking for and yes my first name was the same but that didn't mean I was him.

"Well do you know his address?" I was asked.

"I never met the bloke and know nothing whatsoever about him," I replied.

I did a lot of sitting around in Crown Court during my time in Nottingham. On one day I saw 10 men sent to prison for life for murder. They had all pleaded guilty and it was like a conveyor belt, a bit like the number of cases dealt with in Cromer, Beccles or Lowestoft but they were for minor motoring offences. Suddenly I became blasé about murder convictions and violence in general.

And that's how it was in the Midlands. When I was working in Nottingham, I think it had the biggest crime rate per head of population in the country and at times it certainly felt like it. I remember being sent out to interview a man whose son had died of a drugs related situation. He lived on a farm. I knocked on the door and was threatened with a shotgun. I got out of there very quickly, found a phone box, rang Derby and told them what had happened.

"Go and speak to the neighbours," I was told.

I don't think I did and told them that nobody was answering their doors. I wasn't being paid nearly enough to be shot at.

Often, I was told to play journalists off against each other. Derby wanted me to be first with a story and that meant sussing out where a telephone box was and, if asked by another reporter whether I knew where a phone was, either sending them in the wrong direction or playing ignorant (which has never been difficult for me).

I often drove around an area if I didn't know it, looking for phone boxes. Of course, this problem doesn't exist today with all reporters having mobiles which negates the need to try and outpace other reporters. I was also told that if another reporter asked for information, I was to take their name and company and they would be billed for it. This went counter to everything I believed in with regards to being helpful.

There was one major national story that I believe I did beat the pack to, and it involved a young girl footballer who was challenging a ruling by the national FA that she couldn't play football with boys. This went to a civil court case where rulings were made about girls playing with boys' teams. Now it is allowed up to a certain age I believe, and the ruling of that court paved the way for the start of an increase in popularity of football amongst women and girls. I remember interviewing chairman of the FA Ted Croker and getting my copy over to Derby very quickly. I think they made quite a killing on selling that one to the national press.

There were lighter sides to the job thankfully. The News of The World newspaper ran a weekly Spot the Ball competition where you had to mark where the ball was on a football photograph where it had been taken out. Actually, I don't think the ball was ever there, a panel of people just estimated where it was and then found the reader who had got the closest with their crosses to the centre of the non-existent ball.

On one Friday evening I was asked to drive out to Worksop to inform a man that he had won the £10,000 first prize and those were the days when £10,000 was a heck of a lot of money. I found the property and rang the bell.

"Go away. We don't open the door after 6 pm," I was told.

I rang the bell again and shouted through the letterbox.

"I'm from the News of the World and just wanted to let you know you have won this week's spot the ball and I have a cheque for £10,000 for you."

"Piss off. This is a wind up."

"No it's not I can assure you. Do you do Spot The Ball?"

"Yes we do but it's a wind-up isn't it?"

I poked the cheque through the door and was eventually allowed in to get details that the News of the World needed for publicity purposes.

So not even good news is sometimes easy to deliver. I never know why it is people refuse to believe something that they have probably dreamt about for a long time. They dream of a man knocking on their door with a large cheque and then, when one does, they tell him to piss off.

There were a couple of other amusing incidents when I was in the Midlands, although one person failed to see the amusing side of one of them.

One was the incident when I was dressed up as Father Christmas in Long Eaton Town Centre and you will already have read details of this.

The other amusing incident was when I played cricket for Long Eaton Round Table against a team from Nottingham Round Table. Having played a bit of cricket in my time, I was asked to open with a Tabler who was a regular cricketer and really rated his ability. In short, he was the key player in our side. I can't remember whether we batted first or second, but I do remember that I ran him out. I hit the ball and went for a run. He was slow setting off (or that's my side of the story) and was run out. Some of the team found it highly amusing. He didn't and I think we lost the game. Again, a similar incident happened many years later but this time I got run out as I will recount later.

There was some fall out from that cricket match from my employers. Technically I was on call to them 24 hours a day, seven days a week, 52 weeks a year and on this particular day I played cricket without telling them where I would be and not being contactable for a few hours. This was in the days long before mobile phones. So, on this Sunday afternoon they wanted to call me out for something or other and I wasn't available. I tried to explain that I couldn't be available to them all the time but it didn't get through and so I think that might have been the point where I realised, I needed a different job.

Throughout my working life I have been on call much of the time in one form or another. Today I often go out without a mobile phone. My sons and grandchildren can't understand why I would do this but there are times when you just don't want to be contactable.

I struggled on at Raymond's. One of the more pleasant jobs was covering football matches and I think sports reporting was one of if not the main part of their business and certainly the most lucrative and regular. I mainly reported on Chesterfield. They have just made it back into the Football League (at the time of writing) after a period in what is known as non-league football which is a strange title as non-league football is made up of leagues, but in those days they were a decent lower league team, always good to watch.

Friends always assume that reporting on football in the lower leagues is much easier than reporting on teams in say the Premier League. I have done both and it certainly isn't the case. In the top divisions, everything is laid on a plate for you (sometimes literally). In the lower leagues you have to go in search. Years later when I was reporting on Norwich City for local and national Media, the Press had our own room. You also had your own reserved seat. There were drinks before the game, drinks at half-time and drinks at the end and managers would come into the Media room to give their thoughts on the games. Requests could be made to interview players as well.

At Chesterfield it wasn't like that. For a start the turnstiles weren't open early and often I had to climb over them with a heavy briefcase carting radio equipment which I had picked up from Radio Hallam. At half time, cups of lukewarm Bovril were put out on a shelf. Sometimes we got them, sometimes passing fans took them instead. We soon got to know the other reporters there as it tended to be the same ones for every game. So, we took it in turns to fetch the Bovril depending on who was free. After the game if we wanted to interview a manager or player, we had to knock on the dressing room door and wait for it to be opened to make our request. Then the groundsman wanted to lock up and so we had to rush through reports and often climb over a wall to get out.

At that time Chesterfield played at a ground named Saltergate. This was subsequently knocked down and they moved to another ground.

A day at Chesterfield might consist of getting there early after picking up radio equipment from a local office, setting up said equipment, doing a preview for a couple of radio stations, sending over regular pieces every 15 minutes for newspapers, doing half time reports and then repeating it in the second half and at the end of the game. There was one thing you didn't have time to do and that was enjoy any of the football. Most of the time you had your head down writing reports or trying desperately to watch the action while speaking through a telephone to a radio station. Thankfully the reporters there always combined to make sure we were all describing a goal in the same way.

The news agency also covered Nottingham Forest, Notts County and Derby County but these were covered either by the sports editor Neil Hallam or one of the two owners who I will refer to by his initials of JT.

One morning I was sitting in the office in Nottingham when the phone rang. It was quite an animated and angry person on the other end complaining about the coverage of football the previous Saturday. This was at Nottingham Forest hence the call going into the Nottingham office of the news agency.

I told the caller that it wasn't myself who had covered the match and it had been reported on from Derby but that didn't quieten them.

"I don't care who it was. I think he was drunk. He was certainly useless, and we never want him to cover another game. The man was an idiot."

Now I had on a number of occasions found that this man was indeed an idiot, but he was the joint owner along with his business partner who we will refer to by his initials KJ. KJ had an unfortunate manner of talking down to me and I presume he did it to everyone else as well as I don't think he singled me out.

KJ would phone me up.

"Have you got a piece of paper handy? Do you have a pen? Then write this down."

Eventually the person on the other end of the phone calmed down enough to tell me exactly what JT had done, and I must say I had some sympathy for him (JT that is). It's very difficult at a football match to hear anything being said to you on the phone. Reporters in those days were often in the open and so the fans shouting and chanting would make it impossible to hear. You often just went ahead with the reports etc and hoped everything was going ok at the other end. I had even experienced this many years earlier when reporting on Lowestoft Town at a much lower level. There was only one phone at Crown Meadow where Lowestoft played. You just hoped that it was free at half-time and the end so that you could read a report over to a copy taker. This had to be done very quickly ready for the local football paper to be printed and be in the shops by just after 6 pm. Once again you would be sending your reports over with lots of noise in the background and not being able to hear anything being said to you by the person at the other end of the telephone.

An afternoon's work in the Midlands would include written reports and live radio reports. Obviously with radio you just went ahead and gave a minute's report. It was different with a newspaper report. You had to go slowly, spelling names and any other difficult words and telling the typist at the other end when a sentence ended, and a new paragraph started. You would do this with a kind of verbal shorthand that saved time e.g "point par" meaning full stop and new paragraph. Often newspapers wanted to put the name of scorers in bold type so you would say something like "scorer Shearer that's S H E A R E R." This would tell the typist to put the name Shearer in bold type and also how to spell the name.

On this Saturday JT had got his newspapers and radio stations mixed up. So, live on air he would have said something along the lines of:

"Derby mounted a strong attack with name of the scorer Kevin Hector that's H E C T O R scoring, point par."

Then he compounded this by rattling off at breakneck speed a piece to a newspaper at a pace the typist had no chance of keeping up with.

I told the caller that if they needed to make any comments, they needed to direct them to Derby safe in the knowledge that if they phoned there the phone would probably be answered by JT and he could deal with the problems of his own performance himself.

I can't say that I really liked many of the people I worked with. The staff at Derby were hard-nosed journos (probably known as Operators). The two owners weren't people that you could like or take to, and the assistant sports editor seemed to have had a personality bypass. The lady who took down information from me was very pleasant however and when I announced I was leaving she said.

"I'm not surprised, you were far too nice for this organisation." I took that as a compliment.

One person I did get on with was the news editor at Derby – Terry Lloyd. He was the brother of Kevin Lloyd who was well known for playing a detective Tosh Lynes in the television soap The Bill. Terry and I became friendly enough for us to ask him and his wife Lynne round to our home for a meal and we had an enjoyable evening.

After leaving Raymond's, Terry joined ITV as one of their main reporters covering news from war zones across the planet. Tragically he was killed in Basra covering the Iraq War. It is suspected that he was killed by what is ridiculously called friendly fire. He was just 50 years of age. Terry was born under two months after me! I often mused on the term Friendly Fire. It didn't of course mean that you were any less dead than if you had been killed by enemy fire but somehow it seemed to be more acceptable. Oh the vagaries of war.

*   *   *

One day the phone went in the office.

"Do you have some paper and a pen. Then write this down," said KJ.

"Get in your car and drive down to the City Ground. They are about to sell Peter Wythe."

Good job I knew about football otherwise this would have made no sense. So, I duly drove down to the City ground, the home of Nottingham Forest. Peter Wythe was a top-class striker. He played 75 games for Nottingham Forest and the rumour was that he was going to sign for Newcastle United, which he duly did.

A number of us reporter types were gathered in the foyer of Nottingham Forest. Now their manager at the time was one Brian Clough. He came through the door in his sports kit. Apparently, he was a keen squash player. He turned on us with a withering look.

Then he went round us individually with the immortal words.

"Who the fuck are you?"

I wanted to say something along the lines of "I'm a human being who would like to be shown some respect as I'm just doing my job. I've been sent here, and I can think of a hundred things I would rather be doing other than being verbally abused by you and anyway I'm a Norwich City supporter and I don't give a fig about Nottingham Forest or Newcastle for that matter."

That's what I wanted to say but I guess it came out as a mumbled name and company.

Next thing I know Mr Clough has got hold of me by the collar and physically thrown me out of the City Ground along with about five others. To date he is the rudest man I have ever had the misfortune to meet (although I can think of one other who later ran him close but I don't think we will go there).

There was no way the five of us were going to go back to our offices without a comment. So, when we saw England goalkeeper Peter Shilton coming across the car park, we went to ask him whether there was any truth in the rumour. Peter was very helpful and confirmed that Wythe was currently in Newcastle having talks with the Geordie club, that was enough for us.

I phoned Derby up and said I had confirmation from a source close to the club that Wythe was on his way and that was good enough for them to flog the story. Incidentally Clough didn't throw one reporter out. It was his mate from the Nottingham Evening Post who he played squash with.

Another interesting story I covered consisted of allegations against the then Sheriff of Nottingham who was an executive of the Nottingham evening paper. He was threatening to cut staff and various other things, and you can see what we made out of that with lots of references to Robin Hood and the earlier very unpopular Sheriff of Nottingham.

Whilst we were in the Midlands, Anne got a job as a careers' officer in Derby, thus being able to utilise her training. She often visited Rolls Royce which is where she was asked a question and thought that she recognised the voice. She turned round to find Margaret Thatcher standing by her left shoulder.

Our social life in those days was firmly based in Derby rather than Nottingham although I do remember what was called a Safari Supper with Round Table which involved having a first course in Nottinghamshire, a main course in Derbyshire and a dessert in Leicestershire. That was three different counties covered by only a handful of miles.

I particularly remember going to see one of my favourite folk/rock groups in Derby. Lindisfarne were good. Lindisfarne were always good but the support act on this occasion was even better. It was a young man from Middlesbrough by the name of Chris Rea. He went on to have a sparkling career, sang about the M25 as the "Road to Hell" and has always been "Driving Home for Christmas" when he hasn't "Gone Fishing." Just a few Chris Rea track names for you there.

Back at work, I knew something had to be done. I was very unhappy and unfulfilled. I continued to subscribe to the UK Press Gazette and saw an advert for an editor for the weekly paper based in Belper in Derbyshire. It sounded ideal and so I applied and soon had an interview at the Belper News.

Before going for that interview, I had a look round the town and it seemed like a delightful place. It reminded me of Beccles in some ways and I instantly knew I could be happy there. My interview was with the sub editor Tim Healey and the owner AC who had bought the paper off the company that owned the Derbyshire Telegraph.

The duo seemed to like me, and I was offered the job and you can't start to imagine the relief I felt when I wrote my resignation letter to Raymond's and shortly after went on holiday to the USA knowing that when I got back there would only be a week or so before I would start work as editor of the Belper News.

I was full of optimism. Sadly, once again nothing turned out as I expected it would. I dreamed of working on the paper for many years and looked forward to selling my house in Long Eaton and moving to Belper. Until I could do that, I drove every day around the outskirts of Derby and into the countryside and onto Belper. At least it was more pleasant than driving to Nottingham.

My main problem with being an editor was the fact that I was still young and inexperienced, Tim Healey turned out to be hugely volatile and walked out when I dropped his regular column which he wrote under the unimaginative name of Sandy Shore. The problem with this column is it tended to be libellous and often just a tirade directed at somebody or other and usually the Labour party.

The owner was a Conservative councillor and he also hated the Labour party. Labour held the Belper seat in Parliament for many years and then it turned into a marginal seat with Labour and Conservative exchanging control on numerous occasions. From 1945 until 1966 George Brown was the famous Labour politician for Belper. He won no fewer than seven elections for the red side of the political spectrum before being beaten in 1970. Four years later Labour won the seat back and for eight years the MP was the delightfully named Roderick MacFarquhar,

Mr MacFarquhar rang the office one day when I wasn't there and left a message to say that the Prime Minister of an Indian region was planting a tree in Belper a week later and he thought it was something the Belper News would be interested in covering. Indeed, it was. I phoned him back.

"Can I speak to Mr Macfarquhar," I said pronouncing his name as it was spelled.

"It's pronounced McFanshaw but call me Roderick," came the reply. I later learned that as well as being a politician he had been a journalist of some note, so we had something in common (not that I would ever claim to be a journalist of some note). I covered the story, and the freelance photographer took photos. I put it on the front page as it made a nice piece for the newspaper – or so I thought.

But no, AC didn't like it and by this time he didn't like me either as Tim H had walked out. How dare I carry a story about the Labour Party on the front page of the Belper News. And it got worse. I went to see two or three newsagents in the town, and they all said the same thing.

"People are coming into our shop to get the Belper News but we are always sold out."

So, what do you do when this happens? Yes, quite right, you discuss it with the printers and decide to have more copies printed. This keeps the public happy and it's also better value for the advertisers as you are selling more copies.

But for some reason this was the wrong thing to do.

"It's good when people can't always get what they want" is all I got from the owner. Then he was named amongst people fined for not having a television licence and I included his name in the list which we published in the newspaper.

Bad move by me. I was sacked. Or more correctly my employment was terminated after my initial trial period ended and I believe that was three months. I guess I should have just kept my head down until such time as something happened with the paper.

There was something else that I couldn't quite work out. It was ok for would-be advertisers to come into the office but members of the public with stories for the newspaper seemed not to be welcome. It wasn't the done thing according to the owner. In my world and, having worked for local papers in Norfolk and Suffolk, it was very much the done thing.

I also got to know one of the local police officers. Sergeant Adrian Evans would bring over the incident book from Belper Police Station and we would go through it to see if there was anything of interest for the paper. We did this over coffee and Adrian was a great source of information which helped both the newspaper and the police. The owner made it known that he didn't like the local police coming into the building which made me wonder whether he had something to hide. It was all very mysterious. Incidentally Adrian ended up as a Superintendent and he certainly deserved all the promotions that came his way.

I made one last attempt to salvage something from my time at Belper. The freelance photographer and I tried to buy the newspaper, but our offer was turned down. I often wonder what would have happened had we been successful with our bid. The photographer still has a business in the town and I have been back in touch with him.

My friend and fellow journo John Andrews was working for Radio Derby at this time and asked if I would do an interview about my dismissal. My answer was immediate: "I'm not sure what I can say and what constitutes slander."

"I'll ask the questions, you give me honest answers from your viewpoint, and I'll run the whole thing past our legal people," John replied.

That was good enough for me and I think the item went out as "new editor of Belper News leaves job after just three months in charge." This all happened in a very short space of time that seemed much longer than three months. Of course, I found it all very unsettling and it was another nail in the coffin for me and the Midlands. I well remember a small group of students coming round to talk about the paper when I already knew that my contract wasn't being extended. It made talking to them quite difficult but of course the show had to go on and I explained what I knew about weekly newspapers which probably wasn't a great deal at that time..

I mentioned that John worked as a journalist/presenter on Radio Derby. He had an excellent music programme entitled "Solid Air" which was named after the track by Scottish folk/jazz singer John Martyn. John (Andrews that is) played varied and different rock music. In fact, music that went wherever his fancy took him.

John also hosted a phone in current affairs programme. Some nights he was very short of calls and so on more than one occasion rang me in Long Eaton and asked if I would go on air to discuss the state of education or various other problems in the East Midlands. I often ended up waffling on about subjects that I knew very little about. I seem to have made an entire career out of that!

But the plain fact was we didn't move to Belper. I wasn't given the chance to grow the paper and I found myself unemployed for the first and only time in my life. That situation only lasted for a month or so over Christmas 1978 and just into the New Year. That was the time it took to discuss the situation with the other half and make a decision to try to return to Norfolk.

I sent off a letter to Eastern Counties Newspapers asking if they had any vacancies and if so could I be considered for one of them. I just wanted to return home to my county of birth. I felt I had already been away for far too long.

CHAPTER ELEVEN – RETURN TO NORFOLK

It must have only been days before I received an answer in the post or maybe it came via a phone call. We didn't have e-mails in those days.

My stock and reputation in Norfolk must still have been reasonably high. Yes, they did have a vacancy for a sub editor in Norwich on the weekly series of newspapers and the job was mine if I wanted it and subject to a meeting with the editor which I quickly arranged. That went fine and I was formally made an offer and we started the search for a new home back in Norfolk. My professional life and certainly my personal life was soon to change and change very much for the better.

I did a lot of travelling back and forth between Norwich and Long Eaton before we found a new home. The original thought was to return to Beccles and a friend of ours was selling their bungalow on the side of the railway. I think the reason we decided not to make an offer on this was due to the distance between Beccles and where I would be working in Norwich. We wanted somewhere a bit closer.

It was obvious that south of the city was the most pleasant and easiest access to Norwich, so we started looking around that area. I had no great wish to return to Hellesdon where I was born as the journey into Norwich would have been a nightmare. I have no idea how or why we settled on Hethersett but, looking back, it was a stroke of real luck. It was probably because we got a load of house details from estate agents and felt that Hethersett was close enough to Norwich but still in a rural area, something that was exactly what we wanted.

One of the homes we looked at was in Buckingham Drive and a chalet bungalow at number 36. We put in an offer which was accepted. I can't remember having any problem with getting another mortgage and so we moved into a village that was our home then and is our home now, although we did make a big move many years ago to the posh end of the village, about a mile away. I probably need to explain the phrase posh end. I believe the family we bought from had the name of Lord (or maybe that was the bungalow in Kirby Cane – memory over years can play tricks). At least we can say that at one point in our lives we bought the house of the Lord.

One of my colleagues on the newspaper lived two doors away from us in Buckingham Drive. Neil Haverson worked in the advertising section of the newspaper but was also a keen writer and one with a great skill as I was to find out. Neil played hockey and one day I'm not sure whether he suggested it or whether I did, he wrote an amusing piece about sport for the paper I worked for. It was funny and featured his family and I suggested he might like to write a regular column. He jumped at doing this and Neil's sports column was featured in the weekly papers for many months and later morphed into a more general column for the Eastern Daily Press newspaper which was entitled Fortress H and which involved his family known to all as Brat Major, Brat Minor and Mrs H. This column was very amusing. A few years ago, a book of these columns was issued under the title "Ink In The Blood" with a launch at Jarrold's Department store in Norwich. Neil kindly gave me a mention for starting him on the road to his regular writing and so I am happy to repay the compliment by mentioning him here in this epistle. There is also something else we have in common. When I finally burst into print with my book on a massacre in Northern France during the Second World War I did a signing session in Jarrolds Department Store.

In the early days of Fortress H, Neil often mentioned me in his column and I believe I was referred to as Radiator Man as I had helped him fix a radiator on one occasion. When we left Buckingham Drive to move a mile up the road, he referred to me as Posh End because we had gone to what he considered to be the posh part of the village. I often implored him to mention me in his column as it was all great fun.

Once again, I benefitted from an excellent boss as I learnt the art of sub editing. Marjorie (and her surname evades me) was very patient and understanding when I made a mistake but gradually, I picked up the art which involved taking the stories from branch offices, reading and correcting spelling and grammar as necessary, writing headlines and designing pages. This was all done on paper as the idea of using computers and publishing software was still some years ahead.

The print industry had gone through a number of changes and moved from hot metal which was a hideous way of putting newspapers together but still a way remembered with fondness by some. It involved exactly what it sounded like – slugs of hot metal forming words and put into the pages that were referred to as galleys. This all gave way to the use of bromide which was basically sticky paper with type on it which was cut up by men and women (but predominantly men) called compositors and pasted onto large pages which were then photographed and turned into print. The printing industry at this time was very male dominated.

The stories we worked on were typed onto offcuts of paper (scraps in other words) and sent via vans, buses and trains as I have already explained in an earlier chapter. We wrote instructions about type size and also headlines onto the pieces of paper and then put the stories into a tube which was sucked along the building and made its way to a mysterious area where the type was set before everything was checked again by a team of "readers." That way very few spelling mistakes or grammatical errors got into the papers. This is no longer the case, and you often find errors creeping into stories.

The standard of writing amongst the journalists we were dealing with was of variable quality – some good and some really bad. Sometimes as press day approached, we worked late into the evening. This was compensated for by having half a day or a full day off on Fridays. During these long days we usually had a break of at least an hour at teatime. This gave us plenty of time to have a meal or a drink in the canteen or to go to the staff lounge to watch television, read or even have a sleep. Then it was back to work.

On one occasion I spent my tea break reading the book "Sophie's Choice" by American author William Styron. This was later made into a film starring Meryl Streep (that's the book and not my reading of it). The language in Styron's book was complex and the section I read on this particular evening was almost poetic in nature.

I then returned to work to read a story from one of the offices that seemed to have been written by an average 10-year-old. There was one chief reporter from a branch office who had been a chief reporter for years and years. A very senior member of staff who was often condescending and talked down to his staff. I believe he referred to himself as "father". This man's copy and writing style were just dreadful and I had to re-write large passages of his work often much to his annoyance. Another thing I remember about this guy is his purchase of ice creams for his staff. The more senior they were the more expensive the ice cream. As they say it takes all sorts.

I have always been fascinated by the way people who don't like each other eventually become firm friends and this happened to me when I became a sub editor. As a reporter in my previous life there was one sub editor I couldn't stand. A call from him would always be sarcastic and difficult. I think he took great delight in speaking down and winding up reporters and if I got a call from him, I grimaced. I got lots of calls from him.

Then I was forced into a situation where I had to work with him, and I believe he was assistant chief sub so technically one of my bosses. Once I found out that face to face, he was no longer sarcastic and he found out that I wasn't the idiot he thought me to be we started to get on well. On our days off we often went fruit picking. I've no idea why we did this as neither of us needed the money and we would often spend it in his social club afterwards anyway. But it was a kind of strange fun thing to do and it also filled the time. This would probably be in the period between leaving the Midlands and Anne joining me back in Norfolk.

I didn't stay as a news sub editor for very long before moving over to sub edit sport, working alongside my friend Norman Hicks who was just a year my senior and whom I had worked with at Cromer. Norman and his young family had visited us in the Midlands. It was obvious that Norman didn't intend being sports editor of the Norwich Mercury Series for ever and I was hoping to get his job when he left, which he duly did.

But I didn't get the job – well not immediately anyway. Another man I had worked with in the Evening News box when I was assistant Whiffler was brought in as sports editor much to my annoyance. He had once upon a time been a sportswriter on the national Daily Express newspaper.

There was a couple of times in my working life when I have been taken aside and told to keep my head down as something positive would happen. I cannot remember on this occasion where this advice came from, but I was given a coded message along the lines of "If you keep quiet and get on with the job you never know what will happen."

And so I did and within a few months I was appointed sports editor of the Norwich Mercury Series of newspapers. The other guy had been brought in as sports editor as part of a plan to get him into the room with a view to him becoming assistant editor, something that happened much quicker than we anticipated.

I loved being sports editor of a number of weekly newspapers. There were quite a lot of them at the time. I can remember the "Norwich Mercury", the "Thetford and Watton Times", the "Wymondham and Attleborough Mercury", the "Beccles and Bungay Journal", the "North Norfolk News," the "Dereham and Fakenham Times" and probably a couple of others that have slipped the memory.

I had an assistant (they changed three or four times during my time as sports editor) and each week we would divide the papers between us and design the pages. We would also take it in turns to spend Thursday evenings in the print area which was known as The Stone. This is where the pages were put together by the compositors for us to sign off the final articles ahead of the newspapers being published.

I like to think that I was successful in improving and increasing the sports content in the weekly newspapers. If additional pages were going begging I would always take them on and often a newspaper would have five or six pages of local sport which is considerably more than they have today. In fact the trend continues to be against localism.

Take the "Wymondham and Attleborough Mercury" as an example. At times I had up to six pages of local sport including features, reports, photographs and much more – all relevant to the area. This year, as I write, the same newspaper had one page of sport which was old coverage of the previous week's Norwich City matches. There was little or no local sport at all. To me that's all wrong and very sad.

At times there was incredible frustration, however. The people who set the type and pasted it onto the pages had a very strong Union and often worked to rule. They were scared of losing their jobs or being forced out of the industry. Of course, their fears were founded when computerisation came in and journalists began to take photographs as well as write words and make up their own pages. I'm not sure that today the role of sub editors isn't superfluous as well.

As a result of all this, a considerable number of stories and a considerable amount of copy wasn't set and, at the end of the week, we had to take a huge amount of it back and see what could be salvaged for the following week – and at times that was very little. So, in effect we could be wasting most of our week, but we were told to carry on working as normal so that we weren't in breach of our contracts. This made me extremely angry. There was nothing worse than doing a week's work to have most of it returned.

This anger was compounded during these times by massive posters that sprang up around the building informing us that "in the jungle the customer is king." It featured a Lion. To me this was insulting. We were being told that our customers, which I took to be our readers, were Kings but we were regularly giving them and expecting them to pay for a sub-standard product. Of course, the wish of advertisers always outranked editorial content and in this context, it was probably the advertisers that were being referred to as the customer.

A few years ago, the "Norwich Mercury" went out of existence and over 200 years of publication of what was one of the first newspapers in the country were wiped out. In 2022, the Wymondham and Attleborough Mercury printed edition went the same way as I've already said. This was another sad day for me as I remember that paper, which just happens to be my local paper, being launched. It had been little more than an advertising freesheet for many a day but I for one miss it and remember what it once was – a good quality newspaper that was actually full of news.

Undoubtedly print media has had its day. At its height and in the days when I worked on it, the Eastern Daily Press was the largest selling provincial daily in the country and regularly sold over 90,000 copies every day. Assuming that each copy was seen by at least two people and often by many more it means that 200,000 plus people from Norfolk and Suffolk would be reading it each day. Now I don't think the sale of the printed version is much more than 17,000 and probably much less, although there is a digital edition and of course the internet has taken over as the largest provider of news.

I seem to remember the combined circulation of the weekly papers hitting 100,000 and the editor cracking out the champagne to celebrate that fact. Some of newspapers had to be bought but others were free.

Eventually the sub editors of the weekly newspaper left our dedicated room and moved into a section of the main newsroom where it was more difficult to concentrate due to the hustle and bustle going on. But we soon got used to it and work continued. There was a change of editor when gentleman Barry Hartley retired and was replaced by somebody nobody was initially happy with. Once again, I will use initials. This man was GN.

I had reason to be grateful to him as he had been the man to give me the chance to become a journalist. He also went to the Norwich School and so we had things in common. At the time of my appointment, he had been on an upward trajectory and indeed was to become editorial director. I would describe him as quite a tough task master and very serious about his work. He didn't have much of a sense of humour either. But that was then and this was now.

GN was pushed sideways, and you might even consider it a demotion, but we were unhappy to hear that he was becoming editor of the weekly newspapers. But the man had changed. He became part of our team, a decent boss and we couldn't believe our ears when he said that his view on work was "get in, get on and get out."

So, life on the newspapers continued in the same vein but work was changing thanks to technology and automation. Printers as such were being "forced or phased out." Now whether this was a good thing or not is a matter of conjecture but suddenly journalists and sub editors had new computers with new software packages and journalists were able to send over their own stories electronically which could then be corrected and slotted into electronic pages and eventually be passed for printing at the touch of a button. Today this has just become the accepted norm but I'm glad that I worked in the industry at a time of great change.

I have already mentioned a two-day course we had to introduce us to the new technology. The first time I used it I have to admit I was all at sea. It was a real struggle, but as I got used to this new style of work, I began to embrace it. It gave us total control over pages and it's the kind of thing I still use today for a number of publications that I will talk about in a coming chapter.

There was one amusing incident with the new technology. Our area was very close to that of the main reporting teams. One of the EDP's top arts critics and reporters was Charles Roberts who wrote under his initials CVR. I liked Charles but he could be rather pompous. He wrote a series of books on Norfolk churches which became very well respected.

I had an amusing run in with him over a concert review. Whenever possible I volunteered to review concerts and events at Norwich Theatre Royal. When Neville Miller wasn't available, I reviewed for the Eastern Evening News. One week I was asked to review an opera. I cannot remember which one. I knew nothing about opera and had no idea whether what I was watching was good, bad or indifferent. I had tried to find out whether CVR, who was reviewing for the EDP, thought it good or not but he obviously worked out what I was doing and stayed tight lipped. When you are reviewing something and in doubt about its quality just throw praise at it and say nice things, and that's what I did.

A few weeks later I received a letter written in Italian from the leading tenor in the opera. Luckily the assistant editor of the weekly papers was married to an Italian lady, had lived there and spoke fluent Italian. He told me that the letter was full of praise for my review and my knowledge of opera. I thought this to be the case as there were lots of "Bellas" in the letter and even I knew what that meant. So, I showed the letter to CVR along with the translation.

"WELL" he thundered "you little whippersnapper. You know nothing about opera."

"On the contrary the lead in that opera states that I know an awful lot about opera."

That letter is long lost but the memory isn't.

There were two other occasions when CVR referred to me as a whippersnapper. In those days I wrote a pop/rock column entitled "Here and Now" (more about this later). He had occasion to comment on something I had written about rock music. It was probably something disparaging about that style of music which he abhorred.

I decided I would get my own back by commenting on a new version of Anton Bruckner's Fourth Symphony. You see as well as rock music I also love the classics thanks to Bernard Burrell and I had been listening to this piece. I think CVR was gobsmacked that I had even heard of Bruckner, let alone had views on the fourth symphony.

Then there was my favourite conversation with CVR.

It was the week when I struggled with the new technology. On Thursday evenings various groups were shown around the building. They saw the whole process of producing newspapers culminating in them seeing the Eastern Daily Press being printed and taking home a free copy.

A group of ladies came over to my machine and I explained the new technology and tried to sound knowledgeable. They thanked me and moved on. CVR who had been struggling with the new technology came over to me.

"WELL," he thundered: "You little whippersnapper you were pretending you knew all about the new system."

"Yes I replied and you know what I bet you £10 that I can go to bed with one of those women tonight."

What I didn't tell him until later was that the group was from Wymondham and Attleborough Ladies Circle and one of them was my wife. Charles retired and moved to France where he died many years ago.

I have mentioned "Here and Now". It was a weekly music column in the "Norwich Evening News" and something I had always wanted to write. I think when I initially went off to journalism college my ultimate dream was to write for the New Musical Express. I don't think my character would have been suitable for that though and the thought of taking drugs has never been on my radar. Today I only rarely drink alcohol and can't say that I feel I have missed much.

Recently I read a book about the history of the NME and it really did seem to be all about sex, drugs and rock 'n roll.

When a vacancy came up to write the "Here and Now" column I jumped at the chance and spent a few years happily covering the pop/rock scene in Norwich. I was joined by John Miles (a journalist and not the singer). "Here and Now" has been mentioned on a number of websites and in some books on the local rock scene, one of which stated that it gave people their local fix of rock music. I wrote this column for a number of years, interviewing a number of rock stars in the process.

I also co-wrote a column on Norwich City Football Club entitled "Eye On City." Thankfully I have kept some cuttings from both "Here and Now" and "Eye On City." I made regular visits to the club's training ground which at the time was at Trowse just outside Norwich and about a mile or so from the office. Today the training ground is just outside Hethersett and about a mile from where we live. I will write more about this in my section on sport.

But the time came when I felt it was right to move on again and looking back it was a good decision as the world of newspapers gradually fell apart. That time came and the day came when I needed to speak to GN. I asked him if I could have a word.

"Not now I'm rather busy," he replied.

"I just thought you should know that I've just handed in my resignation," I said.

At that point he listened. I had a feeling that I had experienced before of being very comfortable in a job but realising that if I didn't make an effort to move on I would be stuck in a rut for a very long time. But there was a difference here. This time I had no intention of moving away from Norfolk and no intention of moving house either (although we did but only a mile up the road).

So when a job came up as Norfolk Police's first ever civilian press and public relations officer, I applied and had an interview.

When I had been writing my "Eye on City" column one of the pieces I put together involved shadowing the police during a Norwich City match. The police gave me access to their match day briefings and I also went with them into the various supporters' pens moving from Norwich City to Wolves fans and finding it quite intimidating. This was in the days when football hooliganism was rife and there were pens for fans all over the ground.

I worked alongside Superintendent Colin Bunn and Superintendent Roger Sandall. They were very open with their views. I asked Colin Bunn what his thoughts were at the end of each game, and I always remember his reply.

"It's a game closer to the end of the season," he said.

As for Roger Sandall – well he later became a very respected colleague, worked in an office two down from me and turned out to be my third cousin as I will explain. He also nicknamed me "Scoop" and if he wanted a word would holler "Scoop" down the corridor.

But for now, I wrote the article which was appreciated by the Police and probably one of the reasons I got an interview for the job.

I now know that I wasn't the first choice for the police job. I wasn't even the second choice but two people either couldn't take up the post or decided against it. As a result, I was offered the job and took it without any hesitation, certain that this time I wouldn't be making the same mistake as earlier and would be taking on a job I enjoyed.

And so it turned out for most of my time with the police.

CHAPTER TWELVE – NORFOLK CONSTABULARY

I was back to thoroughly enjoying my job. Every day I would travel from home to Norfolk County Hall where the police had their headquarters at the time. Initially this would have been around the Norwich ring road and then the Southern Bypass when it was built. I had a parking lot at county hall which was a bonus and somewhere to park at the weekends if I wanted to go into Norwich which was about a mile away. It was also just a short walk from the football ground. The journey to work took between 20 and 30 minutes depending on the volume of traffic and the journey home gave me a chance to wind down after some tough days.

Eventually a new headquarters was built and that was even more convenient as it was at Wymondham just over two miles up the road from home. There we had a press office which was staffed by three people.

I remember well the day the new HQ was officially opened by the Queen and Duke of Edinburgh. For that day much of the building was freshly painted. As someone remarked "The Queen must think that there's a massive repainting programme for every public building in the country as everywhere she goes there's the smell of new paint."

Nobody was allowed to take their car into work for security reasons and so a normally full car park was completely empty.

The day before, a lovely furry sniffer dog went round all the offices trying to sniff out anything that could be dangerous. The one that came to our office went straight to my bag and took out a very dangerous object, my cheese sandwiches. Cheese can be a dangerous thing. Exploding cheese can be a killer! It probably had pickle in it as well, although I probably never found out as I had to bin the lot and go to the canteen instead.

It took me some time to get into the job as it was a new position, but slowly things slotted into place. When I started in 1989, I was part of the community relations department, and we were a very tightly knit group of both police officers and civilians. We used to go out socially as well. In those days working in an office could be fun and we had plenty of laughs although much of our work was of a very serious nature.

Overall, I enjoyed my time working for Norfolk Constabulary although I did struggle in the last couple of years when it all became about spin rather than working with the Media as it had been for the previous 15 years. I always looked upon my role as assisting the Media and certainly not managing them. Trying to manage the media is a futile exercise and I had experienced both sides of the coin. People referred to me often as a "poacher turned gamekeeper."

The things I remember mostly about that work were the high-profile cases where I was part of the investigating team. In fact, I used to tell friends that during my time with the police I was involved in a number of murders. I then have to explain that I was performing the function of Press Officer.

I think it is appropriate here to talk about my part in just a few of these investigations which often saw me appearing on television and/or radio and which have formed the basis of talks to a number of groups since and indirectly led to my gaining a master's degree in professional development from the University of East Anglia.

I start with the murder of Norfolk prostitute Natalie Pearman which is the case where I probably got the closest to a family that has lost a loved one through murder. Natalie's body was found on Ringland Hills on the outskirts of Norwich. This is a beauty spot often used for picnics and is close to a river. As soon as we got word that a body had been found, the police's media team swung into action as part of the senior investigation team.

We were asked to speak with Natalie's mother Lynne and stepfather and the first thing we wanted to broach with them was the possibility of making an appeal for information through holding a press conference.

In a situation like this, I was never sure how the bereaved would respond. Lynne immediately agreed and so we arranged the conference which turned out to be the first of a number. Lynne made it known to me that she would be happy to do any publicity that might help to find her daughter's killer. Natalie seemed to have gone from a normal friendly and well-adjusted teenager into somebody "falling in with the wrong people" and turning to prostitution and drug abuse. I think in some way the family may have blamed themselves for being partly responsible. Natalie was described by one policeman who had dealt with her as being "as hard as nails" and "the toughest person I have ever come across."

Over the next many months, I visited Lynne and other members of her family at their home in Mundesley on the North Norfolk coast. I sat in on newspaper and magazine interviews and continued to generate publicity for them in the local press, on local radio and on local television.

Sadly, to date nobody has been caught and held to account for Natalie's murder and appeals for information continue to this day. I guess it is now looked upon as a cold case but I know there is still hope that the mystery of Natalie's killer will be solved.

The second murder I remember vividly came over a Bank Holiday weekend. Thomas Marshall was a 12-year-old boy whose body was found dumped at the back of a lay-by near Thetford which was some considerable distance from his home in Happisburgh (pronounced Hayesborough), again on the North Norfolk coast.

I was called out to meet Thomas' parents John and Carol on a Bank Holiday and explained about how important maximising publicity was. It sounded rather trite to be talking about press conferences and publicity when a couple had just lost their only son.

I don't think the parents took part in a press conference on this occasion, but they were happy to go along the press information road. I remember, having spent the morning with them at their home, coming to my own home and going along to the local pub in Hethersett. Everyone was laughing and having a good time, but I had to force food and drink down and didn't feel like being there at all. I wanted to scream "stop laughing and enjoying yourself" to all those there.

Ultimately Thomas' killer was discovered. It was a local shopkeeper, and it was an outstanding piece of police work that helped catch him.

The shopkeeper was a top suspect but there was no real evidence against him until the backroom of his shop was searched and the U bend from the sink was dismantled. Among the usual gunk that you would associate with that area there was a bead from a necklace. This was found to be identical to the beads on Thomas' necklace that the killer used to strangle him. The necklace was a very unusual design and came from Germany. The detectives were able through a visit to Germany to establish that the bead found in the waste pipe actually came from the necklace owned by Thomas.

I was in Crown Court in Norwich the day that Thomas' killer was sentenced to life imprisonment. We were all geared up for making a statement to the Media outside the court at the end. This was being done by a senior police officer and one of Thomas' aunts. Before going ahead with this we needed to check whether the killer was going to lodge an appeal which would have stopped our press statement. I asked the defence barrister. He looked at me and said, "I really don't think so." In other words, he had just defended somebody he knew was as guilty as sin. I have touched upon this kind of thing in a previous chapter on my time working in Beccles. Sometimes the law really is an ass, but I guess it's still the law.

I came across Carol and John Marshall a couple times more. Once was on a coach holiday to Germany which they were also on and the other was when I was being shown around the Norfolk Records' Office where John was painstakingly restoring old documents. It was a very involved job which he seemed extremely suited to. It took me some time on the holiday to remember who they were. I knew I knew them from somewhere but took a while to work out just where that was.

The investigation into the Thomas Marshall murder gave me the opportunity to go on BBC Crimewatch. It was an interesting experience. Four of us drove down to London. It was me and three police officers. I cannot remember who drove, but it wasn't me. We got to the studios in time for refreshment and then a run through of the programme where we could listen about what was going to happen and the Detective Chief Superintendent in charge of our murder could run through the statement he was going to make. This was very different from what happened when the programme went live in the evening. Three of us were answering phone calls that were coming in following the various appeals. The main problem was once the phones started ringing, we had no idea what was taking place on camera. Also, we had to take calls on other crimes that we knew little about. I didn't take one call on the Marshall case. At the end of the programme we were put up at the BBC's expense in an hotel at Paddington. I didn't get to bed until 2 am and was up at 6 am to undertake telephone interviews with Norfolk radio stations and other Media.

One of my favourite jobs (if you can call a serious attack as a favourite) involved a young lady by the name of Karen Newman. Karen had been trapped in a house with her violent brother-in-law and was stabbed over 70 times. She played dead and managed to call the police on a mobile phone. Thankfully Karen survived her ordeal despite having to spend some considerable time in hospital. Karen's niece and the daughter of the man responsible was also in the house and also survived the attack.

One day I was sitting in the office when the phone rang. It was Karen on the other end. She explained that she was the victim of the stabbings. I believe the story had been covered in the local press but not to any great lengths. Karen asked me what the best way to tell her story in the media was. I asked her whether she was happy to do media interviews and she replied, "yes as many as possible" and so started a little journey with Karen. Obviously, the press were delighted to have access to her and to understand what had happened. Her attacker was sent to prison and later committed suicide.

At that time press and public relations officers from throughout the country came together once a year for an annual conference which included talks and presentations and the sharing of experiences. Somehow this always seemed to be in greatly attractive places such as Port Rush in Northern

Ireland or at the coast. But it was always in November and so sometimes the weather wasn't great.

I was asked to contact Karen to see whether she would speak at one of our conferences and she immediately said yes. I believe this one was in Lincolnshire. Karen was due to talk mid-morning with another speaker following her and talking about image on television (including how Margaret Thatcher used to spend hours getting her image just right).

I introduced Karen, gave a little of the background to what had happened and the investigation from the police point of view. Then Karen took over and entranced the audience with details of her ordeal. She held nothing back and at the end of her presentation there was a barrage of questions.

I have spoken before about the quiet person, the person that never pushes themselves forward and the person that often becomes overlooked. Often these people are the deepest thinkers. During Karen's presentation I kept an eye on the audience – all of whom of course were police employees. One young lady seemed to be totally uninterested in what was going on. She shuffled around and seemed bored with the whole thing.

We finished our presentation, having run over time due to the number of questions being asked. There was a 10-minute scheduled break before the next presentation by the university professor on image. During the short break this professor, who came from Middlesbrough and sounded exactly like Paul Daniels, came up to us and called over the conference organiser.

"I cannot and do not want to follow that presentation," he said. He wasn't being awkward. It was simply that he felt so emotional that he just couldn't talk about something as flimsy as image. Then the "bored" lady came over, grabbed Karen and gave her a huge hug. She was in tears and told us that she had been so affected by the presentation that there were hundreds of questions that she wanted to ask but none would come out of her mouth. Always think about the quiet ones. They can be the deep ones.

Things were re-scheduled; we had an early lunch, and the professor did his presentation after the break. Karen and I did a few training sessions for new press and public relations officers as well after that and it always went down well. Karen went on to do work with Victim Support which, as its title suggests, supports victims of crime.

I too did work with Victim Support, supporting their ideals and helping them with publicity. I still have a booklet where Karen Newman is photographed on the front page with another big supporter Sally Whittaker who is now better known as Sally Dynevor and even better known as Sally Webster in the ITV soap opera Coronation Street. On that cover they look so alike that they could almost be twins.

Another major crime I got involved with in a roundabout way involved one of our own Chief Inspectors whose stepson had been murdered whilst he was at university in Warwick. John and Berni Davies wanted maximum publicity in order to find out who had killed their son with a hammer. I believe that the murderer was eventually caught. I believe that a flatmate was eventually charged with the murder.

There was also a nasty double murder deep in the Fens but still in Norfolk where a mother and her daughter were bludgeoned to death in a robbery that went wrong. This resulted in early DNA analysis being used and there was another piece of excellent detective work. Once again, the murderer was caught. I spent quite a few hours standing out in the chill of the Fens holding impromptu media briefings. This was an interesting thing to do. I would drive up in my car to a spot where the media were congregated, get out of my car and immediately be surrounded by cameras and microphones. I don't say it phased me, but it was a tad disconcerting as many others have found over the years.

It did teach me one thing though. From the time my car drove up I was probably being filmed. So, there was no laughing and no caustic comments to journalists I knew well. It all had to be very serious and professional because I was dealing with a very serious situation.

There was one other murder that I found particularly sad and which, like Natalie Pearman, has never been solved. That was the killing of Johanna Young at Watton. Her body was dumped in a local pond. Johanna seemed to be just another ordinary teenager. The police had a main suspect but no real proof to convict them. I spent many hours either in the police station at Dereham or Watton dealing with the Media in the mornings and then returning to county hall in the afternoon to answer queries on other matters. I never lost my sense of awe or my wonder at being part of police major incident teams. Sadly, Johanna's killer has never been caught and may still be living in Norfolk which is a sobering thought.

I was delighted at the police when I was told they wanted to send me to university to gain a master's degree in professional development. Going to journalism college, I had not had the opportunity to gain a degree. The University of East Anglia was organising a new project entitled COMEX which stood for From Competence to Excellence. The idea was that I would attend the UEA on Wednesday evenings and then carry out work-based research with a resulting dissertation on something that would benefit the police.

But first I had to do an introductory module as I didn't have an entry degree for the Master's. This wouldn't give me a bachelor's degree (BA) but would give me an Advanced Certificate in Education. It meant weekly sessions and a 10,000-word essay which I wrote on Beat Policing, advocating a return to more community-based policing in Norfolk. I also looked at the role of the Family Liaison Officer in serious crimes, something I felt very strongly about. At that time the role seemed to be fulfilled by anyone who was spare at the time. I advocated that this should be a specialist role and only undertaken by people specifically trained.

In my role I had worked alongside a number of Family Liaison Officers. They were the police officers assigned to be with families and look after them when the unimaginable happened. My conclusion was simply that family liaison officers needed to be highly trained people.

I remember a very amusing incident on that initial introductory module when I was hit over the head by another student who was upset by something I said. She actually took what I said the wrong way and later we had a good laugh about it and got on fine.

I said that some people led quite boring existences and did the same thing every day or every week. I took as my example my father who went to work, came home, read the newspaper and watched television before going to bed. The next day he went to work, came home, read the newspaper and watched television before going to bed. She took this as me being snobbish and criticising another person's lifestyle which is exactly what I wasn't doing. I was simply pointing out that some people were satisfied with this style of existence and didn't ask any more from life, whereas it would have bored me and wasn't the kind of life I wanted.

I got through that module and went onto the master's level where there was a group of nine or ten. The problem (or maybe it wasn't a problem) was it was me and eight or nine ladies. We all got on well, but I think only three or four of us stayed the course and ended up with a degree. I'm still in touch with most of them.

I was really interested in my subject matter as I took a lengthy and involved look at the way victims of crime and their families deal with the Media. Now many people see the Media as the big bad boys and girls but in my experience most of the direct victims of crime like Karen Newman and the families of those murdered wanted to deal with the Media and co-operate with them. I wanted to find out why and so approached many of those I knew, and they very kindly agreed to be interviewed with a tape recorder present.

The result was a lengthy dissertation which I found difficult to write, not because of the subject matter but because of the style I was asked to write in. It didn't come naturally. As a journalist I had been trained always to attribute quotes and to give a balanced view of all sides of an argument/story. Writing in an academic way, everything was depersonalised, and interviewees were referred to simply by letters as in Interviewee A and Interviewee B. This didn't come naturally to me, especially as all those I interviewed were happy to have their names used.

I put together a first draft which was read by a personal mentor. I wrote it pretty much as I would a very long newspaper article.

"I would love to put this in but I'm not sure it would get you a degree," was his response.

I wanted that degree and didn't want to fail so I re-wrote it all in academic language and passed.

I have mentioned that lots of the pupils dropped out, not being able to deal with the workload. Many had a problem that surrounded writing such a large piece of work. Writing at length has never been a problem for me as this autobiography is probably testimony to. Writing comes naturally to me (one of the few things that does).

On one evening we were asked to write 1,000 words about the brick wall opposite. Some of the other students found this difficult but to me it was just another chance to show that I had some writing skills.

Then there was a really surreal evening when our lecturer (also a woman) for some reason asked us to write 1,000 words on getting a penis caught in a trouser zip. It was I suppose meant to be an exercise in creative writing and I think it might have come from a magazine article she had read.

I could say without fear of contradiction that in that lecture room I was the only person that had ever suffered that painful experience.

"What did it feel like?" I was asked.

"Bloody painful," I replied.

"It's not the getting it stuck in the zip that's as painful as getting the little blighter out of the zip," I added. I cannot remember what anyone wrote on that evening. It's probably that I was still in shock at the subject matter and it reminded me of the day many years previously when I had stood in the town centre in Harlow asking people about which birth control method they used.

I re-wrote the dissertation into a format that was academic and duly passed which made me feel very proud. As a result of the work, I wrote articles for the Victim Support magazine and Police Gazette and was invited to be a keynote speaker at a medical conference where I was on stage with consultants and the Coroner for Norfolk Bill Armstrong who I had come across on a number of occasions. He lived in Wymondham and was a real gentleman. I think my talk about the pressures that victims of crime could be put under by the media and how victims could get the best from the media went down well as I got several smiley faces on the feedback forms and an overall score of eight out of 10. It's a talk I have never given again for no reason other than I have never been asked and I doubt whether I could reproduce what I said anyway. I find this with a lot of talks I do on various subjects. After I have given them, I forget what I've said.

I have put all my university work on my personal website and if you have any interest in reading it, head over to www.peterowensteward.weebly.com and just follow the links.

A few years ago, I was contacted by a university student from New Zealand who asked my permission to quote passages of the dissertation for her own finals. I was delighted to give that permission. I love sharing what I love doing and take it as a huge compliment when people want to use my photographs or text. I am certainly not precious about what I write. So, if you want to quote anything from this book, please feel free to go ahead, although the story about the penis and the zip might get you into hot water (literally)!

One of the strangest jobs I had whilst with the police was going over to Great Yarmouth one day because the town had been caked in semolina. Yes, you read that correctly. I even had to look this up again on the internet as I wasn't sure when writing this that it had actually happened. But it had.

It happened in October 2006. Two tonnes of semolina fell on Yarmouth following a freak accident. A silo at Pasta Foods on Pasteur Road overfilled and blasted the grain into the air, covering the town in a white film of semolina flour.

And when the fire brigade tried to clean it up with water they just turned it into a gooey mess. I don't think anyone took out a spoon to start eating it though.

I also spent quite a few Bank Holidays sitting in Great Yarmouth Police Station in case there was trouble at the annual scooter rally. Back in the 1960s Yarmouth was one of the seaside resorts subjected to violence between Mods and Rockers. The scooter rally was an offshoot of that, although only Mods were featured with their scooters. They took over one of the town's car parks and there were thousands of them. Usually, it all passed without too many incidents, but I was always glad when it was over. I can't remember ever having to leap into action.

Not only was I sent to university to get a degree (which was a good idea), but I was also told to attend Dutch lessons on a Wednesday afternoon. This was in the days when police services at home and abroad were looking to forge partnerships beneficial to all. Our Deputy Chief Constable at the time decided that a number of employees should learn Dutch with the idea of some form of exchange with Holland. I may or may not have mentioned before that I have no ability to learn languages. I always found them difficult at school and certainly in my forties I wasn't going to find it any easier.

Our tutor was, not surprisingly, a Dutchman. He only spoke to us in Dutch which I found confusing and I was useless at it. An exchange never came to fruition and today the only thing I can say in Dutch apart from hello and goodbye is "Can I have a cheese sandwich please" and "This is my jacket." Neither is any use unless of course you are in Amsterdam and want a cheese sandwich or to point out the obvious about your jacket.

It was all futile anyway because virtually every Dutch police officer speaks fluent English. I did arrange to go to Amsterdam for a few days to meet my counterpart as part of a holiday for myself and my wife. He pulled out at the last minute but informed us that he had arranged a two-night stay in the centre of Amsterdam. So off we went by air from Norwich and by train into the centre of the city. We found the hotel. It was small but no matter. The problem came when we tried to go to bed. Our room was over a disco that went on until 3 am. It was horrendous and impossible to sleep. We complained to the front desk, and they gave us a refund when we told them we hadn't been informed about the disco. We found a very nice hotel in a leafy suburb for our second night's stay.

With any job however much you enjoy it, there always comes a point when you feel it is time to move on. I think most people know when that is, and I certainly did. I could write a book on my time working for Norfolk Police but it's time to move on with my story yet again.

The time came when I had the chance to take early retirement and I jumped at starting a new chapter in my life and having more time for voluntary work (see coming chapters).

I didn't have too long to wait for another opportunity to present itself. A Norwich-based emergency media company was looking for freelance staff and I was glad to take up their offer. To facilitate this, I decided to start my own small pr company which I called Postscript Media for two reasons. Firstly, the shortform for a Postscript is PS which are my initials and then, when writing letters (old fashioned letters written on paper with a pen and then sent by what has become known as snail mail), people always use the PS for the most important part of the letter. You know the thing. Five hundred words of absolute waffle are followed by

PS – Forgot to tell you we're expecting a baby

PPS- Forgot to tell you that last month we won a million pounds in the National Lottery.

So, myself and my very small company (one member of staff - me) became an emergency response facility and I continued with that for a number of years, even working two days in the office in Norwich. The company mainly supported the oil and gas sector in emergency situations, dealing with the Media (something I was quite experienced in doing). The company had numerous retained staff throughout the country.

I used to visit Shell Oil and other companies in Norfolk – mainly at the Bacton Gas terminals. On one occasion I had to visit Shell and took my wife, my cousin and her husband with me. The idea was they would go for a walk whilst I was at Shell.

I duly went in for my meeting and then met them at the end. They had been stopped by armed police who thought they were acting suspiciously in a highly delicate area. I don't think the police believed them when they said I was at Shell for a meeting with the CEO – but that was the truth.

I may have mentioned that golf isn't the sport for me and I will develop this in the chapter entitled My Sporting Life. But each year one of the oil companies (I believe it was Perenco) held a golf tournament. Our company decided to put in a team. Two genuine golfers stepped up but one of them couldn't make the day through one reason or another and so I was asked if I played golf.

"Yes very badly," I replied.

"Well you're in the team with Bruce," I was told.

Being only two of us, we teamed up with two other oil company employees to make a four. Bruce had a handicap of 36 and my handicap was not being able to play golf. The competition was played under Stableford rules which I don't have enough space to go into but in very basic terms meant that the more useless you were at golf the more your handicap (or in my case lack of it) went in your favour. Ultimately this meant that I was given a number of strokes on each hole and could just attack everything. If I had a 30 foot putt I could just go for it. If it went in it was a bonus and if it didn't, I just picked up my ball and went onto the next green.

We were the last foursome to go out onto the course and when we got to the 18th green it was getting very very dark and we were lucky to finish. But somehow with all the handicap strokes taken into account we won and that was due to the other three and not to me. Our prize was a brand-new putter worth over £100 in the days when £100 was a decent amount of money.

As I went to shake hands with Perenco's CEO who was presenting the prizes he just looked at me with a strange grin on his face.

"Bandit" was the only word he said. To the uninitiated the word bandit in this context indicates somebody who is much better than their handicap suggests. I also got a trophy to put on my shelf.

Winning trophies was something I had never been good at. My two sons had loads for football, but I had always avoided them but gradually I built up a collection of my own as you will find out if you continue to read on.

I am at this point bringing my working life to a close, although not entirely. I eventually left the emergency media company and, for the first time for many years, I didn't have to be on call all day every day. It was quite a relief to know that when the house phone or my mobile phone rang it wasn't somebody calling me into work. Having two pensions (one a works pension and the other what used to be known as the Old Age Pension) life wasn't too hard.

Then one day I got a call from the then editor of the Eastern Daily Press newspaper who lives in the same village as myself. He wanted to know whether I would be interested in doing some freelance work within Hethersett, covering events in the village for the newspaper. It took me approximately five seconds to jump at the chance.

For me working life had gone full circle and I was back doing what I really loved doing – being a journalist, in other words a keeper of a journal and a recorder of daily life. I also used my skills to start or take over various voluntary publications and websites, but more about those later in my section on voluntary work.

Up to now the main gist of my autobiography has been growing up and then work, although I have brought elements of my private life into the work pages. But now it is time to turn to something I am very proud of and that's my community involvement that has had me referred to in the Eastern Daily Press newspaper as "Mr Hethersett." When friends comment on this I say that they can just call me H.

Work had its moments and of course it paid the bills and gave us the lifestyle that we now enjoy, but it is the voluntary work that has given me the most satisfaction. I always say that work all too often consists of aggressive people all too keen to stab you in the back in an effort to get your job. When it comes to voluntary work this just isn't the case.

I got so far in my working life and no further because there were always others willing to push for promotion and make more noise (remember the quiet ones I always say). In the voluntary area I have at times found it only too easy to get to the top and that has culminated over the years with my rising to the head of a number of groups and organisations and generally being appreciated for the skills that I possess, whatever they may be. I have found the whole thing much more satisfying.

I first toyed with the idea of public volunteer service in Cromer and developed this a bit in Beccles when I joined the Round Table, the town's twinning committee and the town football club.

As a child I never joined groups such as youth club or cubs and scouts. Arguably the first "club" I joined was Round Table. It was at Beccles when the owner of a local garage – John Gale – asked whether I would be interested in joining this organisation.

I was in Round Table in Beccles and then Long Eaton and then Wymondham before leaving well ahead of my 40th birthday when men get chucked out for being too old. They then join something with the original name of 41 Club which is a more social gathering than Table.

But the reason I never got to what was called "chucking out" was because the charity failed to live up to its caring reputation. In 1981 I had what Queen Elizabeth II once called an Annus Horribilis. My wife had a miscarriage, I ended up in hospital after suffering a very painful hernia and my mother died. And all I got from Round Table was a letter reminding me of the fact that according to rules if I missed three consecutive meetings I could be expelled from the organisation. I might have been a little at fault for not informing them of the things happening in my life but there are times you feel people and organisations should be more aware of what is happening with their employees and/or members. The first reaction to somebody missing on a regular basis shouldn't be to beat them but to find out if there is a particular problem.

The letter pointing out my lack of commitment angered me and I contacted the chairman and that resulted in the social secretary coming to see me full of apologies. After that I never felt the same about the organisation and handed in my resignation (note resignation and not retirement on this occasion) shortly after.

Before that I had been part of the area committee responsible for publicity. This culminated in a rather ridiculous event when the national conference for Round Table came to Great Yarmouth. Our area was responsible for organising what became something of a bean feast. The national president had his own area where he could invite named guests. This was all too elitist for me, and I wasn't happy when one of my functions was to prevent unwanted guests getting to the president and only admitting those with passes. I guess it's my socialist tendencies coming out here as all Round Tablers should be equal. I was glad when that event was over. We all had to wear badges containing job descriptions. The hall, and it may well have been a marquee, was divided into two sections imaginatively entitled A and B. My wife joined me as part of section A and we were Stewards in more ways than one. The badges we wore included a top line of our name followed by a bottom line with the words either A Steward or B Steward referring to the section we were looking after. So Anne had a badge which said

A Steward
A Steward
I had a badge which said
P Steward
A Steward

All very confusing.

But now having given you a flavour of my voluntary work, I move on to section four of the autobiography which deals with more these areas and many of the interests that have helped to form my middle and later years.

PART FOUR – OTHER ASPECTS OF LIFE
CHAPTER THIRTEEN – A SPORTING LIFE

BEFORE entering on a chapter about my proudest achievements which all involve my activity within various communities, I must write a chapter about sport. This of course will be in addition to all the sporting bits and pieces that you will already have found dotted about this book. I will also be developing this section into a stand-alone book which will form part two of my autobiography.

Sport has been a huge passion and part of my life from my earliest days until the present time. It has been my hobby, my love and, for a time at least, my career.

I have no idea what draws me to sport apart from always being competitive. My parents weren't greatly interested in it, but I soon found it was my first love in life. I can't remember the first time I kicked a football, the first time I hit a tennis ball or the first time I bowled a cricket ball or ran round an athletics track but many of my proudest achievements involve sport. Over the years I have spent thousands upon thousands of hours playing sport and probably much more watching it and writing about it.

I never made the Kinsale Avenue junior school football team but plenty of my mates did and so, when the team was at home, I went to support them. I also remember playing football at the school although, as I've said I never made the team. Not sure why that was as I felt I was good enough. I used to be friendly with the school's captain and would go round his house and kick a football around.

But I did make the cricket team, although there wasn't one. That may sound rather strange and will need some explanation.

The school didn't have a cricket team, very few if any junior schools did, but we did play amongst ourselves in the summer. I loved batting and scoring runs and our teacher Mr London knew this and so took it upon himself to bowl at me. I couldn't score runs against him, but neither could he get me out. So, one day he paid me a compliment.

"If we had a cricket team, you would be my captain and opening bat," he said. Funny how such things stick in your mind.

So let's stick with cricket for the time being. In the spring and summer, I spent most of my spare time as a youngster over the Recreation Ground in Hellesdon playing cricket. You would just turn up and there would always be people there for an impromptu game. Me and my mates also recreated test matches. I remember trying to bowl like South Africa's Eddie Barlow and trying to bat like Australia's Ian Redpath. You would not only take on these people's names but would also try to play like them. A friend of mine was a very fast bowler (he probably wasn't that fast but to us he was scary). He would pound in and let fly on a surface that was rutted and dangerous enough at the best of times. We wore batting gloves and pads but never wore helmets. I don't think they were invented in those days. To this day I have never worn a cricket helmet. That's not bravery but just the fact that nobody wore them in what I would stupidly refer to as "my era" whatever that was.

All this playing and practice put me in good stead when I went to grammar school. I was picked to open the batting for the Under-12s and also played for the Under-13s before, as I have already said, swapping cricket for tennis. I returned to play cricket for my house at school and well remember going into bat at around number six when we needed something like 12 runs off three balls to win a game. That obviously meant three boundaries in a row. I was facing the school's fast bowler and one of the fastest ever to play for them. His name I believe was Van Ree or something like that.

I was soon back in the realms of Mr London. Van Ree didn't get me out, but I didn't score any runs and it was all I could do to just stop him hitting my wicket. I went back to the pavilion.

"Why didn't you hit out?" I was asked by a teammate.

"Mainly because I never saw the ball," I replied. Is it any wonder I took to playing tennis?

I have already recounted how I ran out Long Eaton Round Table's star player and my games of cricket became few and far between until we moved to Hethersett and I joined the local club. At the time Hethersett played on the local park with changing facilities in an old, dilapidated building (more on this later). The pitch often verged on the dangerous and one man virtually ran the club being captain, secretary, chairman, groundsman and many other things. Let's call him Tony because that was his name.

At this time the club played mainly friendlies and this guy opened the batting and opened the bowling. He was never averse to playing out a draw. I remember one match on a Bank Holiday Monday when I gave up an entire day to play a two innings match between the Chairman's XI and the President's XI. We played all day with one of the teams being set a target to win.

Our friend opened the batting and solidly defended and ensured the match ended in a draw. He made no attempt to win the game. I guess it was a matter of honour for him not to lose, but for me it just made the day pretty pointless.

On one occasion I was actually sent in to run him out as he had scored 17 runs, all in singles. I was quite a fast runner in those days and so hit the ball and called him for a quick single. I ran full pelt up to the other end only to find that he hadn't moved. He had his hand firmly in the air and bellowed

"NO."

I had to turn round and try to get back and was run out by half the length of the pitch. The plan to run him out had backfired badly.

I do admit that this man probably saved the club from extinction on more than one occasion, but to me what he was doing wasn't really in the spirit of the game. I played a few seasons sporadically for the team and then had a break before returning many years later and trying to play again.

One of my proudest days was playing in the same team as my youngest son Matthew who was picked for his first game for the club. He couldn't have been more than 12 and we were playing somewhere in the country in South Norfolk. I think it was in the Diss area. I ended up batting with him and manged to hit 30 or so runs including hitting a six into a cornfield.

Matt went on to become a much better cricketer than I ever was and has played for Hethersett for almost 30 years, winning a number of trophies along the way. He turned into a very powerful all-rounder, bowling at a reasonable speed and becoming a punishing batsman who could turn a game by launching a serious attack on the opposition.

As for me, well it all ended on a park in Lowestoft. I went into bat and got hit on the ankle. It was immediately very painful. The guy I was batting with obviously didn't realise how hurt I was despite my using several expletives. So, he hit a ball and called me for a quick single. I could hardly move let alone run 22 yards and once again was run out by some distance.

It took well over three months for my ankle ligaments to heal. I decided once I had recovered to give it another go and was fielding in the slips when the ball caught the edge of a bat and shot down towards me. I didn't get down quick enough and the ball smacked into my other ankle, damaging ligaments once again.

That was the point when I realised that my eyesight wasn't as sharp as it could have been and so I retired there and then, although I did make one final appearance for the club in another Chairman's v President's game. Batting at number 10 in order to make the numbers up, I was out for a duck (nought) in the first innings but did manage to put on 15 for the last wicket in the second innings although all the runs were scored by my partner but at least I had managed to keep my end up if you'll pardon the expression.

So ended my cricketing playing career. But what followed was much more important to both me and the club.

Cricket in Hethersett has a proud history stretching back over 150 years. Over that time hundreds of men have played for the club and today there's a thriving youth and ladies and girls' section as well.

Over 20 years ago, it was decided that the club should leave the village for a number of reasons.

Firstly, the facilities at Hethersett were dreadful with the pavilion not fit for purpose. Secondly the pitch at times bordered on dangerous and, being on a public park, was often used for football and even had people cycling across it. Thirdly the club was offered a purpose-built home at Flordon by the Ellis family, three of whom played for the club.

So Hethersett moved to a new home at Taswood Lakes where it played on one of the most picturesque grounds in Norfolk. There are two pitches, surrounded by lakes and woodland and it's out in the country Very soon the club had a clubhouse and changing facilities better than it could ever have dreamed of in the village. Flordon is a 20-minute drive from Hethersett. In keeping with its new surroundings, the club changed its name to Hethersett and Tas Valley. When my son announced that the club would be moving, I was very much against it leaving the village.

"Just come and look at the facilities we now have," he said.

So, I did and just one look was enough to convert me. Hethersett just couldn't compete. In addition, the club entered the Norfolk League and worked its way through the various divisions before getting promoted to the Norfolk Alliance – the top Norfolk league. There followed more promotions until in 2022 the club realised a dream by reaching the Premier Division. This is the top division in Norfolk cricket with only the East Anglian Premier League above it and that league features teams from Norfolk, Suffolk and a few more counties. In our first season playing at that level, we finished sixth, which was a remarkable achievement with a number of talented young players. Sadly the following season we were relegated but it won't be long before things look up again – and that I'm confident of.

Alongside that success the club has a thriving junior section and now ladies and girls' teams and that allowed us to obtain the highly prized cricket charter mark for excellence a number of years ago and I am proud to have done the work towards this.

With my playing days behind me, I joined the club's committee as club development officer and then spent two years as club chairman before handing over the reins and being made an honorary vice president, a position I will continue to hold for as long as I'm around.

Ultimately the sport of cricket has been good to me, and I hope that in some small way I have been good for it. Saturday afternoons in the summer will often find me sitting in the sun in Flordon, watching the cricket and possibly having a short snooze and maybe a pint of beer or glass of wine. My youngest son loves cricket, my eldest son can take or leave it but I have been to watch test matches with both of them and more recently with my grandson who is representing Norfolk and is a canny leg spin bowler.

And so, to football. I have covered quite a bit about football in previous chapters but not my involvement as a coach. So here goes.

We journey way back in time to the early 1990s when my two sons went to Cubs. They went to Cubs primarily because they wanted to play for the football team. There were two cub packs in the village and they came together for the football team and played against other Cub teams. Hethersett didn't have anyone to run them and so I offered. It didn't take me long to make that offer. So, for two years I coached and ran the Cubs' team, and we were pretty successful. The main problem was dropouts, and I don't mean weird people or youngsters letting the team down. I refer to the ridiculous rule that said that on your 10th birthday you were out of the team. It could mean that at the beginning of the month you had a sparklingly good team but by the end of the month you were scrambling around to find 11 players. In those days boys and girls of all ages played 11-a-side for 30 minutes a half at Cubs level. Today football has changed, and youngsters start with smaller sided games with smaller goals.

At the same time as taking the Cubs team, I popped down to Woodside School on Friday lunchtimes to organise a football game for their top two years. I was able to do this thanks to having most Fridays off as a sub editor on the newspaper. There I had some very talented young footballers and really wanted to continue with my coaching.

Today coaches have to take qualifications, they have to be vetted, they have to be able to dance and lift weights (I made the last of these up). In those days none of this existed and so I just went down and tried to teach the kids a little about the game. I certainly think that having qualifications is a good thing and certainly acts as a safeguard for the youngsters.

Both my boys were very keen footballers. From an early age I had them out on the road passing footballs to them and trying to teach them the rudiments of the game. Luckily, we lived at the bottom of a cul-de-sac and so there were no traffic problems. Both went on to become better players than I ever was.

In 1989 my friend Mel Perkins decided to start a new football club – Hethersett Jubilee. It took its name because it was initially based as part of the Hethersett Jubilee Youth Club. When that association came to an end the name was changed to Hethersett Athletic. That was just a name and had nothing to do with athletics, although it did cause some confusion in some areas. Mel started the club mainly because his youngest son was not very good at football but was very keen. He couldn't get in any team and so Mel built one around him. In their first season they lost every game, but Mel was determined to continue and I decided to join the club a year later and run a team which included my youngest son alongside the other team. My eldest son was playing for another team in the village.

Most of my players had played for the Cubs team and so I knew them well. I had some very talented players, and I took that team from Under-10s through to two or three seasons as adults. Along the way we won cups and did well in the leagues.

Hethersett Athletic continued to grow and new teams came in below ours as we began to fill in the gaps and offer competitive football to more and more youngsters. The club flourished but there was no firm structure. So we created one and I became the club's first chairman with Mel as secretary. We developed a committee structure and went from strength to strength with our one club ethos.

After something like 15 years as chair I decided to hand over to someone else and took on the role of assistant secretary for a while. During my time as chair, Hethersett became the joint first team in the county to be awarded the prestigious national Clubmark. Norfolk FA once said that we were one of the three best run clubs in the county, which was a great compliment to our efficiency as a club.

Meanwhile my sons were making their own mark. Both went to the Hewett School in Norwich for sixth form and both played for a hugely successful school team which mixed it with and beat the best in the country. They even went to the USA and won a major international tournament.

Describing that would take a book in itself. They beat a top-ranking youth team from Liverpool and many others.

A few years ago, I decided to pull back from my day-to-day involvement with the Hethersett club and was made an honorary life member. In addition, I am one of only two people to win the Lee Thompson Memorial Trophy twice. This is awarded annually for the person making an outstanding contribution to the club. The other person to win it twice is founder and current club president Mel Perkins, my mate. The trophy is in memory of youth team player Lee Thompson who was tragically killed by a car on his way home from a night out in Norwich.

I have already talked about my time as a sports editor and mentioned that I wrote a weekly column about Norwich City entitled "Eye on City". It gave me the chance to get to know some of the Norwich players of the time. Some players are difficult to interview, and some are very easy. I remember vividly a very young teenage player being signed from Liverpool. His name was David Watson, and, over the years, I watched Dave change from a shy homesick young man into a leader. There are two Dave Watson's who have played for England and so this might be a bit confusing. Our Dave was probably the lesser known of the two.

I was the first journalist to interview him, and it was quite obvious that he had no idea where he was or what he was really doing. Eventually he became team captain and a fine player who insisted on calling me Pal in a broad Scouse accent. In fact, I think he called everyone Pal.

Alongside Dave Watson was Steve Bruce who has often been described as the best player never to win an England cap. Those were the days when players were picked for England according to ability and caps weren't given out like confetti. There is no doubt, however, that Bruce should have played for England. He went on to have a glittering career at Manchester United and then became a successful manager.

My main memory of Steve Bruce was his being pushed into fronting the Media after Norwich had won the Milk Cup at Wembley. He was nervous and very humble. I came across Steve on numerous occasions whilst I was writing the column, and he was always very open and very friendly. Another favourite was England international Joe Royle who always used to make the tea when you asked for an interview. Joe was a lovely guy who liked to talk about other things other than football and I spent happy hours talking to him at the training ground. Others who were always approachable included John Deehan and Mick McGuire both of whom supported a little fete we organised each year at a farm near Hethersett.

Both were happy to referee a five-a-side football tournament although their contracts prevented them from playing, which was probably just as well.

I became a Norwich City supporter around 1959. I know the date because that's the year when Norwich as a third division club reached the semi-final of the FA Cup. This was a big deal for a club from the third tier. On the way the Canaries beat the likes of a star-studded Manchester United team which included some of the greatest names to have ever played the game including one Bobby Charlton. Norwich won 3-0. Sadly, they lost the semi-final to Luton Town after a replay.

I vaguely remember the football but what I mainly remember about that semi-final was the tacky replica FA Cups. These were on display in a Norwich department store (Curls) and would only be sold if Norwich beat Luton in the replay. My grandmother promised to buy me one if Norwich won. When the result came through, the replica cups were packed away – presumably to be shipped to Luton. Luton lost in the final to Nottingham Forest.

But this time I put a successful curse on Luton Town Football Club. My one on the Norwich Speedway housing site didn't work but that on Luton Town did as they went through some very rough times and dropped out of the football league for a time before bouncing back and they are now in the same league as Norwich, having spent one season in the Premier League. Somewhere along the line I must have withdrawn the curse. The next day after that Luton defeat, I was on a train with my parents. We would have been going either to London or Great Yarmouth as those were the only places we visited. It was still in the days of steam trains and those little individual compartments that took six people who had to face each other. We were facing this woman who said she came from Luton. I believe I tried to hit her. It was my one and only instance of being a football hooligan. I guess for a six- or seven-year-old it was all too much.

I became a Norwich supporter from that point onwards and have been ever since. I have stood on the terraces, sat on the terraces, reported on the club for the Norwich Mercury and the News of the World (freelancing for them on match days). I must have an aside here. One day I was reporting on a match for the N of W. Norwich had been well beaten and Cyrille Regis had scored four goals. That game was probably against West Bromwich Albion.

I was sending over my report to the newspaper without knowing that Mr Regis was sitting behind me, being interviewed by a radio station. In those days you had to rate each player and give them a mark from four out of 10 which was atrocious to 10 out of 10 which was out of this world. Cyrille Regis may have been the only player I ever gave 10 to.

In my report I used the phrase "Too Hot to Handle Regis" and as I said it I got a tap on the shoulder and turned round to see a smiling footballer.

"Steady on" said Cyrille as he burst into a broad grin. I bet he used that phrase himself when he got home.

Football has continued to play a huge part in my life. I have so many fond memories of running youth teams, of going all over Norfolk and further afield.

I remember one match when I was coaching an Under-13 team. We were playing at Bircham Newton. My team was full of talented youngsters and by half-time we were 6-0 ahead. It was an easy team talk at half-time. "Just continue playing how we have been and let's see if we can get double figures," I said. Nowadays I think youth teams are instructed to ease up when the score mounts up, but my competitive spirit says, "grind em into the ground" and in saying that I'm only partly joking.

We scored virtually from the kick off to make it 7-0. Then it started to go wrong. 7-1, 7-2, 7-3, 7-4, 7-5 and then 7-6 with about two minutes to go. I have no idea what went awry but I took off two attackers and put on two defenders in an attempt to stop the other team equalising and somehow, we held on. Funny game football. The other thing I remember about that game is it was on my birthday and so I imagine I needed a lay down when I got home and before the birthday cake was brought out.

Other things I remember include one of our players in the Cubs when we were winning 20-0 going to stand with our goalkeeper. "What were you doing?" I asked. "I thought I'd have a chat because he seemed lonely," came the reply.

On another occasion our team was taken to an FA hearing because two of us ran onto the pitch without permission. It was a particularly bad-tempered match between Hethersett and Norman Old Boys. It was usually a pretty bad-tempered game when you played Norman. On this occasion one of the Hethersett players was fouled and seemed to be in trouble. Our excellent physio Vicky Potter and I shouted to the referee but when he ignored us, we decided to run onto the pitch without permission. Our player had indeed swallowed his tongue, but thankfully Vicky's quick intervention saved the day. At this point the referee decided that rules were more important than saving a life and showed both of us a red card and reported our club. He later sent off a Norman player and didn't realise that player came back on when Norman made a substitution. When our club came up before the inquiry we got off on all charges after saying that we would do exactly the same thing again if a player's health was at risk. Football can be a dangerous game. I also remember being involved in organising a number of junior five-a-side competitions for our Hethersett Club. In one of these a youngster also swallowed his tongue, and he may have even stopped breathing. Thankfully a doctor was present, and it ended happily with the boy making a full recovery.

Some of the pitches our club played on were agricultural to say the least. At times we had to compete on what were not much more than ploughed fields, often containing cow pats. Often dog mess had to be scooped off pitches before they were fit to play. Sometimes there was glass on the pitches as well.

But there were so many good memories from those days. Memories like standing out on Southwold Common with the wind whistling across from the sea (the coldest I have ever been) and the day we got new sponsors – The Murderers Arms in Norwich.

We contacted the FA to make sure it was ok to have Murderers printed on our shirts. They said that if they were our sponsors, it would be ok. Each season we played a team from the Winfarthing Fighting Cocks. They played at the back of the pub in Winfarthing and were a tough team made up of tough guys. On their shirts they had Fighting Cocks in large letters. You can imagine their reaction when we came out with the word Murderers in large letters on our shirts. I think we out trumped them. I think we might have beaten them as well.

I also vividly remember the first game my boys ever played at adult level. Again, we were playing a team of tough nuts who took no prisoners and believed they were going to wallop all these young boys. I think we were 8-0 up when they had a player sent off for stopping a goal-bound shot with his hands. Then a second player was sent off for a terrible tackle. At this point their captain decided to fall to the ground writhing in agony in an attempt to get the game abandoned due to them having only eight players on the pitch, The match was abandoned but the game was awarded to us and the opposition received a hefty fine – such is and was local football. I could write an entire book on this subject alone and maybe one day I will to go with my coming book on sport..

Other outstanding memories from my football involvement include the day our club played at Carrow Road, the home of Norwich City, in the final of the Norfolk Sunday Cup. We came up against a very strong team from King's Lynn who were the trophy holders and lost 5-0. But the scoreline didn't matter. We just enjoyed the day. We hired a coach to take us to the ground despite it only being eight miles away. We all had the same colour suits and matching ties and our supporters had scarves specially made for the final – I still have one in my garage.

The King's Lynn team turned up in cars wearing jeans and scruffs, while we really looked the part. This was commented on by Norfolk FA.

The other thing I was really proud of was fostering and promoting the girls and women's game. We had one of the two best ladies teams in Norfolk – Norwich City Ladies being the other. We won the Eastern Region Cup three years in a row, but they wouldn't let us keep the trophy as is usually the case when a club completes a hat-trick. But enough about football.

*   *   *

In 2010 I had the idea of bringing all the sports and fitness groups in Hethersett and the surrounding villages of Little and Great Melton together for the mutual benefit of all. It wasn't the first time that a sports association had been in existence, but this was the most successful attempt. Along with some other village sporting activists we invited all the clubs we could think of and had a launch event in February 2011. We obtained quite an extensive grant from South Norfolk District Council and then awarded small grants to our member clubs. We were able to pay for renovations, pay for start-up youth teams and offer support to a variety of clubs playing a variety of sports. In addition, we were able to bring everyone together around a table.

The sports association continued in existence until COVID lockdown after which a couple of meetings were called but failed to generate the interest that had previously existed. I was chairman of the association which was known as HAMSA (Hethersett and Meltons' Sports Association) until just before lockdown and I am proud of what we achieved in uniting all those interested in sport, health and well-being. I feel we performed a very useful function at a time that function was definitely needed.

One day out of the blue I was contacted by Active Norfolk and asked whether I would be their sports co-ordinator for Hethersett. The main function was to support the ideals of Active Norfolk and to organise teams for the South Norfolk and possibly the Norfolk County Games. This all brought the village together in a wonderful way with the idea of enhancing the fitness levels of local residents.

The games were held all over Norfolk with the winners of each area coming together at the University of East Anglia. Hethersett regularly won the South Norfolk competition, but it took us many attempts to become county champions, something we eventually achieved in the last ever games before the funding for them was withdrawn. So, in effect we will forever be the reigning county champions.

My task for Active Norfolk was to arrange players to represent the village in the various sporting activities which included five-a-side football, rounders, badminton, tennis, athletics and many others – in fact a full sporting gambit. I loved doing this and took an immense pride in how people of all ages came together in the name of sport and friendship, although it was still very competitive.

In 2010 Hethersett Parish Councillor and member of our Hethersett Sports Association Shane Hull came up with the idea of organising events in support of the London 2012 Olympic Games. This all tied in with the sporting ethos we were trying to set-up in the village.

We organised so many events that we were given a special achievement mark and had a personal visit from Sir Keith Mills who was chair of the organising committee for the London Olympic Games. We also received a letter of support from Lord Sebastian Coe and were later made the first village in the country to be awarded a Prime Minister's Big Society award and the village also received other awards as well (see my later section on awards).

In support of the London Olympics, we had five-a-side football tournaments, a come and try sports event, a swimming marathon, a Hethersett's Got Talent competition, a church service, a concert and much more.

Again, this all brought the village together and is something I am very proud to have been a part of. The Olympic legacy in our village continued for many years and is still alive today with Hethersett Athletic still hugely active, along with many other sports clubs and organisations.

So, what of my other sporting exploits.

Golf – Golf to me has always been a foreign country. I have had lots and lots of lessons with professionals but never improved and I now accept that I'm never going to get any better and have officially hung up my clubs. Actually, I gave them away to a friend who is threatening to return them as they are right-handed and he is left handed. I do remember one lesson where I hit a stonking drive straight down the middle of the course.

"Why can't I do that every time?" I asked.

"If you could do that every time you would be a pro golfer," came the reply from the professional who was giving me lessons.

I think my golf ability is summed up by an incident that happened on a nine hole course near my home. I got to the tee on a par three. The green was on two levels with the pin on the lower level. We had to wait as a threesome of young men were ahead of us. They finished the hole and waved us through but stayed on the edge of the green to watch our shots. I popped my ball on the tee and hit a nice straight shot that went onto the higher level of the green, spun backwards and dropped onto the lower level, finishing a couple of feet from the pin. I got a round of applause. They waited until we approached the green and one of them said.

"Don't suppose you could give us some lessons."

I just smiled and they waved us through onto the next hole which was over 500 yards long. I took 15 shots! I think you would call my ability at golf spasmodic at best and downright awful at worst. Stick some water on a course and I will be attracted to it as if it is a magnet.

Squash – I played this regularly when working at Beccles and was part of the sports' centre's ladder league. That was a competition where you could challenge the person above you or could be challenged by the person immediately below you. That way you could move either up or down. On one occasion I was challenged by a fellow Round Tabler who was one place below me in the ladder. I beat him but it was a tough game and afterwards I sat in a pool of dripping sweat in the changing room. I didn't even have enough energy to have a shower at that point.

"Blimey you must have taken quite a beating to look like that," someone said.

"No I won. You should see the other guy."

I was always strictly average at squash, as I was at badminton and table tennis. I have played table tennis in a number of leagues but never really improved one iota.

Darts and snooker were two other pastimes I have never been able to come to terms with. Watch either being played by professionals on television and you immediately say: "I could do that. It looks simple." In reality it is anything but simple. At Thursday lunchtimes on press days when I was a sub editor, we had a long wait and a long evening ahead of us and so a few of us used to go to a snooker hall where I gave a very good impression of somebody who had no co-ordination.

I was just as useless at darts. Every year the Norwich Mercury Newspaper held a very prestigious tournament which was imaginatively called "The Mercury Cup". Being sports editor, I got a team together and we entered this knockout competition, always getting knocked out in the first round. Finding treble 20 was always an impossibility for me. Finding a one was simple.

Athletics – I was always a short distance sprinter at school rather than a long-distance runner. I enjoyed athletics but gave up running quite some time ago when it began to hurt.

Swimming – Oh no not swimming. I have touched upon my fear of the water, and I didn't learn to swim until I was 40 and that was under sufferance. Today I can swim but only badly. As they say "I can get by."

We had an auction at the local Methodist Church. I think we paid for the rector of the time to come to our house and do some heavy gardening. He was a strong guy and certainly wasn't phased by a piece of unkempt waste ground at the bottom of our garden which we had just purchased. He reduced that to something manageable.

Anne also bid for one-to-one swimming lessons with the Middle School's swimming teacher who was a friend of ours and this would be in the school's swimming pool. Soon I was swimming widths and she had me sitting on the bottom of the pool. I felt it was one of my best achievements as I had always been so frightened of even the idea of swimming. Today I rarely swim as I can't say I enjoy it, but at least I now know that I can.

But almost enough about sport. I won't mention enjoying going to horse racing at numerous tracks from Yarmouth to Newmarket, or watching tennis at Wimbledon and the fact that we once had a visit to the tennis venue and were pictured sitting behind the press conference table where so many great champions had sat in the past and continue to do so. Then there was test cricket at Lords or Trent Bridge, football at Wembley Stadium. Let's just say I've eaten up many miles attending sporting events both in this country and abroad (horse racing in Australia, baseball and American Football in USA, cricket in New Zealand, ice hockey in England and much much more).

But before I leave the sporting theme, just a mention that for a number of years we acted as landlord and landlady for a succession of Norwich City Academy footballers. These were young men who were either having trials with or whom had been signed as youth players by Norwich.

Some of them stayed for a couple of weeks, some for a few days and some for the whole year. At times hosting was difficult, at times it was a pleasure although there is only one of our "lodgers" who we see regularly and with whom we stay in touch and that is Harry Barker who our sons refer to as our third son.

The only one of our lodgers to make it into the big time is Carlton Morris who, at the time of writing, is playing for Luton Town who I mentioned previously. Carlton stayed with us for just two weeks whilst he was either having trials or his usual landlords were on holiday. He was a very respectful young man with a beaming and flashing smile that lit up his face. This is something I remember well.

And I can't leave the sports section without mentioning two major events that brought a huge amount of publicity to the village and which involved Hethersett and the Meltons Sports Association. The first was an off-route visit to the village of the official London Olympic flame. This was the first and only time to date that the flame has detoured off the official route. It took place at 6 am in the morning when over 2,000 people turned up to see Shane Hull walk round the playing field of Hethersett High School (now Hethersett Academy) with the Olympic flame and a heavy police escort. Again this was in recognition of the number of events organised by the village in support of the London 2012 Olympic Games.

The other major event saw the Tour of Britain cycle race flash through the village in 2015. The streets were once again lined and there were promotional flags everywhere as the riders hurtled along Queen's Road and Great Melton Road and out into the country. It was one of those "blink and you'll miss it moments." I did manage to take a lot of photographs, one of which is one of my all time favourites with one of the riders looking straight at me with a broad smile on his face.

But enough about sport. To read more you will have to wait for the second volume of my autobiography. For now, let's move on.

CHAPTER FOURTEEN - AWARDS and PRESS COVERAGE

This is the section of my autobiography that I really struggled to write as it's about awards that I have received over the years and rather sounds like the chapter where I puff out my plumage and tell everyone what a jolly good chap I am.

This is not the intention, but I felt that I couldn't ignore the accolades and awards that have come my way as they are part of my life story and please treat them as such.

*   *   *

But first let's look at some of the awards won by Hethersett in the past two decades. I am proud that I played a part in most of these awards either directly or by nominating the village. So here goes:

2006 Eastern Daily Press Pride in Norfolk Community of the Year

2008 Eastern Daily Press Pride in Norfolk Community of the Year Runner-Up

2010 London Olympic Games Inspiration Award

2010 Eastern Daily Press Event of the Year Runner-Up

2011 Active Norfolk South Norfolk Village Games Winners

2011 Active Norfolk County Village Games Runners-Up

2011 Eastern Daily Press/Active Norfolk Sports Village of the Year

2011 Eastern Daily Press/Active Norfolk Sports Champion of Champions

2012 Active Norfolk South Norfolk Village Games Winners

2012 Active Norfolk County Village Games Runners-Up

2012 Eastern Daily Press Pride in Norfolk Community of the Year

2013 Prime Minister's Big Society National Award

2013 Active Norfolk South Norfolk Village Games Winners

2013 Active Norfolk County Village Games Runners-Up

2013 Active Norfolk/Eastern Daily Press/Radio Norfolk, Norfolk Sports Village of the Year

2014 Active Norfolk South Norfolk Village Games Winners

2014 Active Norfolk County Village Games Winners

2014 Active Norfolk/Eastern Daily Press/ Radio Norfolk Sports Village of the Year runner-up

2016 Active Norfolk/Eastern Daily Press/ Radio Norfolk Sports Village of the Year runner-up

2020 Stars of Norfolk and Waveney Village/Town of the Year runner-up

The citation for the 2012 Eastern Daily Press Norfolk Community of the Year (Over 5,000 Population) reads as follows.

"Hethersett is far from a dormitory community for Norwich based commuters. With a growing population currently standing at 6,000, Hethersett truly has a village feel. For the last three years, the very active Olympic committee has organised more Olympic-themed sporting and cultural events per head of the population than anywhere else in the UK. This achievement was recognised with a visit by the Chairman of London 2012, Sir Keith Mills, and a truly unique off-route visit by the Olympic Flame during the Torch Relay.

"Hethersett is also proud of its village hall and playing field, run by volunteer trustees. The playing field committee organised a Diamond Jubilee Fayre which was well attended despite the weather. The Hethersett Environmental Action Team (HEAT) organises regular litter picks, tree and ornamental features, maintenance, promotional walking and energy conservation. The latter was supported by the Energy Saving Trust's Green Communities Programme by winning a £20,000 grant to install measures to reduce domestic energy use for vulnerable households. HEAT also recently completed a biodiversity survey, publishing a book called "Wild about Hethersett."

* * *

In 2012 I nominated the village of Hethersett for a Prime Minister's Big Society national award after reading a plea from Prime Minister David Cameron to create a Big Society. My motivation was the fact that in

Hethersett the Big Society had been operating for decades and so this idea was nothing new for us. I felt that the thousands of volunteer hours put in by hundreds of people should be recognised further afield than just in Norfolk.

Early in 2013 I heard that Hethersett had become the first village or town in the entire United Kingdom to receive a Big Society award and this gained a considerable amount of coverage in the local Media. This culminated in my travelling to London along with my wife and fellow village activists Shane and Lorraine Hull for a reception and presentation at 10 Downing Street where we were presented with a certificate on behalf of the village by David Cameron. We also received a rather cheap and nasty plastic trophy which now resides in a cabinet in Hethersett Library along with many other trophies and certificates.

These trophies also include Hethersett's very own Olympic torch designed along the lines of the official torches. Returning to the Prime Minister's award, at Christmas that year we received a card signed David, Samantha and family from 10 Downing Street. We didn't send them one. The visit to Downing Street definitely had its amusing moments like the young people who were winning an award and insisted on doing cartwheels around one of the state rooms and the fact that the PM walked into our little group and said, "hello I'm David Cameron." To which I wanted to reply, "yes we know who you are."

I have already mentioned the Norfolk Village Games but here are the dates.

Hethersett entered the Norfolk Village Games for the first time in 2011. Despite competing against market towns with much larger populations, Hethersett and the Meltons won the South Norfolk Village Games in 2011, 2012, 2013 and 2014 and were runners-up to Downham Market in the county finals in both 2011 and 2012. In 2013 we were runners-up in the county finals to Diss, but in 2014 were finally crowned county champions. This was of great importance as it was the last year of the county games.

Hethersett was named Active Norfolk/Eastern Daily Press/Radio Norfolk Sports Village of the Year for 2013. I represented the village in my capacity as chair of Hethersett and the Meltons Sports Association and picked up the trophy at a special presentation evening at Norwich Forum on November 6th, 2013. The trophy was presented by Norwich City and England international goalkeeper John Ruddy who I have to say didn't drop it, although he was known to spill a few things in his time playing for the Canaries.

*   *   *

I have also been fortunate to receive a number of personal awards.

In 2012, I received a Queen's Diamond Jubilee Inspiring Achievement Award for services to Hethersett over 20 years. I won the award for what was described as "an outstanding contribution to Hethersett over the past 20 years." Also in 2012 I was named Hethersett and Tas Valley Cricket Club Clubman of the Year. I was particularly honoured to receive the Inspiring Achievement award at a special presentation evening at the John Innes Institute just outside Norwich.

The citation for the award read as follows: "To recognise an individual whose achievements have been judged to be far-reaching by the panel but whose achievements do not fit into other categories e.g bringing the community together, long service, community spirit etc.

"Peter has been Chairman of the Hethersett Athletic Football Club for the past 19 years. The club caters for both male and female players across all age ranges from under-10s through to adult sides. Peter successfully championed the introduction of a women's team to the club.

"He is also involved with the Hethersett and Tas Valley Cricket Club, where he has taken on the role of club development officer. He successfully applied to the ECB for clubmark accreditation which involved many hours of work.

"Peter was responsible for the formation of Hethersett and the Meltons Sports Association and organised Hethersett's entry into the 2011 Norfolk Village Games which saw them come in second place.

"Since its inauguration, Peter has been a vital part of Hethersett's hugely successful Olympic Committee. The three years of events and fundraisers in the run up to the Olympic Games was recognised when the Olympic flame was brought to Hethersett in June 2012."

*   *   *

In 2013 I was named a Champion of Norfolk at the Royal Norfolk Agricultural Show and received a certificate from television personality Jake Humphries. My wife received the same accolade.

In 2014 I was a runner-up in the Sport Volunteer of the Year awards organised by South Norfolk Council as part of their Community Awards.

In 2015 I was awarded the Lee Thompson Memorial Trophy for outstanding contribution to Hethersett Athletic Football Club. I was previously made an honorary life member of the club.

In 2018 I was awarded the Lee Thompson Memorial Trophy for outstanding contribution to Hethersett Athletic Football Club to mark my retirement. I was very proud to be only the second person to win the award twice.

In 2019 I was made an honorary vice-president of Hethersett and Tas Valley Cricket Club after retiring as club chairman and development officer.

In 2020 I was honoured to be made an honorary member of the Royal Norfolk and Royal Anglian Regiment Association. This honour was bestowed on members of the Le Paradis Commemoration Group in recognition of our work to bring the death of 97 soldiers from the Royal Norfolk Regiment, the Royal Scots Regiment and others to public prominence and to raise awareness of Le Paradis Massacre of May1940 during the Second World War. More about this later.

Possibly my proudest moment came in 2024 when I was given the Lifetime Achievement Award by South Norfolk Council to mark more than 20 years of service to the village of Hethersett.

With the awards has come a considerable amount of coverage in the local Media, again something that I cannot ignore. This Media coverage has been wonderful and, at times, highly embarrassing in its praise of myself. For whilst you read this you must remember what I'm always saying – I am one of the quiet ones.

I always look upon the individual awards that I receive as awards for the entire community and the many many volunteers that give unceasingly of their time and effort to make our village and area a wonderful place to live.

CHAPTER FIFTEEN - SAMARITANS

People often tell me that I'm a good listener but I'm not sure that's true. It's something I like to think is true but at times I often fall short.

I have mentioned my interest in the Samaritans from my time in Lowestoft when they re-printed an article I had written for the Lowestoft Journal for a national publicity campaign. In addition to that I read the Monica Dickens book about the Samaritans "The Listeners" which came out in 1970 and the television series that followed entitled "The Befrienders" in 1972.

I think the thing that attracted me to The Sams, apart from wanting to help people, was the organisation didn't specialise in specific areas but just listened to people from all walks of life and on all subjects. In addition, Samaritans didn't offer solutions but just a kind and supportive listening ear.

When I was working as a sub editor in Norwich, I decided to apply to become a Samaritan. I filled in forms and had an interview and was accepted onto the branch's training course which took place at the Samaritan Headquarters in Norwich.

It was quite a tough course as you would expect. They had to ensure that they had the right people. At least two people on my course dropped out after realising that they needed the help of the Samaritans rather than becoming one.

We were subjected to some quite intense scrutiny before I was accepted as a trainee Samaritan. That meant working alongside a mentor for a number of months before becoming a fully-fledged Samaritan Volunteer.

Well, I got there in the end and soon began to fly, becoming a mentor myself, a member of the branch committee and publicity officer for the whole of East Anglia. The only reason I left the Sams was because of a conflict with a new job as I will explain.

I eventually became part of the training team for new recruits, and I loved this. I took over as a drunk from another Samaritan by the name of Henry. Those who know me know that I drink very little, and I can honestly say I haven't been drunk once in the last 40 plus years. But I had to play a drunk for training courses. It was the kind of over-the-top role I needed to have employed when I made my one and only attempt at amateur drama. But that was in an Oscar Wilde play as I have mentioned and that just didn't lend itself to an over-the-top show.

Being a Samaritan drunk certainly did lend itself to something of a show. I put on some very old and dirty clothes and drank a can of lager to ensure I had a beery smell. I then chucked some beer on my clothes along with some methylated spirits. The training session was in full swing and at an allotted time I hammered on the door.

They made sure it was opened by a female trainee. I lurched into the room swearing with a barrage of four-letter words and leering in a leering sort of way. In other words, I was very coarse and all the time the trainee was being watched to see how they coped with "this difficult customer." Some coped well, others didn't. Some even recoiled which didn't surprise me at all.

My favourite part was the after session debrief. By this time, I had tidied myself up, cast aside my dirty clothes and they suddenly realised that I wasn't some middle aged drunk but a reasonably intelligent guy who was one of their own number. They talked openly about how they felt threatened by me. That was certainly a new experience. I had never threatened anyone before, apart from the lady on the train who came from Luton!.

In those days being a Samaritan was all hush hush. I don't know whether that's still the same. It was difficult being a press and public relations officer for an organisation when you were meant to be secret squirrel. Mind you I was found out on a couple of occasions.

At the time I was a member of a village group called Candlelight. This was just couples connected to the Methodist Church who got together for social occasions. We called ourselves Candlelight because at our first meeting there was a power cut and we had to continue with candles. Occasionally we would invite speakers along and somebody suggested asking for a speaker from the Samaritans.

"I doubt we would get them as I'm sure there's a big waiting list," one member said.

And he was right. We had a guy who dealt with talk requests and there was a long waiting list. But I pulled a few strings and got somebody and informed the next meeting that a speaker from the Samaritans could be at our next meeting.

"How did you do that?" I was asked.

"Just contacted them."

It didn't take a genius to work out what had happened. I know they rumbled me, but they were very good in not mentioning it.

So now I return to the sarcastic sub editor who I thoroughly disliked when I was a reporter but who I made friends with when I worked alongside him. One day a reporter in one of the branch offices had written a story. My sub editor mate phoned them up.

"I think we need a comment on this from the Samaritans," he said.

The reporter rang the Samaritan office and were given my work number which I had left with them in case they had any Media inquiries which I would deal with.

They gave me a list of questions the reporter had asked.

I immediately put a comment together and walked down about three desks and give it to my sub editor mate.

"Here's the comment from the Samaritans on that story," I said.

He twigged and I admitted my involvement with the organisation.

"If I need any other quotes at any time I'll come straight to you," he said.

I enjoyed my work with the Samaritans, although enjoyment isn't probably the right word. I got to know some callers who I would speak to on a quite regular basis. When I joined, we used our first names and had a number after them which constituted the number of Sams who had gone before. I can't remember what my number was, but it was in the hundreds if not thousands. It was a difficult system which got changed so that we just used our first names and a number according to how many there were using the same name. So, I became Peter 3 because there were two other Peters slightly senior to me. When they left there was no promotion, however, so I would never become Peter 1 or Peter 2 but would always remain Peter 3. If another Peter joined, he would automatically become Peter 4. It all sounded a little like The Prisoner television programme.

Callers could ask to speak to a specific Samaritan and would be told when that person was on duty. We used to do shifts of two or three hours at a time. I worked during the day so my duties would be either in the evenings or at weekends. Although duties were of short duration you would never terminate a call and so they could be extended considerably.

Every so many weeks I was expected to do an all-night stint which I found difficult. You would share the session with another person and there were beds available, although it was difficult to sleep knowing that at any time the phone could go and you could be listening to a person through the night. Then often you had to go to work the next day which could be exhausting. The Samaritan centre was just five minutes' walk from the newspaper office where I worked.

The anonymity situation was quite a tough one. We had people regularly visiting the centre and would give them coffee and have a chat and, of course, listen to them. On one occasion I realised that a person needed to go to Accident and Emergency at the hospital which was just a minute's walk away. When we got there, they took the name and address of the person I was with and then asked me my name and address and relationship to the patient.

I was quite evasive but eventually had to tell them where I came from. On another occasion I had to hand a call over to another volunteer when I realised I knew the caller and that it was somebody I worked with.

Not only did I have to keep quiet about being a Sam but my wife had to join in as well. If somebody rang for me whilst I was on duty, she had to say something senseless like "he's down the pub." Not that I'm suggesting that going down the pub is senseless of course.

As I have already documented I eventually left the newspaper and started working for the police. I was hoping I could still continue with my Samaritan volunteering. That is until one night the police rang me on my home phone in the middle of the night. They either wanted to call me out or make me aware of something. I was on a night duty at the Samaritan office.

Can you imagine what they thought when my wife told them that I wasn't at home, and she didn't know where I was. I suddenly realised that Samaritan volunteering and my new job weren't compatible and so I had no option but to resign from the Samaritans. I always kept it in the back of my mind that I would one day retrain and join again. But over the years this just bever happened and now I'm afraid it never will although I still very much support the organisation and all the good work it does.

CHAPTER SIXTEEN – SCHOOL WORK

Originally, I had entertained ides of becoming a teacher until the writing bug struck, but I continued to have an interest in education. When my boys went to their first school, I took football on Friday afternoons, but it was when they went to what was Hethersett Voluntary Controlled Church of England Middle School and what later became Hethersett Junior and then Hethersett Primary School that I really became involved in education and school life.

It all started when I was asked to join the parent teacher association (PTA). I became vice chairman or chair of vice as the chair put it.

It was hard work, but we didn't half have some fun. The highlights of the year were the summer fete, the Christmas craft fair and the Christmas turkey supper. The latter was always oversubscribed with a waiting list every year. The day after the event people would book for the following year.

Turkey supper was just that. A turkey roast supper followed by a disco in the decorated for Christmas school hall. This was always preceded by the immensely popular craft fair which was resurrected in 2022 after a gap of over two decades.

The summer fair was tremendous fun. Each year we had a gunge tank which was an elaborate toilet style kiosk which dumped crap on a person- usually one of the teachers who pretended to complain but who knew very well what was happening.

I always wanted to be gunged and the only way to be assured that this would happen was to make it known that you really really really didn't want to be gunged. Worked a treat one year. I was ceremoniously led to the gunge tank, sat on the toilet and this sticky, gloopy blue mess descended on me. I pretended that I hated it but absolutely didn't. What I did hate though was the post gunge hosing down with cold water that made me cry out. The main ingredient of the gunge was mashed potato and in those days that was large packets of Smash (who remembers that?)

The other idea we invented for the summer fair was to send four members of staff or people connected with the school off without a penny on them. They were then driven blindfolded to various areas of Norfolk about 20 miles from the school. They were dropped off and it was a race to see who could get back the quickest. Meanwhile people were asked to guess who would be back first. It usually went ok as the quartet would thumb a lift or borrow a bike etc. One year it backfired when the fete was over before any of them got back!

The most memorable or maybe infamous event at one year's fair was the appearance of the Red Barrows' Formation Team, and yes, I do mean Red Barrows. Members of the PTA dressed up in antique flying gear – all leather and goggles – and did formation dancing with wheelbarrows. The formations were based on those of the legendary Red Arrows. Hundreds of hours of practice went into our display (ok that should have read tens of hours). We weaved in and out with great movement and made intricate patterns and it was very hot in those leather flying suits. Thankfully no wheelbarrows were hurt in the intricate manoeuvres. We made the local press for that one and then the problems started. Fetes and organisations started ringing the school to see if we would perform at their events.

We did a couple but then decided to call it a day. It was just too uncomfortable in those outfits, and we only had them on a short-term loan as well and certainly couldn't afford to buy any ourselves.

I stayed on the PTA whilst my boys were at the school and then decided I would like to get even more closely involved and so stood for election as a parent governor and was lucky enough to come top of the poll. In those days I pretty well knew all the parents and most of them knew me.

Being a governor in those days at that school wasn't a comfortable affair. There were certain undercurrents and a number of problems, and the governing body was run by a cabal or a clique as I referred to it. This consisted of a quartet of the older Governors who seemed to sort out most of the decisions amongst themselves outside meetings. I was even accused by these people of passing on school secrets to certain parties. It was all hush hush James Bond style politics with a small p. There was also discontent amongst the staff, and I felt the school was not in a good place but doing something about it was more difficult.

There were a couple of other younger governors who were also unhappy at the way decisions were being made. One day I received a phone call from one of these younger governors asking me whether I would stand for chair of governors if they supported me. Whether they saw me as a stalking horse, as a means of breaking the cabal, or whether they thought I would do a good job I have no idea.

I thought about it for some time before agreeing. They had obviously been doing a bit of canvassing of the Governors. The existing chairman was standing again and I'm sure was expecting to be re-appointed unopposed. He looked very surprised when I was put forward and seconded.

Before the annual meeting I was told by my supporters that they had worked everything out and I would receive eight votes to the existing chairman's seven. It was an embarrassing agm for me as one of my so-called supporters gave their apologies and wasn't present. I believe they were ill.

All the other Governors voted as expected in the election and that meant the existing chairman and myself were tied at 7-7. The problem was in the case of a tie he had the deciding vote and of course he voted for himself.

I had always got on well with the guy and he was quite magnanimous in saying that he would do one more year and then move aside for me to take over and he kept his word. And so, we started with modernising the governing body much as Stuart Andrews had done all those years previously at the Norwich School. No more meetings going on for four hours, I imposed a two-hour limit and when you do this the agendas always seem to shrink and members stop waffling. Trying to make decisions at 11.30 at night has never been a good idea. Many of the governors had completed a day's work and all too often important matters went through on the nod without being discussed properly because it was too late, and people were too tired.

I was chair of governors for a number of years, working alongside two excellent heads in Tim Strugnell and Andy Whittle. Tim in particular was an outstanding Head Teacher and loved by the staff. "Best boss I've ever had" was a regular comment made. I instigated regular social gatherings between governors and staff to try and improve the understanding of the various roles.

There were a number of excellent governors on the board during my time as chair. One of these was Norfolk's Chief Constable. Carole Howlett took over as temporary chief constable as a stop gap measure. She was anything but a stop gap. She was one of these people who light up a room simply by being there. She had been a Governor in her previous job, and I asked if she would consider becoming a community governor at our school. She agreed and stayed until she moved away from Norfolk on retirement.

I will always remember that at one of the staff/governors get togethers we were going round all the governors giving our names and what we did for a living.

Carole simply said, "I'm Carole and I work with your chairman." That's what being humble sounds like. At work she was very much my boss.

Of all the things I feel I achieved as chair of governors, the two I'm most proud of were firstly getting an ancient Design and Technology block, which was known to contain asbestos, knocked down and replaced with a new purpose-built classroom complete with kiln and secondly saving the swimming pool when it was under threat of closure. Much of the credit for the latter should go to my vice-chairman Chris Doggett who fought hammer and tongs to save the building when, at times, we looked to be beating our heads against the proverbial brick wall.

I had a love-hate relationship with that swimming pool. My boys had learnt to swim in it and so did I. I don't think I've mentioned where I believe my fear of water came from. I can put it down to a day at Great Yarmouth as I must assume that I wasn't born with a fear of water. On this day I went into the sea on my own for a paddle. I couldn't have been very old. There was a family quite a way out and they beckoned for me to join them. I ran towards them, and the beach suddenly shelved downwards. I lost my footing and went under and panicked, taking in this horrible salty water. I'm sure there was no reason to panic but I can still smell and taste that sea water. I was pulled out spluttering.

From that day onwards I hated being in the water and refused all attempts to teach me to swim. There were occasions when I went to the swimming pool a couple of miles from my home but I hated the smell of chlorine and everything about swimming.

As I grew older, I added learning to swim to my bucket list but kept putting it off, having vivid memories of that day at Yarmouth. Then came that auction of promises mentioned in another chapter.

After the designated one on one lessons bought by Anne, I joined a beginners' group in the pool on Thursday evenings. Again, this was fun. Everyone was at the same standard as me, apart from ones that were even more afraid of the water than I had ever been. Another very pleasant part of those Thursday evenings was the noise that found its way into the pool.

The Norwich Pipe Band (bagpipes that is) were practising in one of the classrooms or the school hall and the bellringers were practising in the parish church. It made a glorious mix of sound.

Anyway, our efforts as governors saved the pool and it's still in use today. Today two of our grandchildren swim there. There were many more issues we dealt with on the governing body, and I like to think that by the time I retired it was a fairly harmonious body, I have always tried to bring people together and genuinely work as a team.

The most difficult thing I had to do during my tenure is telling parents that their child couldn't be educated at and attend the school. It was one of those situations where I could see both sides of the issue. Each year group had two classes. We had 32 in each class which meant we were fully subscribed and full. But more parents wanted their children to join. So, we reluctantly upped this number to 33 per class which meant two more children could be admitted. But at that point we had to say enough was enough as teachers couldn't teach classes any larger and we had to think about their welfare as well as that of the children. That meant turning parents down. They appealed against decisions but what else could we do? We didn't have the space for additional classes, and some were already meeting in mobile classrooms.

After many years as chair of governors I was beginning to feel a touch stale and the straw that broke the camel's back was allegations from one set of parents that their son was being bullied. I spoke at length about this with the Head who told me that their son was doing the bullying and not the other way round. So, I spent a couple of lunchbreaks either on the playground or watching from the head's office.

And it was obvious who was doing the bullying. But we had to deal with the parents as though their son was being picked on. We couldn't refute their claims. I've never been quite sure why we couldn't, but it did leave a nasty taste in my mouth. I left shortly afterwards but not exclusively because of that incident. I was just getting tired keeping up with all the reading and all the legislation. It's one heck of a job running what amounts to a business as a volunteer.

I still have a tremendous love of the school which is now a through age primary with many new classrooms. I still remember the day we had an OFSTED inspection, and we were rated as "Good" with some areas outstanding including the general management of the school."

I also vividly remember a number of school trips I went on whilst a governor at the school. These included a couple of visits to the Hippodrome Circus at Great Yarmouth. We took a coach full of children and always had seats in the front, around the ring. That meant we were very likely to get picked on by the clowns. On one occasion another member of staff was hauled into the ring and had to take part in a boxing bout after being wrapped in bandages and toilet paper. I got away very lightly. All I had to do was try to catch popcorn in my mouth from a machine. I got off lightly.

The Great Yarmouth circus is I believe the only permanent circus in the country. It is still going and a unique selling point is the floor of the big ring slides back at the interval to reveal a swimming pool from where the second half takes place. Nowadays there aren't any clowns.

When we had grandchildren we quickly introduced them to the circus. Elliot loved it from the age of three or four, but Poppy had to be taken out on one occasion because she was upset by the noise and smell. She has long got over that and we are back to taking them both most years.

I also remember going with a number of pupils and some members of staff to see a recording of the television cooking show "Ready Steady Cook" which took the form of a competition between two cooks who would prepare a meal and the audience voted for which they considered to be the best. You did this by holding up boards that either had on them red tomatoes or green peppers.

We got to the studio in plenty of time and went through what would happen. There were a couple of mishaps on the way when I got on the wrong underground train but managed to get off again before the doors shut thanks to the shouts of the children and staff. Also, a member of staff had a fear of heights and had to be led with eyes closed across Waterloo Bridge. But back to the competition. The two cooks (one of whom was Brian Turner but the identity of the other escapes me) got to work.

Before the start of the recording everyone is asked if they have any problems, whether they feel ill or have any allergies etc. A big guy wearing a Welsh rugby shirt was with his wife. The lady told the programme organisers that everything would be fine unless a plaster was brought out to cover a cut. Her husband was likely to react badly to this, she said.

The show started and midway through Brian Turner nicked his finger. It was only a small cut, but he called for a plaster. One was immediately placed on his finger at which point the man in the Welsh rugby shirt, who was a very well-built guy, keeled over.

The recording was stopped, and we all had to go onto the stage whilst he received first aid and was taken away to sit quietly to recover. It wasn't the cut or the blood that upset him but the plaster. Apparently, this is called Pittakionophobia. Whilst on the stage we had a chat with the host Fern Britton and one of the children asked Brian Turner whether he enjoyed doing the programme. I will always remember his answer which was delivered in a broad Yorkshire accent and went something like this.

"Son. I get picked up from my home in a limousine, I come here, do the show, meet all you lovely people, get treated to a top-class meal and then get taken home again by car. Oh and they pay me as well. What do you think?"

Eventually the recording got underway again. I remember we had to vote twice for either the green pepper or the red tomato. After the first vote they added each up and then asked us to vote a second time when they already knew the result. That gave them the chance to say "It's very close but the green peppers just have it." Unless of course the red tomatoes had it and then they would say "It's very close but the red tomatoes have it."

Many years later my wife got a similar response to that of Brian Turner. We were looking around racing stables in Newmarket and met Sir Michael Stoute. My wife, being a racing fan, asked for his autograph and gave him her programme for the day along with a cheap pen.

"Madame," he said. "I will be delighted to sign your programme but one of the benefits of making a lot of money is having a good pen." He took out an expensive looking pen and signed the programme. I like to think he was trying to be funny rather than being rude. He didn't give her the pen of course. Many years later at the Epsom Derby we saw Sir Michael walking the course and my wife shouted to him, asking if his horse in a particular race was going to win. He just nodded. It duly came first.

But back to the school trips. I went on a four-day trip to Boulogne so that the children could try out their French "Ou Est Le Toilet?" One enquired. Then there were trips to London to see the musical Cats. On one occasion we had a young boy in a wheelchair and the only way to get him out of the theatre at the end was via the stage door which took us past the actors, most of whom were obviously dressed as cats.

Some of them came to talk to the children. One lad said to a male cat:

"What do you do when you go home?" Back came a very quick reply.

"I have a nice saucer of milk and then curl up for a sleep." I thought that was an excellent answer.

I did other school trips as well – supporting Anne when she was teaching at nearby Cringleford School, I went to How Hill, which is a nature study centre on the Norfolk Broads. Like all residential school trips, it was fun but hard work, particularly at night when the youngsters were far too excited to go to sleep. But we did get trips on the Broads and the grounds are/were marvellous.

*   *   *

I have documented elsewhere my master's degree at the University of East Anglia. That wasn't the end of my university work. Many years later I saw an advert from Newcastle University for a distance learning diploma in life coaching. It was something that seemed to fit in with my counselling interests and so I signed up. Primarily it consisted of research, interviews, essays and much more and I passed. It's something that I've never really used since then but qualifications are never wasted.

So, when I saw a diploma in sports psychology up for grabs I did the work for that as well. This was relatively easy as I used my youth football teams as my focus. The essence of the two diplomas was positive thinking and it's something I always try to employ but am aware that often I fall very short.

And that really was the end of my schoolwork. I can't see myself committing to anymore although I still attend school fetes and events and my family is full of teachers. Anne was a Primary School teacher for many years, our eldest son is a secondary school teacher, and our daughters-in-law are both teachers.

CHAPTER SEVENTEEN – PARISH COUNCIL AND PUBLICATIONS

After a few years in the village, the idea of being a parish councillor appealed to me, but it was some time before I decided to stand for election.

I put my name forward when I knew very few people and very few people knew me. I did no publicity at all and not surprisingly came last in the poll.

"Why did you stand," said one of the councillors at the count?

"I've no idea," I replied and at that point I really didn't have an idea. Perhaps I was just trying to test the water.

I used to attend parish council meetings in my early days in the village because of 1/ interest and 2/ I sent information to the local paper – a return to my roots.

How times have changed. In those days I had to ask permission to take a laptop computer into meetings and it was refused. I'm not sure why but I suspect they were suspicious of what I was using it for, and they felt it was noisy and disruptive (what nonsense). Now meetings can be recorded, and any number of people take along laptops, mobile phones and tablets to help them with minutes, agendas and reports. In fact, as I write this, the council is in the process of going paperless.

A quick aside here: How language and the meaning of words has changed. I told my granddaughter that I was off shopping to buy 100 eye pads. She looked incredulous expecting me to spend thousands of pounds on electronic goods whereas I meant a packet of eye pads with which to bathe my eyes. Similarly, I told her I was going to pick up my tablets and she thought I meant an electronic device which was in for repair while I was talking about my pills for hypertension or high blood pressure (yes I have to take them). But back to the parish council.

Many years after my first aborted attempt to join the council there was another vacancy that could be filled without an election if only one person came forward. I was the only person to apply so was appointed.

During my time on the council, I found it disappointing that our powers were extremely limited. I also found it difficult abiding by certain rules that would exclude me writing what I wanted to for various publications.

So, when it came time to elect a new council I decided to retire. The chair said it was the best thing I had done. That wasn't a criticism it was just her way of saying it freed me up to report on the council in an honest and unbiased way and I do that to this day. I have always emphasised the difference between retiring and resigning. I consider when I leave groups I am retiring. That has a soft feel to it whereas the word resign sometimes implies a certain amount of angst.

So now I must turn to publications:

As technology began to improve, ability to put together publications became easier and easier. For many years living in Hethersett, I had this idea of writing and editing a magazine for the village. The local Media played at covering the village with a few stories here and there. I wanted to put together something dealing with the village's history, writing features, reporting news and campaigning over village issues.

I didn't take this idea forward until one day when I decided to launch a website about the village. I had been closely involved with websites when working for the police and at one point had the fancy title of Head of E Communications. Early on I saw the possibility of the internet as a promotional tool and worked with Radio Broadland to put together a small site featuring crime appeals for the police. It may not sound much now but at the time it was something of a big deal.

I ran all this past the then Chief Constable who said something like "Get on with it then." That culminated with my running the police website for a number of years. I have to say this particular Chief Constable had no interest or knowledge of technology. One day he was given a mouse to use with a new computer and ran it across the computer's monitor and he wasn't trying to be funny.

I set up a website for Hethersett village. But a website wasn't a publication in the accepted sense of the word. In November 2015 I wrote and produced my first Hethersett Newsletter which was just eight pages and the lead story was about the theft of lead from the parish church roof.

Gradually the publication grew and grew and a few years later I was producing 150 pages a month. This then slimmed back to its present size of somewhere between 70 and 100 pages. It has appeared exclusively online ever since. I would love to have a printed edition, but it is very doubtful that I ever will due to the costs and time involved in distributing it. After a few editions we re-named it Hethersett Herald. When I was with the police I started a newspaper style publication for them which was entitled Norfolk Guardian.

I was also approached by the Norfolk Family History Society to see if I would take on the editorship of their quarterly publication "Norfolk Ancestor." They didn't quite put it how I would have liked as they said.

"You are our last chance."

It became evident that if I didn't take on the post the magazine would cease to exist. I had been interested in Family History for some time and history even longer and this seemed to be a good way of combining the two. Along with taking on the editorship I was made a trustee of the society and so began to get a handle on the internal workings of the organisation which has members all over the world. In all I wrote and edited well over 30 magazines and only gave up in 2023 when a new volunteer came forward and I reverted to being Publicity and Public Relations Officer. I subsequently retired (that word again) from that position but am still a volunteer at the society's headquarters in Norwich and today volunteer on the front desk when the headquarters in Norwich is open and also look after the society's Facebook page.

Then I was approached to edit another publication. The Hethersett "Good News" magazine has been in existence for over 150 years and is church based. It started life as a small insert at the back of a national magazine full of home-spun philosophy and hints. Gradually it became a Hethersett publication but was home made for many years before professional printers were called in. Today as I write this, Good News is put together using Publisher software and then printed by a professional company before being distributed by an army of volunteers.

Again, I was told that I was pretty much their last chance, and the publication was in desperate danger of folding. I was delighted to take this on and, hopefully, improve its content and the way it looks, which was my aim. I cannot look after any publication without trying to improve it.

Today it has a circulation of just over 1,000 and runs to 32 pages and is fully supported and funded by advertising and small subscriptions.

My love of publications goes back to the days when I used to read comics and even put together my own. Now I do it on a voluntary basis which I have to say is hugely enjoyable but time consuming and at times hard work. It is something that gives me incredible satisfaction.

CHAPTER EIGHTEEN – WEDDING DAY

As I mentioned, this autobiography is not in chronological order, and I am jumping around a bit. And so to my wedding day.

Saturday July 24th, 1976 – The Day I Got Married

At the time in my personal diary, I called this "the most important day of my life and certainly the one that has meant the most to me and will mean a completely different style of living from now on."

That might be a touch trite but it's how I felt at the time.

I seem to remember I slept on a mobile bed at a friend's up in Yorkshire on the eve of the wedding. The following memories are taken direct from my personal diary written at the time.

"Despite the impending excitement I slept well and only got up half an hour earlier than in the past two days. I had a bath and then put my old clothes on and had breakfast.

"Everybody seemed to think I should have felt nervous, but at that point I certainly didn't. While others got ready, I quietly read a book and it wasn't until I finished getting ready and got my suit on that the nerves started.

"I was ready by 10.30 am and that meant walking round and round the house trying to kill time before setting out at 11 am.

"We took both cars to the Darrington**. Mine was being hidden away and Mike (my best man) followed to pick me up and take me back to Knottingley.++

"It was when we were halfway back that I realised I had left my camera in the car. So others were dropped off at the church and we went back to pick it up and we were still back at the church on time and it was 11.45 am.

"The first thing was to go into the vestry and pay the fees and then we took up our places at the front.

"Anne was just about on time and looked pretty in her lovely wedding dress. I had bad nerves just before the service, but once it got going, I was okay. In fact, it was all slightly hazy to me as if everything was slightly unreal, although of course it is a unique occasion which will never be repeated.

"After the ceremony there were plenty of pictures to be taken by the official photographer and all the friends and relations. In fact, there must have been well over 100 people in the church.

"The photographer took ages, but eventually we got away and drove in Peter's*** car to the Darrington Hotel for the reception. It was quite nice there although of course still being in something of a daze it was impossible trying to take it all in and get round to meeting everyone. We tried our best, however.

"First was a sherry reception on the lawn and then we went in for dinner. The meal itself was excellent, plenty of good hot food. Eventually we got to the speeches. There was a funny one by Peter, a nervous one by me and Mike's (I'll pay him back for that in four weeks' time)+++

"By that time, it was time to leave and unfortunately it was pouring with rain. It was an isolated shower though and by the time we got back to Knottingley it had stopped. Luckily the weather for the service was nice and bright without being too hot. We drove back to Anne's after I had picked my car up. Loads of people followed and came home for tea. By the time we got there it was hectic once again trying to see everyone and grabbing some food.

"By the time we had taken the toilet rolls off the car (about the only trick the multitudes played) it was 5.45 pm when we set off on our honeymoon. During the day Malcolm Robertson had said it would take six hours to Scotland. That was a daunting prospect, but luckily four was nearer the mark although the drive was still long enough, and we were both very tired.

"We found Peebles without much trouble and when we got there asked a bloke the whereabouts of the Cringletie House Hotel. Co-incidentally he saw my Beccles sticker**** on the back and told us he had been stationed there in the war.

"With his directions we had no trouble finding the place. It was a big rambling building in the country and quite superb. We booked in and ordered a pot of tea for our room and then went to bed after washing for our first night together as man and wife."

The order of service at Knottingley Parish Church was as follows:

Entry of the Bride to "A Whiter Shade of Pale" (Brooker/Reid)

HYMN – Thou God of Truth and Love

THE MARRIAGE

THE ADDRESS

THE SIGNING OF THE REGISTERS

HYMN - O Perfect love all human thoughts transcending.

BIBLE READING: Philippians 4, vv 8-9

Finally, brothers, whatever is true, whatever is noble, whatever is right, whatever is pure, whatever is lovely, whatever is admirable - if anything is excellent or praiseworthy - think about such things.

Whatever you have learned or received or heard from me or seen in me - put it into practice. And the God of peace will be with you.

PRAYERS

HYMN: Lord Jesus Christ You have come to us

THE BLESSING

Wedding March - Mendelssohn

NOTES

* - Mike was a school friend of mine. He was my best man.

** - Our wedding reception was at the Darrington Hotel, Darrington, in West Yorkshire.

++ - Knottingley. The town in West Yorkshire where Anne comes from and where we were married in the parish church.

*** - Peter was Peter Harris who became my brother-in-law. He is the husband of Anne's sister Joan. At the time of writing this autobiography, Peter has just turned 90.

+++ - Mike was married to Jeanette in Norwich a month later and I was Best Man. They were subsequently divorced and Mike re-married.

**** - At the time of our wedding I worked and lived in Beccles, Suffolk.

It was an interesting wedding as we had no less than three officiating clergy.

Anne as I've said before was and still is an active Methodist. The Methodist chapel in Knottingley had been pulled down and worship was conducted in a hall (it still is).

She did not want to be married in a hall and so we went to the parish church which is set in its own grounds. The service was conducted by the vicar The Rev Stuart Pearson, the Methodist Minister the Rev Ralph Lowery and another Methodist Minister the Rev Michael Wedgeworth.

I remember chatting to Stuart Pearson before the day. We mainly talked about cricket, and he had stories about Geoff Boycott who lived close by. Mike Wedgeworth was a friend of Anne's from university, and I remember often discussing politics with him. He lived in Barnsley, and we still receive Christmas cards from him and his wife and family. He was a chaplain at the University of East Anglia when Anne was studying there. He subsequently dabbled in politics before becoming chief executive of one of the northern councils.

Ralph Lowery was the local Methodist Minister. I wasn't too happy with his inclusion as I had months previously walked out of one of his services when he attacked pop/rock music for being evil and also verbally attacked the Beatles. I don't mind opinionated people unless their opinions are founded out of ignorance as was the case with this man,

I cannot remember much about the service. I mainly remember what Anne looked like because I have a photograph of her on her wedding day just above my computer desk in my study. I remember my mother and father missing part of the sherry reception after getting lost trying to find Darrington. It shouldn't have been difficult because the hotel was just a few miles down the main A1. Today it is by-passed.

Two other guests - George and Allison Perrin - missed the service because they went to the wrong church and, not knowing anybody, assumed they were at the right one until the wrong bride and groom arrived!

I remember the rain and the afternoon tea whilst many of us watched Knottingley play cricket on the field opposite where Anne was brought up. I remember virtually nothing about the drive to Scotland except thinking we were well on the way to Scotland when we reached Scotch Corner only to find we were still nowhere near.

One other thought surrounds the playing of "Whiter Shade of Pale." It has been one of my favourite pieces of music ever since my schooldays and it was a quiet nod towards my old music teacher Bernard Burrell. We gave the music to the organist the week before the wedding. I don't remember meeting him and we probably didn't.

But oh, my goodness. He had probably never heard the music as what he played was unrecognisable. I should imagine that when he got home, he threw our sheet music into the bin.

CHAPTER NINETEEN – HAPPY and SAD DAYS

Everyone has happy and sad days in their lives, and I am no different. There are days of sheer joy that are life changing and days of abject sadness that will live in the mind forever.

There are relatively few of these days as they rise above or fall below the days that could be deemed slightly good or slightly bad. They are real life changing happy and sad days. I have to start with the sad and then turn to the happy. But you've already read about one of the happy days – our wedding. But let's start with a sad day.

My lovely mother died in November 1981. She was just 61 years of age. I don't remember her being ill at all as I grew up, but I do remember her finding a lump in her breast which was diagnosed as mastitis. I'm not sure whether this was a misdiagnosis or not, but she subsequently developed breast cancer which spread throughout her body.

I have never really written about my mother before writing this book. I was close to her. She was a kind person who would do anything to help anyone. She was friendly and looked after me as a I grew up. When we left the shop, she got a job as a cleaner at my old primary school and loved the interaction with staff and parents.

I remember silly little things like chatting to her as I wiped up the dinner things. I have always had the idea that her and my father didn't have a harmonious relationship and she went home to her mother on two or three occasions but always came back. Of course, I never knew what that was all about.

One of the great sadnesses in my life (I used to call it a regret, but you can only regret something you have or have not done, and I had no control over this) is that my mother never met her grandchildren. She died just three months before our first son was born. We knew that she was seriously ill but tried to keep her going so she could at least see her first grandchild. Sadly, she couldn't hang on.

I remember she went off on holiday with my father but had to come back after feeling unwell. I spoke to her on the phone just after she had received the diagnoses of breast cancer, and I don't remember her having any treatment.

She died at home. The strange thing is I remember very little about her funeral although I could look it up in my diary but, even after all these years, the memory of her death is still very painful for me. Towards the end of this epistle, I have written a piece to my mother which is just a way of summing up my life and finishing off this autobiography as well as coming as close to talking to her again as I can get..

Another sadness (again not a regret because I had no control over it) is that I am an only child. I would have loved to have had a brother or sister or even one of both. I remember vividly sitting on the stairs in the shop (I remember sitting on the stairs a lot – perhaps it was my happy place) and listening to raised voices coming from the lounge. I caught just a few snippets of this conversation, but it soon became apparent that my mother wanted another baby but my father didn't and, as was usual, he got his way. I have no idea how or why this conversation has stayed with me for over 60 years, but it obviously left its mark. Maybe I feel that he never really wanted me although my mother always said otherwise. I remember on one of those washing up sessions with my mother (she always washed and I always dried) that I complained that my father never did the things with me that fathers and sons did and that I didn't feel that we had a good relationship. I remember to this day her reply.

"He would be really hurt if he knew you felt that way."

I doubt that she ever mentioned the subject with him, however.

Recently somebody said something that to me summed up being an only child.

"The problem growing up with no brothers or sisters is you have nobody who has shared your experiences of childhood and nobody you can talk to about them."

I always got on with my father because I didn't know any other way. He had his good points. He worked hard, put food on our table and did play games with me occasionally. But by and large he was a very self-centred man and very selfish, always putting himself ahead of his family although he did help neighbours out when they had problems that needed technical help, like repairing televisions and toasters. He was also a keen gardener as was my paternal grandfather. In fact, he spent most of his life when not working either in the garden or watching television.

Sadly, as he got older, he became even more self-obsessive. Towards the end of his life, he became very lonely, although he did have a few lady friends including a long-term relationship that we were happy to encourage. At no point did I compare his new love to my mother. I don't do things like that.

A typical response from my father came when he was still living at home. I had just been given an award for my community work by South Norfolk

Council and I knew it would be featured in that evening's newspaper. We walked round to the local garage which was just a handful of yards away and bought a copy of that newspaper. We took it back and showed him. I believe Anne said something along the lines of.

"Peter's got an award and there's a report is in tonight's Evening News."

His response was something along the lines of

"Oh right. I'm just wondering whether I should have ham or cheese in my sandwiches tonight."

Somehow that seemed to sum him up, more interested in what he was going to have in his sandwich than something I had achieved. I think I got used to this kind of thing and it truly didn't worry me, although in my sub consciousness it may have had an effect.

When we lost our first grandchild (continue to read to get more on this) his response wasn't to ask how my son and his wife were or how we were but to turn it round to himself.

"Oh so I'm not going to be a great grandfather," was what he said.

That was a typical response, everything was about him and as I was growing up it always was. He decided where we went on holiday (London or Great Yarmouth) and he took little or no interest in me when I was at school or in later life. He gave me no guidance and little support and I can't ever remember him talking to me about school or looking at my work. In fact, we had to support him. I guess I should claim that to be another sadness.

As always there are silly things I remember about him like on one visit to London it was decided that we would go out for the evening. My mother wanted to go to the theatre in Drury Lane to see My Fair Lady. He wanted to go to see a film entitled "The Russians are Coming." We went to the latter. I do remember going to see My Fair Lady at a later date so he must have agreed with that. It was the classic adaptation starring Rex Harrison as Henry Higgins and featuring Stanley Holloway. I must say though that "The Russians are Coming" was a funny film. I watched it again a few years ago and it still made me laugh.

ANOTHER SAD ONE

And now I have to turn to the saddest day of my life. This even eclipsed the death of my beloved mother.

We were at a quiz in a pub in Wymondham with our youngest son and his wife so you can see I have wound the clock back many years. They dropped a few hints during the evening, and we eventually cottoned on that Emma was pregnant. Oh, the sheer joy all round that sadly would ultimately turn to huge sadness.

Everything went fine until the time of the birth approached and Emma couldn't feel the baby moving. Being worried she went to the hospital as a precaution, only to be told that there was no heartbeat and that the baby had died. As if this wasn't bad enough, Emma then had to be induced and give birth a few days later to a fully formed baby, which was a boy. They called him Oliver.

I slept at their home the night before the delivery as they didn't want to be on their own, something I understood. We also went to the hospital to see them after the baby had been stillborn. By this time the hospital had moved from close to Norwich to the outskirts and even closer to where we lived.

There was something hugely tragic to see our son and daughter clutching their dead baby and I find myself tearful as I write this. I had to turn away and stare at the wall. It was the only time in my entire life that I have known uncontrollable grief. And that uncontrollable grief went on for weeks and months. We had some kind of hospital chaplain visit us. She told us how cute the baby looked, and I just wanted to scream out "yes but he's dead." Her presence did absolutely nothing to make me or the others I suspect feel any better. In fact, if anything it made me feel worse. In my mind she was representing something that had denied us something so precious. This isn't a view that I have now, but it was certainly a view I had at the time.

I tried to get some solace by going for long walks, but nothing seemed to work. I have often been looked upon as somebody that can keep his composure under any circumstance and in many ways that is true. On the surface I will seem to be calm and collected. Underneath it all I may be anything but. But this face is something I show to the world. I have been asked to read eulogies at funerals because "you are the only person that can do it without bursting into tears." And so, it has been.

But not at the funeral service for our first grandson. Oliver is buried in the local churchyard in Hethersett and for a long time I couldn't visit his grave. Every time I walked anywhere near the churchyard I would mentally say:

"I love you little man and I will always remember you."

The funeral service was led by the Rev Di Lammas who was Rector of Hethersett at the time. She hit the spot when she said, "Oliver will never hold his mummy's hand, he will never play football with his daddy but he will always be remembered."

Those words were a comfort to me. Going back to that delivery room and that chaplain. She started talking about being with Jesus etc and tried to bring us comfort. Sadly, what she was trying to do brought me no comfort at all and I even resented her being there.

On my walks I kept listening to a new album by Nick Lowe entitled "The Old Magic." There was one song on that album called "Stoplight Roses" that I played over and over. The lyrics had no relevance to my situation. They were about people who try to sell you flowers when your car stops at red traffic lights. But somehow that song takes me back to those horribly sad days. I have no idea why.

But now we must fast forward one year. Oliver was delivered stillborn on September 1st, 2011. Exactly one year to the day on September 1st, 2012, our second grandson Elliot Oliver Steward was born. His middle name is in remembrance of his brother.

Obviously, we were delighted when Matt and Emma announced they were expecting again. Of course there was a huge amount of trepidation. Would the pregnancy be ok or would there be a repeat. I was heartened by reading that after a stillbirth, 99 per cent of subsequent pregnancies go ahead without any problems. But there was always that concern and that one per cent.

If I had been a religious man, I would have prayed. I'm not but I believe I still did pray. And this time everything was fine. It was strange that Oliver and Elliot share the same birthday, but I took this as a sign that Oliver lives on in Elliot and that Elliot is more than just one person.

And of course, Elliot's birth was one of the happy days as was the day his sister and our first granddaughter Poppy was born under three years later. Both have been a source of huge pride and love for me. At the end of 2023 they were joined by our fourth (we always include Oliver) grandchild when Lyla was born to Chris and Alicia. And they will be joined by another before too long. Let's call him or her Bump.

More Happy Days

Just a few months after my mother died, our first son was born. It was all gloriously planned. I think we always took it as read that we wanted children. I couldn't contemplate life without them. We enjoyed our life as a young married couple, but the time came when it felt right to start a family.

Anne had a few miscarriages, which we learnt was quite normal, but then became pregnant and everything went swimmingly. She suffered from low blood pressure, and I remember Christmas 1981 when we were enjoying a meal at a Norwich restaurant when she suddenly keeled over. We had to sit by an open window (and it was very cold) until she recovered. I think the drop in blood pressure was something to do with the sudden intake of food as it happened again when we had our second son. Again, this was in a restaurant (I cannot remember where, but I know we were on holiday). The owners were very concerned because they thought it was their food. We had to assure them that it was normal, and she would soon recover which she did.

But back to the first birth. I have mentioned that in 1982 I was training for the Black Dog Marathon which centred around Beccles and Bungay. On February 23rd I did my longest training run. Training was going well and, on this evening, I ran round and round the village for about 18 miles and then ran home. Not to put too fine a point on it I was seriously knackered but very pleased to have run that far.

My training stopped that night but for the best of reasons.

Shortly after getting home, I had a drink and went to bed. In the early hours of the morning, I was woken up by Anne who was having Labour pains. I repeat I was absolutely knackered. Please remember that as I go on.

I phoned the hospital, and they told me to make her a cup of hot tea and then if the pains continued to come in. At that time the Norfolk and Norwich Hospital was virtually in the City Centre of Norwich. Today that site and the old buildings are flats and ironically, we considered moving to one many years ago but then decided against it.

Babies were born on the delivery floor which was the ninth floor of a tower block and it was just down from the Samaritan centre which I have talked about earlier. Going into labour in the middle of the night wasn't as bad as it sounded. Being on the edge of Norwich, the hospital never had enough car parking during the day, but this wasn't a problem during the hours of darkness. So off we set.

We took the lift to floor nine. I couldn't help wondering why the delivery floor was at the top of the block and not on the first floor. How many people had given birth in the lift because they couldn't wait to go up all those floors? How uncomfortable was it to be nine months pregnant and in pain and going up a lift and what would happen if the lift got jammed? So many imponderables.

But we made it to the delivery room. Thankfully these were the days when fathers to be were allowed to be at the birth. Gone were the days when other halves had to sit in a side room with a pile of musty magazines awaiting the announcement of whether it was a boy, a girl or a duck.

I sat at the side of the bed. I won't bore you with all the grizzly details. Anyone who has been through the delivery of a baby will know exactly what I mean. It was a lengthy process but thankfully no complications. In those days you didn't have the option of knowing the sex of the baby before it was born. If this had been possible, I think Anne would have turned the offer down, but I would have wanted to know.

It was a boy. We had talked about names and a boy would be called Christopher and a girl Claire. In addition, a boy would be given my second name as his second name. At the time I assumed that the name Owen came from a Welsh connection, but I have subsequently found that it was the surname of my Great Great Grandmother. I don't know whether she had Welsh blood, but she was certainly born in Norfolk.

Christopher Owen Steward was born on February 24th, 1982. I sat there and when one of the nurses said:

"Would you like a cup of tea and some toast" I immediately said "yes please."

"Not you, your wife," she replied.

I did get a cup of tea though.

They later told me that I had been one of the calmest partners they had ever had.

I told them it wasn't calmness, but I was so tired from running and being up all night that I could scarcely move.

Actually, I was pretty calm as it wasn't me going through the birth. I was just there to make pathetic comments like: "you're doing well" and "just keep breathing." As if not breathing was an option.

In those days new mums stayed in hospital for a few days. I believe Anne was there for three days before she came home with the baby. It was when I got home and started to make telephone calls that the emotion began to come. I spent most of the morning on the telephone. I had been given a couple of days off work.

With the phone calls made, I got some sleep and then went back to the hospital to see my wife and new son.

The next day I went back to the hospital. One of the nursing staff took me aside.

"You know your baby and wife are fine," she said.

"Yes, is there a problem?" I replied.

"No, it's just your wife has been visited by three church people and we were getting a touch worried that she thought something was wrong."

I must have laughed out loud. Anne was and is a committed Methodist. The ministers were our village Methodist Minister the Rev Brian Dann, the second was a retired Methodist Minister who was still active and a personal friend, the Rev Trevor Hughes and the third was the Methodist Minister from Beccles whom we knew well from our time there, the Rev Al Loades. All turned up wearing what are colloquially known as dog collars.

I was able to set the nursing staff's mind at rest. The other thing I remember about the birth is the enthusiasm of a young midwife who told us it was her first delivery and she insisted on staying on to see the birth long after her shift should have ended and even though others told her to go home.

And that was one of the happiest days of my life.

So let's stay on the same theme and push the clock forward just under two years and the birth of our second son – Matthew David. Again, we had names ready. Matthew for a boy and Claire for a girl. With the boys' names we chose two that we not only liked but which wouldn't seem and sound silly as they grew up. As a little boy Christopher was called Chrissy, now it's Chris. Same with Matthew who has been Matty and is now Matt.

I know that I got the first name Peter because my mother had a friend who had a teenager whose name was Peter. I believe his surname may have been Moore. Isn't it funny how random facts remain in the memory? This Peter was a charming young man and she remembered that when it came to naming me. I have always been happy with the name, although I also like my middle name and would happily have been known as Owen.

A similar thing happened to me, and it was one of those on the surface irrelevant things, but it made me want to call one of my sons Matthew. I was playing tennis with a friend in Eaton Park in Norwich. A man and his young son were on the court next to us and they were having tremendous fun, laughing and thoroughly enjoying themselves. I had no idea who these people were. I had never seen them before and never saw them again but the fun they were having was infectious and I thought when I have children, I want to be a dad like that, and I also want a son named Matthew like this little boy. And so, I later kept that promise.

On the day of Matt's birth, I hadn't run 18 miles and it was a much more orderly event. I believe Anne had been in hospital a couple of days earlier with pains but had been sent home when nothing happened. Then something did happen, and we had two boys.

There have been many more happy and sad days during my life. Many of them have been included in this book. For now it's time to move on again.

PART FIVE – BITS AND PIECES FROM A LIFE
CHAPTER TWENTY ONE – Odds and Ends From A Life

Inheritance

When my father died, I inherited his bungalow. He had hidden the fact that things were falling apart including the boiler not working and underground pipes being cracked. He always came to ours for visits and we rarely went to his. So, it was only when he had to go into a home that we found out the extent of the repairs needed. This surprised us as he was always quite a fastidious man in his dress, very neat and tidy.

We spent quite a bit of money on repairs and then let the bungalow out to people we knew. I used to go over to do the garden, but it was a losing battle. When these people bought a home of their own, we decided to sell the bungalow and I was hugely relieved when I received an acceptable offer, and the sale went through smoothly. There was still plenty that needed doing.

I had hoped that one day we would be able to live in Cromer again and so it came to pass. We had sufficient funds to be able to have the luxury of buying a holiday home in the seaside town. I have mixed feelings about the purchase of second homes, as I know many people do. Huge swathes of Norfolk and Suffolk have properties owned as second homes or holiday places and one of our favourite places Southwold is a large town with only about 900 permanent residents, the remainder being holiday lets or second homes.

We tried to buy a flat at Overstrand Heights on the outskirts of Cromer but that fell through. So, we bought a two-bedroom flat in a retirement block which turned out to be rather a mistake. There was nothing wrong with the flat which was very pleasant. It had a nice lounge/diner and two largish bedrooms and a modern bathroom. The main problem was it felt like an old people's home, and I don't want to demean homes, but we weren't ready for that quite yet.

Apparently, we became the talk of the place and rumours abounded that we would sublet to "undesirables." We never had any intention of subletting as it was against the rules, but you know how rumours build. I told our neighbour, who was much more sensible, to spread the rumour that we were taking in three families of illegal immigrants, and we would be stabling three horses in the garage.

"I don't think I'll do that because some of them will believe me," he said.

We had this flat for a couple of years before deciding to sell. Selling proved difficult. One woman made us an offer which we accepted, then pulled out and then made us another offer which we turned down as we didn't trust her motives. I believe she then came back a third time, but we no longer entertained her. Eventually we did receive an acceptable offer from a much more trustworthy family and so we packed the furniture up and left.

In the meantime, we decided to buy a caravan on picturesque Kelling Heath neat Weybourne in North Norfolk and chose the van which was actually declared to be a lodge and a plot of land to put it on. It seemed perfect. We were right in the forest, a good 10 minutes' walk away from the village square/centre, so nice and quiet. And best of all you could look across the fields and see the North Sea in the distance. The problem was this was in the Spring and by Summer the trees had all their leaves back and we couldn't see the sea, or should that be sea the see? Nevertheless, it was an enjoyable place to be even though when the leaves came off the trees our decking got completely covered and our gutters were filled with detritus.

But it was a good move. Friends and families have been able to enjoy the caravan/lodge and, in the summer, the park is alive with owners, people renting the caravans and people camping there. The park is about a mile from the beach at Weybourne, although beach is a wrong term as it's all shingle and stones. We had thought about having a property at Kelling Heath before buying the flat at Cromer and probably would have been better going down that route.

So once again we spend time each year living in North Norfolk and travelling on the Coasthopper and Coastliner buses along the coast. We have even walked a considerable amount of the Norfolk Coastal Path and will continue to enjoy this beautiful part of the world for many years to come and in particular the beautiful open Norfolk skies that seem to go on forever.

A Daily Blog

I have already mentioned an abortive effort to start writing a daily diary which was then followed by a real attempt that started on December 23rd, 1972, and which has been running ever since.

The same thing happened with a blog. Over the years, with the improvements in technology, I made a number of attempts to start a blog and two or three were aborted. I kept one going for a couple of months, but it was always a false start.

But, when in 2020 we suffered lockdown through the COVID pandemic, I made a genuine attempt to write a daily blog and it started to take off. At the time of writing, I have completed almost 2000 blogs and have no intention of stopping.

The blogs started as an outlet when I had more time on my hands than I would have cared for. We couldn't see or visit people as everyone will be only too aware. Anne lost two brothers during the pandemic, and we couldn't travel to their funerals. I know many other people shared the same horrible experiences. Various enquiries have suggested that the pandemic was handled badly by the Government, but this biography isn't here to make political comment. I leave that to my blogs which occasionally do become political in nature.

I wanted to share what skills I might possess to help people and that for me meant writing. Writing is what I am, and writing is what I do.

At first, I used the blogs as a means of keeping people informed about what was happening in our village, what was closed and what was open. This went hand in hand with my e-magazine which continued to be published throughout lockdown. No groups were meeting, and people were almost trapped at home, but there was always things to report and I began to have a hope that Hethersett Herald and Peter Steward's Daily Blogs would act as a record of some very strange times. I think this is something that I managed to achieve.

So, each day I would go out for my one permitted piece of exercise which usually meant about two miles around the fields of our village, carefully ensuring no meetings with other people and occasionally shouting to friends and people we knew and from whom we had to keep our distance. In many ways it was a frightening time and one I hope we never have to repeat.

I posted the blogs on my website and then on my Facebook page and they began to become popular and attract more and more people whom I called my bloggettes. With popularity ever increasing I decided to launch a dedicated Facebook page which I called simply Peter Steward's Daily Blog. The comments kept coming and were very humbling.

It is my intention to make this autobiography part of a trilogy of self-published books about my life. Volume Two will feature my involvement in sport which I have already touched on and Volume Three will be about my holidays and trips. In addition, I hope to bring out at least one volume of my blogs with the first covering the first year of lockdown.

As an appetite whetter for the lockdown blogs volume here are a couple of those early blogs. I have to say I am very proud of the response to the blogs and the lovely comments I received and continue to receive.

19th March, 2020

There's nothing happening but everything is.

That may sound like something of a contradiction, but it does sum up the current situation in Hethersett.

I spent quite a bit of time this morning re-writing large sections of Hethersett Herald to reflect the current situation in our village. It's now more of a case of what is open and functioning rather than what is shut. I couldn't help but muse on the fact that news is likely to be in short supply over the next few months. The cancellation of VE Day celebrations is particularly sad as this would have brought the village together and been a piece of village history. But then I realised that what we are living through at the moment is exactly that - a piece of village history.

I can imagine a conversation between two elderly people in 50 years' time:

"What do you remember about growing up in the village?" asks one.

"Well I remember when we had that there virus thing, when everyone had to stay indoors. That was a rummin," replies the other.

The Coronavirus will obviously take its place in Hethersett folklore - but not for some while of course. Today we have to live through it and stay safe.

Today has brought news that the parish council office in the village hall will be closed to the public until further notice. Schools of course will shut as from tomorrow, although they will stay open for children of key workers and children at risk. We are still waiting to hear exactly what that means.

Popped into Hethersett Library which is still open and also read many Facebook messages expressing thanks for how the majority of people are behaving and supporting each other during the crisis.

And there is some good news. Popped into Church Farm shop to find the place thriving and a hive of activity. It seems a long time ago that we spoke to Jake Willgress about how takings had slumped because of the road works and traffic lights. Now we are seeing the other side of the story. The shop is providing a valuable local service. I just hope that when things calm down and we return to normal that people will continue to patronise and shop at local outlets which are serving them so well during the crisis.

Jake told me that he had sold a week's worth of bread in a morning. He and his staff are working hard to keep things going and also undertaking deliveries. Emergencies can bring the best out of people and let's hold onto that thought as we go forward.

AUTHOR'S NOTE: Church Farm is now nationally recognised and has won a number of local awards.

24th March 2020

I find it quite amusing when the national news concentrates on one town and village and heralds it as doing something unusual or ground-breaking regarding self-help during the current crisis.

Hethersett has been doing that since the start of the pandemic. So many people in our village have been working so hard to ensure people are kept informed of what is going on and everyone has access to food etc.

The questions now seem to surround the word lockdown - the latest buzzword. No we aren't in lockdown. We can still shop for vital supplies; we can still go out for a walk/cycle ride/run.

But the fact remains that providing you don't have close contact with anyone outside your immediate household, you cannot spread the virus. The quicker we abide by the rules, the quicker we can all get back to normality. It's only when you experience something like this that you value the freedom that we usually have - the freedom to go out for coffee, go to the shops, play sport, visit families and friends, the list is endless.

Thank goodness for the internet in these tough times. It helps us all to stay informed and also continue to function in many areas as normal. I think if Broadband went down, we would lose an essential lifeline.

Travels and Holidays

Growing up, I used to enjoy family holidays, but they were strictly limited. The only two places we ever holidayed were London and Great Yarmouth. I don't remember ever going anywhere else. Great Yarmouth was where my maternal grandparents and many ancestors came from. Going further back many ancestors came from North Norfolk and these are the places where I have always felt very much at home. Take Salthouse on the North Norfolk coast for example. It's a small coastal village and it's a long way down to the beach from the main road. There's a church, a pub, a shop and not a lot else. But I have always been drawn to the place and that's long before I found that many of my ancestors came from there.

The church at Salthouse holds regular art exhibitions and at one we got talking to one of the artists who came from Norwich.

"Are you interested in church graffiti," he asked?

"Yes I am," I replied and indeed I had been ever since going to a lecture on the subject a few years ago. In medieval times, builders and craftspeople would leave their calling card with drawings on stone etc that might then be covered up and which are gradually being uncovered.

"There's some interesting carvings in the wood of the choir stalls. I think the youngsters in the choir must have been bored by the long sermons," said the artist.

We took a look and amongst the names scratched into the wood was my great great great grandfather Dew. I immediately had a picture of him in his choir robes scratching out his name for posterity. It somehow made me feel very close to him to think that all those years ago he had sat in the same place where I was now sitting. It's a good job that he had a short surname otherwise it would just have been his initials and that would have been much more difficult to interpret.

Great Yarmouth was always a draw for me. Initially we went on the train but then, when we got a car, we went via the back roads as my father would never go down "the death trap" known as the Acle Straight which is a stretch of the A47 which cuts its way through the marshes and leads directly to Yarmouth. Today I always go the back roads, not because the Acle Straight concerns me but because the road across the Broads is much more picturesque and takes you through the village of Filby where each year they have a remarkable floral display that seems to go on for miles. It's the best way I've ever found of ensuring vehicles keep to the 30-mph speed limit as everyone slows down to look at the flowers. Taking that route also brings you into the back entrance to Great Yarmouth and saves having to fight your way through the town centre traffic.

We never stayed overnight in Great Yarmouth. It was always day trips. The trains at times were ridiculously crowded. I have seen a photograph of Norwich Station with the queues snaking around the pavements outside the station. It was always a crush. Now you can easily get a seat on a half full train to Yarmouth. I remember too that return trains were always crammed full as well as people piled onto the platform at Yarmouth Vauxhall station.

The station is some way from the sea front. There used to be another station along the seafront, but this is no more and is a car park.

At Yarmouth we would walk up and down the golden mile, perhaps visit the Pleasure Beach, sit on the beach, eat at one of the seaside cafes where the smell of chlorine from the washing up was overpowering. I still remember that smell. You would sit on long wooden benches around the edge of these places, and we would always eat ham rolls. If I have a ham roll today it still takes me back to those days. There are still plenty of these cafes, but they have all long been modernised and now you sit inside or outside around modern tables and benches.

We would watch the bowls (that's bowls as in the sport and not as in the receptacle that you eat out of) – never play but just watch. Then we would go home again, never down the main road.

When we went to London we went for a week. We always went to the same bed and breakfast place in Clapham Common, getting off the Underground on the Northern Line and making a short walk. Days would be spent in central London. I particularly liked visiting Trafalgar Square to feed the pigeons. They have long gone but in the 1960s you could buy bird food to feed them. They eventually had to go because of the mess they were making on surrounding buildings, not to mention on the model Lions in the square itself. We regularly went to London Zoo and I also remember going to Heathrow Airport in the days when you could go onto a roof of one of the buildings to watch the planes taking over. We never flew anywhere, just looked at those who did.

Sometimes we would stay or visit my cousin and her husband in Tunbridge Wells. We would get the train from London. Always the train, we never took the car. I always referred to the couple we stayed with as Aunt Gladys and Uncle Tom, although Gladys was my grandmother's brother's daughter which made us cousins. Tom would always call me "boy" in an affectionate way. I went to stay with them at the time that I proposed to my girlfriend, then to become my fiancée and subsequently my wife. Anne came over and we have a photo of us all in the garden of their house. I went up to London during that visit and bought an LP by the Carpenters and another by America. Both were very tuneful. Tom liked classical records and not pop, but he listened to what I had bought and agreed it was very tuneful. I've never worked out if he genuinely enjoyed the music or was just being polite.

Gladys was Tom's second wife. His first wife had died. He was a civil servant in Whitehall. I loved him dearly and his typical London friendliness and sense of fun. I have a vivid memory of being driven out to a pub called the Spotted Dog just outside Tunbridge Wells in Penshurst. We had our photographs taken under the pub sign and I still have a couple. Almost 60 years later I returned to visit this pub. We had lunch there and I had another picture taken outside and used these in one of my blogs.

I vividly remember one day as a young boy, I was sitting on the wall of the fountain in Trafalgar Square when I toppled over backwards into the water. The only thing hurt was my pride, but the water was very cold, and I had to sit in wet clothes on the train all the way back to Tunbridge Wells.

I don't think my mother and father ever considered going anywhere else other than London or Great Yarmouth. I did have the chance to go with school to Greece and I believe my grandparents offered to pay but I preferred to stay at home. I also turned down a school trip to Spain or it may have been Switzerland or even France but for weeks after had to put up with friends going on and on and on about what a good time they had when I hadn't a clue what they were talking about and became more and more bored.

Same kind of thing happens when I'm in a group of people who are all reminiscing about a past that I had no part in. You know the kind of thing.

"Do you remember old Ted Smith."

"Yeah what happened to him."

"I think he married Louisa West. Do you remember her?"

And so on and so on and so on. Everyone is enjoying talking about people that you do not know and probably never want to know.

I'm sure the first time I went abroad was when I was working on the Lowestoft Journal. I went to Spain with a couple of friends, one of whom I had been at school with and one I had become friends with through supporting Norwich City.

We went to Lloret De Mar. It was bog standard disco Spain, not really suited to a person like myself who never liked discos, although I did pop over to a pub in Norfolk on Saturday nights when I was in the sixth form at school and they had a disco which I enjoyed, although we spent quite a bit of our time drinking at a pub down the road.

So I went to Spain and got horribly drunk on sweet rum and blackcurrant. I have never drunk it since and in writing this I can still smell and taste that sickly sweet mixture. Who remembers those vessels that had a long spout? The liquid was poured onto your forehead and the idea was to let it run down your nose and into your mouth. Quite a bit must have gone in because I got well and truly drunk and I can honestly say that is the last time I got well and truly plastered.

The three of us also went to Butlins at Skegness where I had an enjoyable week apart from one night when we were threatened by some yobs and had to lock ourselves in our chalet and pee in the sink. Those were days before en suites, and we were too scared to go to the washing block. I can honestly say that was the one and only time I have p----d in a sink. Obviously, a shower is another matter altogether.

My life of travelling eventually really took off. I have already recounted my fateful trip to Russia, something that was to change my life for ever. I remember when I got back from that trip, I felt rather empty for some time and suddenly found I had a taste for seeing other countries and experiencing other cultures. So, the following year I decided to go on another exchange trip (once again there was no exchange element to it), this time to Romania where I came across some of those who had been on the Russian trip. By this time Anne and I were engaged but I went on my own.

The trip was nowhere near as enjoyable as that to Russia. This was in the days when Romania was still ruled by the evil Ceausescu regime. His picture was everywhere. The leader of our group was nowhere near as approachable, and I found the capital Bucharest to be monolithic and unattractive. We did get to go to Transylvania and spend some time by the sea where we had a barbecue on the beach but had to put the flames out because there was a fear they could be seen in Russia. I have never understood what threat a few barbecues posed to the Soviet Union but I guess you never know.

Then of course we got married and our travels began in earnest starting with a honeymoon in Scotland and then venturing much further.

Before writing this book, I got a list of all the countries in the world and worked out that we have visited at least 47 and possibly more. I have a variety of memories from our travels like running through Heathrow Airport with a two and four year old and just catching the plane to Spain after missing the turn off on the M25, I remember the incredible beauty of Switzerland and Austria and travelling first class on their trains that always left dead on time and always arrived dead on time apart from our train to the airport which broke down.

Holidays for us are often not holidays but experiences, such as visits to Egypt, Morocco, Vietnam, Cambodia, Turkey, Australia, USA and New Zealand. Some are full of history such as much of Europe. Very few over the years have been a relaxing sit by the pool holiday.

Talking about our travels would take a book in itself and it is my intention to make that book three of my trilogy where I will develop and relate stories about what I have told you here. For now just let me say that we have stayed in many different styles of accommodation from the basic to the luxury – in hotels, in bed and breakfast guest houses, in tents, in cabins, in French gites, in castles and in many more places. Here's a little more flavour of what is to come in what will be the not too distant future.

For over a decade we have been holders of the Holiday Property Bond which I can thoroughly recommend. HPB has high class properties throughout the world and in particular in the United Kingdom. They are always of the same high standard with excellent facilities.

Those who know me will know that I'm very partial to a wind up and a practical joke or two. One of my favourites was a wind up in New Zealand many years ago. I like to employ Socratic Irony which I believe is pretending that you know very little about a subject when you know a reasonable amount about it. Socrates used to employ such tactics to get people to talk about themselves. They thought he was a bit of an idiot. I think Louis Theroux employs a similar strategy.

Anyway, after a very very long flight we landed at Christchurch Airport on the South Island of New Zealand. It was a lovely city, sadly badly affected by a major earthquake a few years ago. We were picked up at the airport by a driver from the hotel where we were staying.

He was quite a chatty chap and we tried our best to sound intelligent despite suffering severely from jet lag which told us that in our minds it was the middle of the night whereas all around us the sun was shining.

As we drove along, we passed rugby fields and I decided to go with a wind up.

"Is that a rugby field," I asked?

He replied in the affirmative.

"Oh I didn't realise that you play rugby in New Zealand. Do you have a national team and are they any good," I asked?

He looked at me rather strangely which probably wasn't surprising.

"Haven't you heard of the All Blacks," he said?

"Are they a team of black people," I replied?

There was a gap in the conversation whilst he stared straight ahead.

"Are you taking the piss?" He said. I think he had got the measure of me by that time.

"Yes sorry. I replied it must be the jet lag. I'm actually a sports editor back in the UK."

For some reason we got on fine over the next few miles until we were dropped off at our hotel. We booked in, had a quick wash and then went out to find some lunch. We walked to the local park which bore a fairly close resemblance to one of the parks in my native Norwich and there in the café we ate fish and chips. I couldn't help thinking that we had travelled over 12,000 miles to sit and do the same thing we might be doing at home. A couple of days later we were on the road and stopped at a small town where they had an art exhibition. It was just like the amateur art exhibitions at home, and we sat drinking coffee, exactly as we would have done at home.

The other thing I remember about that day was going for an early evening (early evening New Zealand time that is) walk to another park and suddenly becoming completely disorientated and not able to think where the hotel was despite it only being a couple of blocks away. Such is jetlag.

New Zealand has a limited ability on the world sporting stage. Yes the All Blacks rugby team is one of the greatest of all time and they aren't too shabby at cricket either. But that's about as far as they go. A few tennis players, a few soccer players, a few athletes.

So I was intrigued when we passed the national museum of sport which was in Dunedin in the North Isle. We had just walked through a market where a stallholder had recognised our Norwich City shirts.

"Do you support the Canaries," he asked?

"Yes we come from Norwich".

"So you go to Carrow Road?"

By this time, I was hugely impressed.

"How do you know about the Canaries and Carrow Road," I asked?

"I watch the championship on television every week," he replied. Appparently he had become a Norwich fan because he liked their bright yellow and green colours.

He suggested as sports fans we might be interested in the museum of sport. So off we went. And I had an ace up my sleeve. A kind of reverse

Socratic Logic where I sounded intelligent (which I know is quite hard for you to believe).

Many years ago, Norwich had tried to sign a New Zealand player by the name of Wynton Ruffer. It was a name that always stuck in my memory. So, I thought I would be a clever bugger by asking them at the desk if they had anything on Mr Ruffer.

"Absolutely. His room is on the third floor," a helpful person behind the counter said very quickly.

I was certain they had misheard me. But no, we climbed the staircase and there it was – an entire room to Wynton Ruffer. He was very famous in New Zealand and actually became minister for sport. I also found the following about his Norfolk connection. This is what Wikipedia had to say.

"Rufer attracted the attention of Norwich City manager Ken Brown, who invited the player and his older brother Shane Rufer to Norfolk for a trial. He impressed and signed a professional contract on 23rd October 1981, becoming the first Kiwi to do so. However, he was denied a work permit to play in England, so he joined Fussballclub Zürich in May of the following year."

Elsewhere in the museum there was a series of rooms dedicated to the Kiwi cricket team and even more dedicated to the All Blacks. Then there was the real claim to fame – a room dedicated to champion lumberjacks and a room dedicated to champion wood choppers. Yes, seriously wood choppers.

I tried a similar wind-up in Scotland many years later. We were staying in the Trossachs and close by was the town of Dunblane. We found it to be a very friendly place. We must have looked like visitors, perhaps it was the camera slung over my shoulder that did it. Two ladies actually crossed the road to tell us all about the town and instruct us where to go (in the nicest possible way). They told us to hurry if we wanted to visit the cathedral as it closed for lunch. They also said the town museum was worth a visit.

Now Dunblane is famous for two things – one good and one horrible. It was the town where a murderer ran amuck in the local school, killing staff and pupils. Two of the pupils who survived that shooting were Jamie and Andy Murray who you will know not for their prowess of chopping wood but for being World Number One tennis players (Andy in singles and Jamie in doubles). They are the good things about the town (or one of them).

So we went to the museum. It was free and very interesting, although I don't remember seeing anything about the Dunblane Massacre/shooting.

Apparently, there was a memorial in the cathedral but somehow, we missed that as well. I found this sad because horrible as it was it was still part of the history of the town.

The lady on the desk obviously recognised us as sports fans.

"You'll find Andy Murray's shoes on the top floor," she said.

"Oh has he lost them," I replied.

"No they're Andy Murray's shoes. He donated them to the museum."

"Oh that's nice I said. Who is Andy Murray?"

I don't think she answered, and we slunk away with our tails between our legs. Apparently, the Murrays own a very expensive hotel in the town. We didn't need a hotel because we were staying halfway up a mountain between Aberfoyle and Calendar. We didn't find Andy Murray's shoes hugely interesting I have to say.

Reviewing Things

Somebody said to me one day.

"You like reviewing things".

And he was right. I have spent my life reviewing music and much more.

"Why," I asked.

"You should review things on Amazon."

And then one day I found an e-mail in my inbox. It was the first of hundreds that would come my way. Usually, they were in very bad English which suggested that they were spam messages. But the first one gave me a code to use at checkout which they said would give me the item free of charge and all they asked in return was a review on Amazon. As no money was needed, I decided to give it a go and so bought the item using the code which indeed gave it to me free of charge. I posted a review, and soon more offers came my way.

In a short time, I became swamped with offers. I was offered all kinds of things from dog collars (not for me I add) to nail varnish, towels to vitamin pills but mainly electronic goods such as speakers and MP 3 players. I reviewed as many as I could and soon noticed that my review ranking was going up and up. Apparently, there are something like 17 million reviewers on Amazon. Most probably only review once. But my world ranking shot up through the thousands and into the hundreds and a high of just over 200. This was a world ranking and so my UK ranking was even higher.

Then Amazon changed the rules amongst allegations that people were giving inflated reviews and high scores in order to get more and more free stuff. The top reviewer said that each day she got home to so many parcels that she didn't know what to do with them. Well, I knew what to do with mine. I gave most away to charities for raffles and sales.

The new rules meant that you had to buy the products and would then be reimbursed. I wasn't into playing that game, but I did enjoy it while it lasted and occasionally, I still get e-mails offering me cat flea remover tablets and the likes.

I have long given up reviewing as it just took up too much time and I had better things to do (like writing books).

Christmas

I've always loved Christmas. As a child I remember the anticipation of Christmas Day, the sleepless night that was Christmas Eve and the best night's sleep of the year (Christmas night into Boxing Day).

I can't remember when I first became aware of Christmas, but I guess it was around four years of age. I don't remember the shop being decorated but I do remember making those looped paper streamers that you licked and stuck together and then put across the room. Then of course there was the Christmas tree that seemed to magically appear each year. Never too big and never overdressed.

And the best thing about early year Christmases is that my maternal grandmother came to stay. She probably bought sausages from Craske's which I have mentioned before.

There was no bedtime hour on Christmas Eve. The evening seemed to go on and on and I was allowed to stay up as late as I wanted as everyone knew I wouldn't sleep anyway.

But somehow, I always did seem to fall asleep before Santa came because by the morning there was a pile of gifts in my room.

There were some presents I remember more than others such as television themed games like "The Army Game" and a nature game where you went in search of collecting animals that were under threat of extinction. I remember the Coelacanth an almost extinct fish and an Okapi, an almost extinct deer. I believe this game was probably Zoo Quest or something like that. It came in a large cardboard container that was more like a massive envelope than a box.

One year I came across a stash of presents hidden in a wardrobe. I can't remember whether I was sneakily looking or just found them by accident but as they were in my parents' bedroom I have to assume I was on the hunt. I saw this long straight thing but shut the door before I could be found out. The next day after Santa had come, I looked at the long straight thing and saw it had a handle and was quite obviously a cricket bat. I just hadn't looked properly when I came across it, probably being too scared of being found out.

My father always seemed to work on Christmas Day morning which was something I thought was unfair but later realised that he had probably volunteered through being paid generous overtime. At that time, he was a television engineer. He always seemed to come home in time for Christmas lunch. So I was left to my own devices in the morning with nobody to play with as my mother and grandmother prepared lunch.

My Aunt lived just round the corner, and she and my father just didn't get on. As I grew up, they did have an uneasy relationship at times and often she and my uncle came round on Christmas afternoon and we sat around the television set watching Billy Smart's Circus followed by the Queen's speech and then probably a pantomime. It was all very dull. And that seemed to go on for years and years.

So in some ways I enjoyed Christmas and in others I didn't. Fast forward many years and I definitely didn't enjoy it. I can remember at Cromer both myself and flatmate John desperately wanted to stay in Cromer for Christmas but we felt duty bound to go home and spend a very boring time with parents watching Billy Smart's circus and the Queen's Speech.

Christmas moves on as Christmas tends to do and it was culture shock time when I got married and we had Christmas in Yorkshire. Anne comes from a big family and there were numerous nieces and nephews and there could be up to 30 people there for Christmas tea. Lots of games and the never used front room sprang into action for one day only.

There were so many people there that we had to have three or four sittings. When our boys came along, we still went to Yorkshire. I remember one of them being so young that we had to tie him to the chair to stop him falling off.

Then as the boys grew, we graduated to stay in the city of York, filling the car up with presents. We hired cottages or flats close to the city centre and there was something magical about being able to walk to the shops and enjoy the singing of Christmas Carols. On one Christmas when the boys were very young, we decided to go to the Christmas service in York Minster. It was pretty full, and we were led right to the front to sit on the floor close to where the Archbishop of York would be giving his Christmas address. We were on tenterhooks throughout the service as to whether the boys would behave themselves. They did.

Today we pretty much stay in Norfolk over Christmas, although we do drive up to Yorkshire for an annual family party and Christmas 2024 was spent on the south coast with our eldest son, his wife and our one year old granddaughter. We go to many Christmas sales and fairs where it is quite difficult to find anything unusual as the crafts always seem to be much of a muchness.

Nearby towns such as Holt and Wymondham do Christmas well with lots of lights and events. Every year I try to remember and reflect on the real reason and meaning of Christmas and I like to allow my mind to wander back to those quieter days of my youth, whilst reflecting on the fact that Christmas today is much more enjoyable than those days when pretty much all we did was stare at a television set.

Romantic Valentines and Jack Valentines

In a mad romantic moment, I was moved to book what was described as a "romantic Valentine's Day mystery tour."

So early in the morning of Valentine's Day in a year that now escapes me we made our way to the coach picking up point in the nearby town of Wymondham. And off we set.

After a drive around parts of Norfolk and even Cambridgeshire to pick up people, we started to go north. My wish was to get to a romantic hotel with a roaring log fire where we could sit, read a book and enjoy a pint or some mulled wine ahead of the included dinner.

We were pretty pleased around lunchtime when we pulled into the historic Lincolnshire town of Stamford. We had been there before, but it was a pretty romantic place and there was probably a romantic hotel with a roaring log fire awaiting us.

But no we were just there for lunch and an hour or so stop. So it was a whistlestop tour of the town and a quick coffee and back on the coach.

We were hoping not to go too much further. And so we trundled into Lincoln. Pretty pleased again. We had been to Lincoln a number of times before but it's always worth a visit and they probably had romantic hotels with roaring log fires. But no, we were just there for a quick afternoon shop. So, we had a quick afternoon shop and then back on the coach.

And on and on and on we went. Over the Humber Bridge (slightly romantic), past Ferrybridge Services (definitely not romantic and about a mile from where Anne comes from), onto the M62 (ever so slightly romantic if you like driving across the Pennines). By this time, it was pitch black and we had no idea why we had gone such a distance and where we were going to end up (well it was a mystery tour). We ended up at a hotel in the back of beyond on the main road near Halifax.

It wasn't very romantic. We were late for dinner and only had time to chuck our overnight bag into a room and go to the restaurant to eat without even having a shower or time to change our clothes. By this time, we were all so tired that I can't even remember what we ate and I was very glad to climb into bed. Perhaps the next day would be romantic…. But it got worse.

After breakfast we loaded up again and set off. A visit to Liverpool would have been good (but no), Manchester would have been acceptable (but no), the small villages around Saddleworth Moor would have been good (but no). We set off in the direction from where we had come from the previous day.

Back along the M62 and into Yorkshire.

"I bet we're going to York", someone said more in hope than expectation. York is quite romantic. We know it well but by now we were running out of options. York would have been good as we have friends there who live in a luxury apartment overlooking the river. We could have taken them out for coffee.

But then it dawned on us just where we were going. OK I know I'm slightly biased against it, but I don't think anyone would claim that Leeds is in the slightest bit romantic. In fact in my book, it's remarkably unromantic (and of course this is my book). There we were on a Sunday morning in Leeds. The shops weren't open for at least an hour and we had four and a half hours to spend. We wandered round and round and eventually did have a coffee and something to eat.

The time really dragged but eventually we had to get back on the coach where at least it was warm if not greatly romantic. One man summed it all up.

"Four and a half hours on a Sunday in Leeds is nowhere near long enough," he said sarcastically.

It took ages to get back home and it was late evening by the time we did so.

But the real sickener and something that at least made us laugh a few years later when we reflected on the day was that, after a few hours' sleep, I was due to take my youngest son back to University and guess where he was studying?

Yes – a return visit to bloody Leeds.

But while we are on the subject of Valentine's let's talk about a character known as Jack Valentine.

Jack Valentine is a Norfolk tradition. Never heard of him? Then you probably don't come from Norfolk although I'm sure he does appear in other parts of the country as well.

As a boy I was always subjected (in the nicest possible way) to Jack Valentine on February 13th although I'm not sure that I was aware of this gentleman's name.

Basically, a visit from Jack consisted of a ring or knock at the door. When you opened the door there were presents on the doorstep but nobody around. Some mysterious person had left presents and this could happen three or four times. Sometimes there were sweets, sometimes it was fruit and once I even got a magic set.

I have now established that many people still have visits from Jack and as always, the internet came to my rescue to show that Jack is indeed a Norfolk tradition.

"Nobody knows where he comes from. Nobody has ever seen him. Nobody has any idea quite how old he is or why he's never ventured out of Norfolk. What we do know is, for the last 200 years or so, on the 13th of February (or Valentine's Eve), Mr Jack Valentine pays Norfolk a visit under the cover of darkness. He works tirelessly all night, silently and unseen, here and there, leaving small gifts on the thresholds of houses. Answer his knock at the door quickly enough and you might spot him – although nobody's managed that quite yet.

"There are two things that are particularly strange about Jack Valentine. Firstly, he's not that predictable with his gift giving. His more affectionate offerings have included vases, shawls, jewellery boxes… even a writing desk or two. On the other hand, he's been known to leave not such nice gifts: coal, or just a small, meaningless scribble in an extravagant box. Sometimes he'll simply knock on the door and run away. Other times he's attached a string to a gift, pulling the present away as the grateful recipient reaches for it!

"The second thing that's strange about Jack Valentine is that he is unique to Norfolk, and Norwich in particular. The tradition of gift giving on Valentine's Eve has been around for years, too, and was big business in Norwich in the 19th and early 20th century. Accounts at the time talk about thousands of pounds being spent on the occasion, and shops here even took on extra staff to help cope with the demand.

"Not much is known about Mr Valentine himself, only that he is a cheeky, traditional character from Norfolk, celebrated across the county with many families continuing the tradition today. However, what differentiates Jack from other Valentine's traditions is that he is all about family. Jack's gifts are multi-generational. He leaves gifts for everyone – young or old; not just for starry eyed lovers."

And so there you have it. Another memory from childhood and something we continue to this day by contacting Jack to get him to call on the grandchildren, although they never seem to believe me when I tell them that I'm a personal friend of Jack Valentine. I do have my suspicions, however, that the Jack Valentine of my youth may have known my grandfather rather well.

I must relate something else amusing that is another random entry in my autobiography.

Orange – A Colour to Avoid

My mobile telephone bill was confusing. Every month there was an amount included for calls from my mobile to my landline. Always an hour in length and always on a Tuesday. I deducted this amount from my monthly payments and informed Orange of what I was doing.

Instead of dealing with me, they put the matter into the hands of a debt collection company.

I had an almost surreal conversation with a man on the other end that seemed to come straight from a comedy show. It went something like this after I had explained the fact that I didn't make any call to my home number as I was always at home at that time on my own with my wife still working.

Him: "Perhaps you had the mobile in your pocket."

Me: "What I made a call from my mobile to my landline?"

Him: "Yes you could have had it on speed dial."

Me: "So you're suggesting that I activated a speed dial key from a phone in my pocket at the same time on the same day of each week and this call lasted for exactly the same time each week?"

Him: "Well it could have."

Me: "So you are suggesting that I made a call from my mobile to my landline at the same time and presumably spoke to myself from one to the other."

Him: "Well you could have done."

By now I'm getting a little exasperated with this man.

Me: "So I'm phoning myself every week, chatting with myself for an hour. I assume you think I'm talking to myself with a mobile on one ear and a landline on the other."

Him: "Well you could be."

I terminated the call at this point as there seemed no point prolonging a conversation with an idiot.

I put all this down in an e-mail to Orange and got an acceptance that this could not have happened and that the charge would be dropped. I got an apology and £25 from them for inconvenience. A day later I switched my provider to O2.

Isn't it strange how these nonsense and largely irrelevant matters stay in your memory and, in my case, get resurrected in written format at sometime in the future?

Charity Walks

It's hard to recall how many charity walks I have undertaken as I'm sure there have been smaller ones, but there are two major ones separated by almost 40 years.

The first in 1986 was a 110 mile walk from London to Wymondham in aid of a special school at Attleborough which is about seven or eight miles from where we live. The second was a 1,500-mile marathon walk in 2022 to raise funds for the East Anglian Air Ambulance.

At the time of the first of these walks, I was sports editor of the Norwich Mercury Series of Newspapers. In that capacity I came across the unique person that was Les King. Les was an unbelievable character in so many ways. Larger than life, he was one of the beating hearts of the town of Wymondham (always pronounced Windham unless you are referring to a village in Leicestershire where it's pronounced the way it is spelt).

I got to know Les through my job. He was known as King of Sport because of his support of boxing, cricket and football locally. He was also heavily involved at the time with Chapel Road Special School at Attleborough and later became patron of the Wymondham-based cancer charity Star Throwers. Les supported many other local organisations and charities, was part owner of Olympic Removals with former Norwich City Football Club captain Duncan Forbes and owner of the Regal Cinema in Wymondham.

I have so many amusing memories of Les. Memories like the day that he was driving and saw me at the top of St Stephens which is one of the main roads in Norwich. Today it's only open to taxis, buses and bikes but in those days, it was open to all traffic. Les was driving round the roundabout at the top of (or the bottom depending on how you look at things) the road. He wound his window down and shouted the first part of a three-part message at me. I say three parts because he went round the roundabout three times as I stood there gobsmacked and trying to work out what he was saying.

As manager of the Regal Cinema, Les did most of the jobs. He took the money, sold the snacks and ice cream and much more. I still remember on one occasion he walked to the front of the cinema and announced the coming programme as the film trailers had failed to load.

"Next week we've got Rocky Four coming. That's like Rocky One, Two and Three but better," he said. He always had a way with words.

I remember on one occasion the cinema was showing a very popular film, the name of which escapes me now. All the seats were filled but Les was anxious that as many people as possible could see it. So he offered to refund the ticket price for any youngster prepared to sit on their parents' lap and then went one better by saying he would refund the ticket prices of anyone willing to leave the cinema and come back for a free showing later that evening. Quite a few people left at that point.

Because I did a lot of work with Les he used to let myself and my family in free – something I was appreciative of but didn't feel comfortable about. So when I mentioned this to him he just made up vague amounts to charge us and always threw some bags of crisps or chocolate in.

On one occasion we took our youngest son and a number of friends for a birthday treat to see a film (again my memory doesn't allow me to remember which one). Les, as usual, tried to let us in free and I refused and put a £10 note on the counter. This was in the days when £10 was a reasonable amount of money. He just grabbed a handful of change which I put in my pocket. When I got home, I found I had more money than I had set out with! This was typical of Les and might have been a contributory factor in the Regal eventually closing its doors although it is still fondly remembered by Wymondham people of a certain age and occasionally still shows films.

Les went on to write three books about his involvement in sport. They were written in a very chatty style and mentioned lots of local people, myself included. The books were entitled King Of Sport One, King of Sport Two and of course King of Sport Three – the last of which was just like the other two but better!

Les was a very generous man as his sponsorship of sport illustrates. A few years before he died, I had the honour of organising a series of cricket charity matches in aid of Star Throwers. These featured my team Hethersett and Tas Valley of which I was chairman at the time and a Norfolk Select XI. I can't remember who won those challenge matches after all the result was irrelevant. It was the amount of money raised that was important.

Les was also a regular at Park Farm Gym and Leisure Centre which is just half a mile from where we live in Hethersett. Les could often be seen sitting in the foyer after a swim with a cup of coffee – something nobody else ever got.

One club member queried this one day:

"Why does Les always get a cup of coffee and nobody else does?" this person asked.

"Because he supplies all the coffee, sugar and milk for the staff," came the reply.

I was in Vietnam when I heard that Les had died. It came as a shock. I knew he suffered from heart problems but had no idea how bad this was. I got the information sent to me via e-mail. It ruined that day for me. He is buried close to the entrance gates in Wymondham cemetery, and I often pass and think about Les and all the fun he brought to our lives.

But back to the walk from London. I can't remember how or why I was asked although I'm sure it would have been through my job. There were four of us on the walk and we ended up splitting into two groups. Les and his mate Buster, whose real name was Alan, pounded ahead whilst me and a police officer by the name of Bernard Daynes lagged a couple of miles behind and went at a slower pace.

Bernard had a handicapped son who attended the Chapel Road School. I was just delighted to be able to raise some money for such a good cause.

What follows are entries from a diary of the walk which Les wrote. They are slightly edited as some of the information is about local people which will be meaningless to anyone reading this. Les turned the diary into a small booklet that had many adverts in and raised even more money for the school – he was a very persuasive man. I hope you don't find this too self-indulgent. This is what the booklet said (and they got it slightly wrong as I have never been an enthusiastic marathon runner).

The four intrepid walkers were:

"Les King, a well-known local businessman and all-round sportsman; Alan Farrow, a keen boxing fan and long-time friend of Les; Peter Steward, sports editor of the Mercury and enthusiastic marathon runner; Bernard Daynes, a policeman, whose son is a pupil at Chapel Road Special School in Attleborough.

"The idea came when Les, Alan and Bernard were having a drink in the ex-servicemen's club one Saturday evening. Les, who has participated in many events for charity, was wondering what they could do next, when Alan suggested a walk from London to Wymondham. Chapel Road School seemed the obvious beneficiary. Not only has Les supported them on several previous occasions but Bernard's son was a pupil there. No sooner had the idea been suggested than Stewart Perkins, Bob Howes and Barney Howes each offered to sponsor them for £100. A few drinks later, the suggestion became a firm commitment - the walk was on!

Next came the hard part - the training. Throughout January and February, despite the freezing weather, all four walked regularly, averaging 30 miles per week. Peter walked to work from Hethersett to Norwich, as well as walking round the ring road. Bernard, Alan and Les walked to Barnham Broom Golf and Country Club several times each week, and also managed a weekly walk to Carrow Road to see their friend Duncan Forbes for a cup of tea before walking back again. Another walk took them from Wymondham to Sam's cockle stall on Norwich Market, where they were rewarded with a welcome dish of seafood. When Radio Broadland wanted to interview them about the forthcoming walk, Les and Alan walked there too! As well as walking, the four also had to decide on clothing, shoes - and ointment for blisters. Success depended on such attention to detail.

"Even the route itself was carefully considered. Les, Alan and Gary Champion went to London twice to reconnoitre the most promising roads where there were paths, not too much heavy traffic and cafes for refreshments. They even calculated the best time to approach Wymondham on the A11 in order to avoid the rush hours. After much thought they decided the 101-mile walk would begin at Woodford High Street in London, going through Epping Forest, Harlow, Bishop's Stortford, Stanstead, Ugley, Quendon, Newport, Littlebury and Great Chesterton. Thence to Four Wentways roundabout, Six Mile Bottom, Newmarket town centre, Freckenham, Barton Mills, Elvedon and Thetford. From Thetford they decided to go past Kilverstone Wildlife Park to Brettenham, through Bridgham to East Harling, round the back of Snetterton race track to Eccles Road, through Hargham Woods to Breckland Lodge, then Attleborough and Besthorpe, ending at the ex-servicemen's club in Wymondham.

"The target was to raise £1,500 and, with the kind help of Christine Cunningham (Norwich Mercury Newspapers), Tim Cowens (Diss Express) and Radio Norfolk and Broadland, the event was well advertised and sponsor money began to come in from a generous public.

"Finally, after consulting David Brooks, weather-man for Anglia TV, they decided to start the walk on Friday March 7th."

What follows is Les' description of the walk.

THE LONG LONDON WALK

Day 1 - Friday March 7th

The alarm woke me at 3 am. After eight weeks of training, walking 30 miles a week, the day had come. Now it was for real. My first job was to pick up my friend Alan (Buster) Farrow at Wymondham, then Peter Steward at Hethersett, Bernard Daynes at Attleborough and finally John Rapley who had kindly offered to drive our back-up car. All aboard, we headed for London, stopping at Frettenham Red Lodge en route for a breakfast of eggs and bacon at 5 am. One and a half hours later we arrived at Woodford, our starting point. On went the foot powder and walking shoes, we found a witness (a Mr Walker!!!) to sign our logbook, then we were off.

The car drove away to our first stopping place. It felt strange to see the car disappear and realise 101 miles of walking lay ahead of us. As we started along Woodford High Street, we looked to see airliners heading for Heathrow - not jet travel for us! Bernard gave the order "no smoking" - out came the glucose tablets instead.

We could see Epping Forest in the distance, and it seemed a long trek through the forest into Epping itself. We had in fact been walking for two hours and it was getting sunny. An hour later we reached the cafe where our car was waiting. A quick break for another breakfast, the flasks were filled with coffee, put into the car which then departed, and we were on our way again, heading towards Harlow. We noticed some aeroplanes and the traffic was building up; luckily, we were walking on paths.

After Harlow came Bishop's Stortford. We all seemed to be going well. Midday found us heading for Stansted where a large airliner was circling in preparation for landing. At Stansted we were met by our car and a welcome "cuppa" from the flasks before continuing to Ugley. By then it was nearly mid-afternoon, and we decided to call a halt at Quendon - eight hours and 32 miles from London.

Our log book was signed by a tramp who had lived in a tent in the woods at Quendon for over 20 years. He was delighted when I offered him a mars bar for his troubles!

We all agreed that our first day had seemed quite easy, as we tumbled into the Mercedes to return home for the night. This was our first mistake. It would have been much wiser to have booked into a hotel or pub for a bath, followed by a meal, but we felt that if people had been kind enough to sponsor us we should not waste their money by having nights out, so we went home each night, returning the following day to the exact spot where we had finished the previous evening. When we arrived home, we were all stiff; our legs felt like blocks of cement. By the time I had dropped everyone off, I could hardly walk. I had a few lagers to refresh my feet, then it was off to a well-earned rest.

Day 2 - Saturday March 8th

Once again, the alarm woke me at 3 am. I felt tired, but after a cup of tea I was on my way to pick up the lads. We all had breakfast at 5 am at Frettenham before heading for Quendon where we got out the foot powder and put on our walking shoes. It was now 6.30 am. Our friendly tramp must have been asleep still in his tent, as the flap was drawn and his dog lay asleep outside.

After arranging to meet our car at Stump Cross, 10 miles further on, we set off once again on the second stage of our walk. Alan strode ahead, while I chatted to Peter who told me how interesting he found his job reporting on sport. We discussed Wymondham Town's chances of a win at Holt that day. Alan picked Hagler to win his fight; Bernard handed round the glucose tablets again!

As we walked through Newport and across a river, we looked over the bridge. Peter suggested we should look for pike --- but alas, we had no golf clubs with us!!!+

We all seemed to be going well. Little did we know that this would be a hard day for us all, possibly the worst day of the whole walk. The weather was sunny and we had a lovely view of Audley End House. All the ducks and wild geese there made us determined to visit it at a later date. Our troubles began as we headed for Stump Cross. Bernard's calf muscles were tightening up and he fell a few hundred yards behind. I was the next to struggle: talking to Peter about golf, I kicked a drain top. The pain shot up to my knee, which immediately started to swell up like a balloon.

Meanwhile Alan was striding ahead - sneaking a crafty smoke now that Bernard had fallen behind! Peter waited for Bernard, while I caught up with Alan. The car was a welcome sight: we needed a coffee break.

For the next 10 miles we had to face the traffic, walking on the road for the first time, so after our quick break we put on our Eastern Daily Press orange jackets. As we set off, with buses, lorries and cars flying past about a yard away, I realised that this was going to be the hardest part - avoiding being hit by a vehicle. It was extremely dangerous, and I would not advise anyone to try this. Alan was tucked in behind me saying we must be crazy; Bernard and Peter were about half a mile back. To make things worse, Norwich City were playing at Wimbledon, so we met all the buses and cars heading towards London. We walked steadily on towards Six Mile Bottom and quiet roads again. Then we had a much-needed bit of encouragement - Duncan Forbes, at the front of the Club Canary bus en route for

Wimbledon, gave us a clenched fist salute. You feel a bit better with encouragement from Duncan.

It seemed as though we would never reach Six Mile Bottom. Alan was thirsty, I was hungry, the walk was becoming boring, and we seemed to be getting nowhere. Then at last we turned off for Six Mile Bottom. At that moment Alan fell over, cutting his hand which bled quite badly. He complained of feeling weak, We got a bowl of cold water from a man cleaning his windows and we fixed Alan's hand. After a drink he was alright, but he then said something very strange. He told me he had "died" and then come back to life. He's the first man I have known to experience this but knowing him it could have happened - he never gives up.

By now my knee was slowing me down. Bernard and Peter were gamely keeping pace behind us. Newmarket seemed beyond our reach, but by 2 pm we were walking through the town centre. Looking into the shops made things easier and we all felt better as we headed towards Frettenham to face the traffic again.

This was the hardest part of the day. We were very tired, there were no paths and the traffic hurtled past. We had not seen our car for hours and were almost completely exhausted by the time the Red Lodge cafe came into view. First priority was a cup of tea (if it had cost £5 I would have paid it!) as we waited for Bernard and Peter who were some way behind but determined not to give up.

The ride home in the car was painful - our legs again felt like cement, and we all had something wrong either with legs or feet. I dropped the lads off as usual, then soaked in the luxury of a hot bath, before dressing my blisters and putting an ice pack on my knee.

We covered 33 miles that day, which meant that in two days we had walked 65 miles - we were winning!

Day 3 - Sunday March 9th

I had a bit of a lie-in - the alarm went off at 4.30 am! After a cup of tea, I picked up the lads and we breakfasted at the Red Lodge before setting off yet again on our walk at the more civilised hour of 7 am. Roger Hansbury, the Cambridge goalkeeper, joined us and our spirits were further boosted by Wymondham Town's 6-0 win over Holt the previous day. Bernard made us envious telling us about the large T-bone steak he had for tea; Alan said he had finished the stew he had prepared before we started the walk!

We were all happy as we headed for Barton Mills roundabout where we would have to face the traffic again, there being no paths until Elevedon. At this point I would like to make it clear that walking on the road was crazy, with the traffic almost bowling us over. When Ian Botham did his walk, he had an escort van in front and behind. We didn't and now we realised the hardest part of this walk was not getting knocked over. Roger accompanied us to Elvedon then left us to return home. Peter's leg was giving him some trouble; it was so stiff that he could not bend it, but Bernard helped to keep him going until we reached Elvedon and the safety of a path to Thetford.

We now began noticing all the wildlife that had been killed by traffic. There was a hare, a fox, several pheasants, rabbits, small birds and even a dog. We passed deer roaming freely in the fields and, as we got bored, we began counting the hares we could see. They were starting to mate, as were the pheasants we saw as we neared Thetford, and even the rooks were building their nests. The jets roared overhead as they headed for Lakenheath and we arrived at Thetford. After walking through the town, it was a great relief to turn into the quiet road that went past Kilverstone Wildlife Park. It seemed a different world - so nice and peaceful with no traffic and plenty of wildlife to see. It was a long walk from Kilverstone to Brettenham and then to Bridgham which must be one of the longest villages in Norfolk to walk through, and on the left was the biggest field I'd ever come across. Alan reckoned that if we were chopping out sugar beet, it would take us a whole day to do a single row.

The weather was still nice (David Brooks had been right with his forecast) and by mid-afternoon East Harling Church came into view - our stopping point for day three. Alan was tired and my ankles were swelling with the extra weight they had to carry! Bernard and Peter were struggling too, but even so we were all looking forward to the final day, confident that the hardest part was behind us.

Day 4 - Monday March 10th

It was breakfast at 8 am at the Poachers' Cafe before being dropped off at East Harling to start the last stretch. Apart from Peter, whose leg was still stiff, we seemed to be getting fitter now. We kept together, discussing the walk, how much harder it had been than we expected. Peter had run marathons but said this walk was much tougher.

The traffic was more dangerous than expected but it was nice and quiet on the back road as we passed the rear of Snetterton race track heading for Eccles Road railway crossing.

We had scheduled to pass Attleborough at 11 am and as we approached we could see the children and staff from the school lining the route with banners, flags and even a small band. What a welcome! It really made us pleased that we had done this walk. Peter was overwhelmed by his first meeting with the children from the school. Bernard's wife was there as well as his daughter Selina who was going to walk the last six miles with us. My parents were there too. The photographers took pictures as we set off on the last stage of the walk. As we left Attleborough, a kind little lady gave us 50p from her purse and then Vernon George's mum rode up on her moped to give us £10. Gestures like this made the walk worthwhile, even though Peter could not bend his right leg at all.

The weather had deteriorated and it was raining as we passed through Besthorpe towards our final two miles of dangerous walking - back on the A11 without any paths. There was plenty of traffic but the only way we were not going to finish this walk now was if we got knocked down!

At last Wymondham Abbey came into view - we were nearly home. A few people took photos as we walked up Damgate Street, then we stopped for a few pictures near the Market Cross. Dave Bedson, the Town football manager, and Leo Parke, the Town captain, walked the last few hundred yards with us to the Ex-Servicemen's club.

As we arrived at the club, several ladies, including Mrs Brenda Ford, the Town Mayor, and Christine Cunningham, the newspaper reporter, plus club members cheered us as we entered the building. The champagne, kindly donated by the Ex-Servicemen's club, was on the bar. Norman Garwood did the honours with the toast, then it was a welcome sit down for a few more pictures ----- mainly of our feet this time!

The walk had been a great team effort, with Bernard, Peter and Alan all doing so well. I certainly would not have done it on my own; it would have been too tiring - and boring.

Mrs Ford kindly gave us a cheque; Christine Cunningham wanted a report for her paper. As we sipped champagne in the place where the ides of the walk was born, we realised it was all over. Off came our shoes. Someone took mine, but what did it matter - I wouldn't be needing them now!

We said we would never do anything like this again, so tiring and dangerous. Still, it had all been well worthwhile.

This is the entries I made in my own diary.

Thursday March 6th

Tomorrow is the start of a four-day adventure - our walk from London to Wymondham for mentally handicapped children at Attleborough. It's quite a challenge and starts at 4 am!

Friday March 7th

The walk started today - and by the end we had covered 33 miles and were as stiff as boards. Got up when the alarm went off at 3.30 am. Had an extremely early breakfast and got ready and at 4 am was picked up by Les King. There are four of us on the walk - myself, Les, Alan Farrow and Bernard Daynes. Bernard is a police officer from Attleborough.

We picked them up and drove as far as a cafe at Freckenham Red Lodge. There we had quite a substantial breakfast. Then drove on to Woodford in London. We started the walk at 6.30 am, ahead of schedule. It was tough going along Epping Forest and then on to Harlow and at 10 am we stopped at another cafe and I had another big meal. Then we walked on and on and on and on getting wearier and with a number of stops at lay-bys for tea from the following car. We ended up doing 33 miles and getting to Quendon. The last hour or so was hell and by the end we had slowed down to almost a crawl and perhaps did a little too much.

We were all glad to get back to the car and were very stiff when we got there. I arrived home at 5 pm. I had a bath to get rid of some of the stiffness. Went to bed early at 9 pm not looking forward to the prospect of getting up and doing it all over again tomorrow.

Saturday March 8th

The walk got harder today. Getting up at 4.30 am was not a particular problem. Had a quick breakfast and then got ready and was picked up by Les King at 5 am. We picked up all the others and drove to the cafe at Freckinham. This time I could only face a couple of rounds of toast and a cup of tea. We then drove on to Quendon.

Started walking at 6.45 am and it was a hell of a day. Walking through the Essex villages for the first 10 miles was okay, but then myself and Bernard had a great deal of trouble from the Stump Cross roundabout. The other two went on ahead. Our only real stop was at a hamburger stall in a lay-by. We struggled on to Newmarket while the others reached Freckenham. We eventually caught them up but I was feeling very tired, very stiff and very sore. I actually fell asleep in the car.

Once home had a hot bath and eased the stiffness and during the evening actually felt quite chirpy. Anne and I went to the King's Head for a meal and drinks. Was home and in bed by 10 pm.

Sunday March 9th

Today was bloody difficult. The walk became one long pain and struggle. I will really be glad when it's all over. Got up a little later - at 5.30 am and was picked up at 6 am. We drove out to Freckenham Red Lodge and had breakfast and then set off to walk. It was very difficult as I had leg pain from the start. Roger Hansbury - the ex-Norwich goalkeeper - walked with us for the first hour or so. Eventually Bernard and I got tailed off. We walked together.

Yesterday when he had problems, I kept him going and today when I had problems he kept me going. The only stops we made were a couple of breaks at the following car for a cup of tea. We got a second wind at Thetford having negotiated the horrible Thetford straight. We then decided to continue along to East Harling - at least we were back in Norfolk!

The last few miles along the country lanes was hell and after nine hours of walking I was practically at a standstill. So, we were glad to get to the car and drive home again. Had tea and a bath and again felt ridiculously stiff. Went to bed early again at 9.15 pm.

Monday March 10th

The day when everything became worthwhile. We finished the walk and met the children for whom we had been walking, including Bernard's handicapped son.

We got going slightly later today. Got up at 6 am and got picked up at 6.45. Drove out to a very smart cafe at Attleborough and had breakfast and then got dropped at East Harling. I had a big problem as soon as we started the walk with my knees giving me hell. But I managed to get into a rhythm. First stop was back at the cafe for a cup of tea and a 20-minute break. Then made the short journey into Attleborough.

When we got to the High Street the handicapped children were there along with Adrian Judd to take pictures - it makes a change to make the news rather than to write it! The kids' love and attitude to life made it all worthwhile including all the pain and problems.

We left Attleborough and I had to get into a rhythm again to walk to Wymondham and it seemed a surprisingly long distance. Eventually made it to the Ex-Servicemen's Club where there was a warm welcome and champagne. I stayed there for well over an hour because there were more pictures to be taken. I eventually got a lift home with Dave Bedson

The Foreword to the Brochure written by Phil Thomas - Headmaster of Chapel Road School was as follows:

"There has been a school in Attleborough for mentally handicapped children for over a quarter of a century. The school opened in February 1960 with only two classrooms. By 1967 the numbers had increased and these early children being now adult needed a separate facility of their own. Thus came the Adult Training Centre in Station Road, where many of the school's young people still transfer at around their 19th birthday.

"Nowadays the school has a new definition, a "School for Children having Special Educational Needs." The variety of children now being taught is very wide. Many of these children are handicapped, some are in wheelchairs. The school has deaf as well as blind and partially sighted young people. Some are physically as well as mentally handicapped. Throughout all its life the school has striven to help parents make their young people as secure and as independent as possible. Lessons are taught in a very wide range of subjects in exactly the same way as in any school. Nearly all children develop literacy and numeracy skills. In any one class one child may be still learning to talk and walk whilst another could be developing computer skills, historical and geographical abilities. Many of the children demonstrate how capable they are. The fact that they are in a Special School does not mean they cannot achieve much, quite the reverse in fact.

"The school has nine teachers and eight welfare staff. Classes are small so that each child can get individual attention. The school is run by the Norfolk Education Authority like any other school.

"One of the features of schools such as this is the wide support it receives from the local community. Over many years the voluntary support has been magnificent, many volunteers having been with us for years. As you are aware Les King, who is the driving force behind this book, is a local businessman. What you probably don't know is how much he has supported this school in fund-raising. Not so long ago he was also a fine Father Christmas. Most recently, the reason for this booklet, Les Walked from London along with Bernard Daynes, Alan Farrow and Peter Steward. We need the support from our friends and all of us at Chapel Road School, parents included, are most grateful for it.

So What Happened to the Walkers?

Over 20 years on from the walk I decided to find out what had happened to the foursome.

As you will gather I'm still very much alive and kicking. I regularly go out walking - but only five or six miles at a time. I stopped being sports editor of the Norwich Mercury Series in February 1989 - just under three years after the walk. The rest as they say is history, although, of course, it's all captured in this autobiography.

Les King was a larger than life character around Wymondham - being president of numerous football and cricket clubs. Sadly as I've already written, Les, who appeared to be indestructible, died a number of years ago.

Alan "Buster" Farrow died a number of years ago too and I do not know what happened to Bernard Daynes.

There were a couple of amusing incidents that Les didn't mention, although I do find his description of having our walk signed off by a tramp living in a tent by the side of the road highly amusing.

At the end of day one Les told us he went home and his wife of the time (I think he was probably married three times) cooked him chicken and chips.

"I wanted bloody steak and I told her so," he told us.

At the end of the second day Les went home and his wife presented steak and chips to him.

"I had that last night," he told her.

I must say at this point that Les was a keen amateur boxer in his younger days and may have been slightly punch drunk from those days.

On the first day of the walk as we drove towards London, we stopped at a greasy spoon café which was probably at Freckenham Red Lodge near Newmarket if my memory serves me correctly. This was a very popular place for truckers to eat and very busy.

Les ordered his meal and ate it. The next day we stopped there again to fuel up. Les walked up to the counter and said:

"Ello dear I'll have the same as yesterday." They obviously had no idea what he had eaten the day before.

Fast forward almost 40 years and I wanted to do another walk to raise money for charity. Let me say at this point that I don't greatly enjoy walking for walking's sake, but I do like a challenge and to me a challenge needs to be difficult but achievable.

So I tried to work out a distance for the year 2022 that would be exactly that – difficult but achievable. I felt 1,500 would fit the bill. The mathematicians amongst you will know that equates to 4.1 miles per day. That doesn't sound a lot but its 4.1 miles when you don't feel 100%, 4.1 miles when the weather is awful and 4.1 miles when you just can't be bothered to go out. Of course it doesn't have to be 4.1 miles every day. You can make up any deficit with longer walks.

I was very pleased that in the 365 days of my challenge there were only six days when I didn't go for a walk. Two of those were during the dreadful storms of February, two when I had so much on that I couldn't fit a walk in and a couple when I just didn't want to go out. That means on 359 days of 2022 I went for a walk somewhere. I must add that walking around the house, in the garden etc didn't count, It had to be specific walks. My longest distance in one day was only 12 miles which pales into insignificance against the 30 miles plus of my London walk – but by 2022 I was much older.

I paced the walk just about right, always being up or slightly ahead of schedule and finished on December 28th – just three days ahead of the deadline. I continued walking and finished the year with a distance of 1,514 miles and raised over £1,500 for the East Anglian Air Ambulance.

Of the two walks, the one from London was the most difficult due to injuries that made me struggle over the last day and a half. The marathon walk was relatively incident free apart from a sore ankle and two lost toenails.

But as I say I'm always looking for a challenge although I think my walking challenges may now be in the past.

I Was The Weakest Link (eventually)

I have spoken about my bucket list of things I wanted to do earlier in this work. Another aim was to appear on a national quiz/game show on television. So, I applied for The Weakest Link.

For those who have never seen the Weakest Link, it's a quiz show that features eight people who are asked questions in turn. Each question answered correctly builds up an amount of money that can be banked by other contestants. If somebody gets an answer wrong the money in that chain is lost.

One of the things about The Weakest Link was the pressure put on contestants by Mrs Nasty – the quiz mistress Anne Robinson who was well known for being harsh, bordering on unpleasant.

After my application I was asked along to a rehearsal in the historic Maids Head Hotel in Norwich where we had to answer some paper-based questions and then do a sample round. Obviously, this was to assess how we would function under pressure, what level of knowledge we had and whether we would be suitable for the show.

I passed the audition as John Lennon would say. They seemed most impressed that at my advanced age I could answer a question about the rapper Eminem. I got invited onto a show which was recorded at Elstree Studios in London.

I could have stayed in an hotel overnight but decided to travel down to Elstree on the day as our recording wasn't until the afternoon. Apparently at that time they recorded three shows each day and we were the middle one. I think I got a taxi to the studio as it was all expenses paid.

We met our fellow contestants in the Green Room before we started. The idea was to chat and get to know each other and perhaps that's the way alliances started to form for the actual quiz. Then we went into the studio where there were hundreds of lights and where everything was very warm. There was a surprising amount of time just to stand around while the filming was checked. This was when you got to know the people standing next to you. A member of staff also popped on and off with powder in case your face was too shiny. Mine never was.

I think I was third to answer questions and in the first round everyone got all their questions correct because they were pretty easy at that point. But we then had to vote somebody off and the person with the most votes was classed the Weakest Link and was out of the quiz.

So how do you vote for somebody when everyone has got their questions correct? I guess that's where the Green Room getting to know you session came in. You don't vote for somebody you have taken a liking to, well not at that point anyway. But somebody has to go and of course you make a mental note of who votes for you so that you might want to vote for them in a later round. Also, you aren't likely in the early rounds to vote for people standing next to you as they are the people you chat to between rounds when the powder comes out.

I think I got two votes in the first round but a woman got three and wasn't amused to be voted off without being able to show what knowledge she had. But she had to go.

Then the whole process started again and after each round somebody was voted off. Often people voted for those they saw as a threat, but I promised myself I would always vote with honesty for the person I genuinely felt to be the Weakest Link.

Of course, there's a buggeration factor in all this in the shape of Ms Robinson. She appeared just as the show was being recorded and disappeared before the end. So we didn't actually get to meet her. Not that I was particularly unhappy about that. Her modus operandi is to attack and ridicule contestants.

I made a bit of a prat of myself but thankfully they cut that bit out. I stumbled about a bit when she asked me about my job and then said I probably wasn't very good at it. By this point my mind was turning to mush. Mind you Anne made a bit of a prat of herself with one of my questions where she mispronounced the name of a rock group. I got the question correct but the producer stopped things and told her how to pronounce the name. She was then asked to ask me the question again and I was asked to take a short time to make it look as if I was thinking and then answer again.

Recording programmes is a strange affair. Many years ago, I was in the audience for an appalling quiz show produced by Anglia Television called Mouth Trap and starring the comedian (alleged) Don McClean who is no relation to the American singer-songwriter of the same name. McClean bounded onto the set, and we were all told when he did this to whoop and holler, cheer and generally seem to be madly and completely out of control.

So on leapt Mr McClean and we obviously didn't whoop and holler loudly enough because we had to do the whole thing again. Then Mr McClean told a joke that was spectacularly unfunny, and we obviously didn't throw ourselves around in hysterical laughter enough. So, we had to go through the whole process again. Second time round the joke was even less funny than it had been the first time.

But back to the Weakest Link. I answered all my questions correctly and ended up as one of the last three. Eventually the final two went head to head in a five question shoot out with the winner taking all the money that had been banked.

In the final round before the head-to-head it was myself against two women and you can guess what happened. We all got a question wrong. By this time, we were all hot and tired. I was asked something along the lines of which character from the children's television show Rainbow is also a word for making a mistake or messing up. Now I had watched Rainbow numerous times with my sons as they grew up. I knew all the characters and of course I absolutely knew that the answer was Bungle. But, as I've said, by this time I was very hot and bothered and said "Zippy" which was wrong.

So it came to voting for the Weakest Link. We all got one vote. I voted for the women who was genuinely the weakest link, she voted for the other woman and the other woman voted for me. She was deemed the strongest link and had the casting vote which meant she could stick with choosing me or change her vote to the other woman who actually had been the weakest link. She stuck with me and I was off the show.

She went on to win something over £3,000. So you could say I had Bungled three grand. By the time we got off the set everyone else had gone. The three of us were taken to the local railway station to make our way home. The winner came from Colchester and so was getting the same train as myself from Liverpool Street. So we had a MacDonalds on the station and she admitted that she had voted me off as I was the strongest contestant. I was quite happy when I found out she was a mature student, and the money would be spent on paying off her debt. She needed that money.

Ironically the other woman could have won if she had answered a question along the lines of which Norfolk based Formula One company also shares its name with a flower. The answer of course was Lotus and the Norfolk Lotus factory is about four miles from where I live. C'est La Vie as they say.

The Weakest Link started in the UK in 2000 but isn't currently aired apart from as a celebrity show.

Remembering the 97

It was a chance meeting on a path in Hethersett that set me on a project that would take up thousands of hours of time over a number of years but something I would feel great pride in achieving/completing.

I refer to my involvement in keeping the memory alive of 97 men who died in a massacre in Northern France in May 1940 during the Second World War.

That chance meeting was between myself and John Head, a man I knew well enough to pass the time of day with if I saw him in the village. Our conversation went something along the lines of:

John: "You're interested in history aren't you?"

Me: "Yes I certainly am."

John then told me of a connection he had with the Le Paradis massacre of May 27th, 1940. His friend Dennis O'Callaghan was the son of one of only two survivors of the massacre – the other being Bert Pooley from London.

John and Dennis along with friend Nick Smith regularly gave presentations about the massacre and the lives of the survivors. John told me that "a huge amount" of memorabilia existed but they didn't know what to do with it.

I suggested they needed a website – and guess who ended up putting a website together. It was a labour of love dealing with numerous original documents, photographs, diaries, maps and much more. As a result of all this the four of us – John, Dennis, Nick and myself – founded the Le Paradis Commemoration Group. The website www.leparadismassacre.com was populated with hundreds of pages, the next logical step was to write a book on the subject.

So John and I set to work with interviews with numerous people and families throughout the country, all of whom were pleased to talk to us and share their own memorabilia. We then extended the website to include details of soldiers fighting in the area around Le Paradis and also steps to have a permanent memorial in the UK to match those in France. This saw the setting up of a Memorial Trustees' group to raise funds for a memorial which now sits proudly in place in Norwich Cathedral Close. Another national memorial is also likely in the future.

Our book is entitled "Hell in Paradise" and we had interest from a number of publishers, one of whom agreed to publish it, stating that they were "excited as it fits in well with our ethos."

In a volte face they then changed their mind and said they were no longer able to take it on. At that point we decided to publish the book independently through the Le Paradis Communication Group with the help of an independent print broker.

As a result, the book was published and immediately received good reviews in a number of publications including the Eastern Daily Press and Norwich Evening News. Our initial run of 500 copies sold out and it was accepted for sale in the book department at Norwich's most famous family department store Jarrolds. The book was also entered in the non-fiction section of the East Anglian Book Awards 2024 but wasn't successful.

I am proud of the part I have played in bringing the story of the massacre to a wider audience and keeping the memory of so many brave men alive and to have worked with descendants to gather together so much information of an event that up until now had been very much lost to history, particularly because many of those who died were from the Royal Norfolk Regiment.

APPENDIX

MY BIRTH CHART

In February 1974, I was working on the local newspaper in Norwich and wrote a feature article on Norwich astrologer Pete Green.

Pete was pleased with the article and offered to produce my birth sign and life pattern analysis.

I have always felt that Pete's analysis was very close to the mark in several areas. I have included in brackets some of my interpretations of where Pete is particularly correct or particularly incorrect. Please remember, however, that this is my own interpretation of my character, and I may be miles out.

Pete started off with the following message: "It should be noted that this section is merely an interpretation of the life-pattern and is in no way meant as a prediction for the future. It simply shows the forces at work on this life unit which may of course be successfully resisted or be altered by other factors."

Then he wrote:

"The initial effect is of a well-integrated personality and one with the tendency to act at all times under a consideration of opposing views, through a sensitiveness to contrasting possibilities. (I like this section as I always endeavour to weigh up all sides of an argument before making a decision. Sometimes I believe I do this too much and it can become a weakness).

"There is strength of will (downright bloody-mindedness some might say), frankness and independence (I would rather say a wish for independence which is at times thwarted) but tempered with caution (how right). There is an addiction to mental and rational interests which strangely contrast with moods of dreaminess and inattention when the mind becomes lost in the world of the imagination (this is spot on. I daydream a lot, I engender the other man's grass is always greener syndrome and sometimes long for the open road and a farewell to care, but then realise it's probably cold and unpleasant out there anyway).

"Despite the outward appearance, there is an underneath deep discontent (covered by my comments above). Personal responsibilities will be heavy, and loneliness and depression will arise from lack of reciprocity from others (I have always wanted to please people, be accepted and loved).

"However, this can be overcome by the natural desire of the mind to realise self. Personal affairs are approached rationally and coolly and there is a keenness to work at educational or literary pursuits. (This is scarcely a difficult conclusion to make as Pete knew that I was a journalist. Over the years, however, I have become more and more interested in education as is shown by my study for an MA degree at university and also my involvement as a school governor).

"Money is best made by ways to do with art, beauty etc but prosperity will come from a close association i.e marriage or business partnership. Legacies can probably be expected. (I feel this is one of the areas that may not as yet have unfolded. My wages have come from anything but matters of beauty). There is a danger in the desire to become grand through money and possessions and a leaning towards extravagance. (I would question this. I love a nice home and pleasant surroundings but would call myself anything but extravagant).

"There is a gentle charm in speech and manner and the mind tends to enjoy friendly discussion, but this can lead to being easily deceived (yes and no here. I am a reasonably out-front person who at times tends to be too open, like in this autobiography).

"There is vision and readiness to change old ways but an unwillingness to submit to routine (spot on).

"Love tends to be intense, secretive and passionate and is one of the ruling factors of this life (not after getting on for 50 years of marriage it doesn't!), but this can be a cause of domestic upsets. There may be some helpful changes in involvement (this report was written about a year before I met my wife).

"There is a strong interest in travel (I have been to many countries) but it does not play a major role in the formation of this particular life pattern (This is very true as nearly all my travelling has been on holiday and not business).

"Eccentricity is shown in ways of taking care of anybody and some success in psychic or occult investigation (still waiting for the latter)."

Pete summed me up as follows:

"A gentle, imaginative life, but with deep inner discontent. Deep, intense love affairs. Ability in the literary arts." Perhaps somebody who knows me might like to comment!

I came across Pete again a few years ago. He was living in the centre of the market town of Wymondham which is about three miles from where we live. He had become the town crier was previously a member of Wymondham Town Council and was very well known about town.

Tragically Pete died following a fire at his home. Just shortly before his death he appeared on the television game show The Chase. Obviously, the programme was recorded. Members of his family gave permission for the programme to be shown after he had died.

MY TIMELINE

October 9th 1952 - Born at Hellesdon near Norwich.

September 1957- July 1963 Attended Kinsale Avenue Infant and Junior School, Hellesdon.

September 1963- July 1971 Attended King Edward VI, The Norwich School, gaining six O' Levels and three A' Levels.

September 1971-May 1972 Attended Harlow Technical College, Essex, to study Journalism.

June 1972-July 1973 Reporter on the Lowestoft Journal, Lowestoft, Suffolk.

August 1973 - March 1974 Reporter and Feature Writer on the Eastern Evening News, Norwich.

March 1974-August 1975 Reporter on the North Norfolk News and Eastern Daily Press based at Cromer: Passed National Council for Training of Journalists' Proficiency Certificate.

September 1975-May 1978 Assistant Chief Reporter Beccles and Bungay Journal, Beccles, Suffolk.

July 24th, 1976, Married Anne Burton in Knottingley West Yorkshire.

May 1978-September 1978 District Reporter for Raymonds News Service, Nottingham.

October 1978-December 1978 Editor Belper News, Derbyshire.

January 1979-1984 Sub Editor Norwich Mercury Series.

February 24th, 1982, Son Christopher Owen Steward born.

January 10th, 1984, Son Matthew David Steward born.

1984-February 1989 Sports Editor Norwich Mercury Series.

February 1989 to April 1999 Press and Public Relations Officer for Norfolk Constabulary.

March 1997 Awarded an Advanced Certificate of Education by the University of East Anglia, Norwich.

April 1999 Awarded Master of Arts degree in Professional Development by the University of East Anglia.

April 1999 to Jan 2001 Head of Media and Public Relations for Norfolk Constabulary.

July 2001 Awarded a Diploma in Sports Psychology by Newcastle University.

January 2002 Public Relations Manager for Norfolk Constabulary.

2003-2005 Head of E-Communications for Norfolk Constabulary.

2004 Awarded a Certificate in Life Coaching by Newcastle University.

2005-2006 Head of Marketing Operations for Norfolk Constabulary.

November 2006 Took early retirement from Norfolk Constabulary to concentrate on other business interests.

January 2007 PostScript Media launched.

2007 to March 2013 Crisis Response Manager for Media and Crisis Management Ltd.

September 1st, 2011 - Grandson Oliver David Steward stillborn.

September 1st, 2012 - Grandson Elliot Oliver Steward born.

February 6th, 2015 - Granddaughter Poppy Rose Steward born.

2019-2023 - Freelance journalist working for local media.

December 15th 2023 – Granddaughter Lyla Louise Steward born.

PLACES I HAVE LIVED

1952 to 1964 157, Reepham Road, Hellesdon, Norwich, Norfolk.

1964 to 1971 31, Middleton's Lane, Hellesdon, Norwich, Norfolk.

1971-1972 123, The Maples, Harlow, Essex.

1972-1973 211, St Margaret's Road, Lowestoft, Suffolk.

1973-1974 31, Middleton's Lane, Hellesdon, Norwich, Norfolk.

1974-1975 7, Corner Street, Cromer, Norfolk.

1975 Upper Grange Road, Beccles, Suffolk.

1976 Waveney House, Ravensmeer, Beccles, Suffolk.

1976 The Flat, Eastern Counties Newspapers, Blyburgate, Beccles, Suffolk.

1977 23, Nursey Close, Ellingham, Norfolk.

1978-1979 95, Lodge Road, Long Eaton, Derbyshire.

30th August 1979-13th July, 1988 36, Buckingham Drive, Hethersett, Norfolk.

14th July, 1988 to present Hethersett, Norfolk

December 2016 to present Hethersett, Norfolk and Kelling, Norfolk.

There is a website to go with this book. You can find this at www.peterowensteward.weebly.com

MY LIST OF INVOLVEMENT:

At the time of going to publication I am involved with the following groups and organisations.

Honorary Vice-President of Hethersett and Tas Valley Cricket Club

Honorary Life Member of Hethersett Athletic Football Club

Founder Member of Hethersett Writers' Group

Founder Member of Hethersett Dementia Support Group

Helper at Hethersett Forget-Me-Not Twice monthly cafe

Owner and Editor of Hethersett Herald e-magazine

Owner and Editor of Hethersett Village Web site - www.hethersettherald.weebly.com

Owner and editor of Hethersett Herald e-magazine web site

Vice-chair of Hethersett Library Friends' Group

Editor Hethersett Good News Magazine

Writer and Editor of Peter Steward's Daily Blog

Volunteer for Norfolk Family History Society

Editor and Administrator of Norfolk Family History Society's Facebook page

Founder Member of Le Paradis Massacre Commemoration Group

Owner and editor of Le Paradis Massacre official web site

Editor and owner of Freda Laycock Memorial Web Site

Editor and owner of Alan Mann, Norfolk Author web site

Editor and owner of Norfolk People web site

Editor and owner of Norfolk Photographs web site

Editor and owner of Norfolk People and Places web site

Editor and owner of Hethersett - A Norfolk Village at War website

Owner and administrator for numerous Facebook sites including Hethersett, Hethersett Herald, Hethersett Dementia Group, Heart of Hethersett Group etc.

Administrator for Hethersett for the Next Door social media site.

Honorary member of the Royal Anglian Regiment Association.

Member of the National Trust

Season Ticket Holder at Norwich City Football Club

In the past I have been

Vice-Chair of Hethersett Middle School PTA

Chairman of Hethersett and the Meltons' Sports Association

Hethersett Parish Councillor

Communications' Officer for Hethersett Parish Council

Member of Hethersett Parish Council's Archive Group

Member of Hethersett Parish Council's Village Development Group

Parent Governor of Hethersett Middle School

Community Governor of Hethersett Middle School

Chair of Governors of Hethersett Middle School

Chair of Hethersett Athletic Football Club

Assistant Secretary of Hethersett Athletic Football Club

Director of Hethersett Olympic Legacy Sports Complex

Web editor for Hethersett Methodist Church web site.

Helper at Hethersett Methodist Church's ladies breakfast

Member at Hethersett Methodist Church Men's Breakfast

Editor of Norfolk Family History Society's quarterly magazine Norfolk Ancestor

Member of the Friends of Woodcote Sheltered Housing Complex

Secretary and Trustee of Hethersett Memorial Playing Field

Village sports co-ordinator for Hethersett for Active Norfolk

Chairman and Secretary of Hethersett and the Meltons' Sports Association

Public Relations Officer and Press Officer for Hethersett Athletic Football Club

Club Development Officer for Hethersett and Tas Valley Cricket Club

Chair of Hethersett and Tas Valley Cricket Club

Publicity and Press Officer for Hethersett and Tas Valley Cricket Club

Coach for various youth and adult teams of Hethersett Athletic Football Club

Coach for various youth teams of Hethersett and Tas Valley Cricket Club

Founder and member of Hethersett Social Running Group

Founder and Member of Hethersett Methodist Church Table Tennis Club

Leader of Hethersett Methodist Church Youth Club

Archivist for Hethersett Dementia Support Group

Editor of Hethersett Hawks Cycle Speedway web site

Publicity and Public Relations Officer for Norfolk Family History Society

Founder and leader of Heart of Hethersett Bereavement Group

Volunteer for Norwich Samaritans

Public Relations Officer for Norwich Samaritans

Community Contributor for Hethersett for the Eastern Daily Press and Norwich Evening News Newspapers and websites.

Committee member of Wymondham Town Football Club

Committee member of Beccles Football Club

Committee member of Lakeford Football Club

Member of Beccles Round Table

Member of Long Eaton Round Table

Member of Wymondham and Attleborough Round Table

Public Relations Officer for Round Table Area Six (Norfolk and Suffolk)

Member of Norwich City Football Club's supporters' group

Editor and owner of Wymondham Coffee Shop web site

Newspaper Correspondent for Hethersett for the Wymondham Mercury, Eastern Daily Press and Norwich Evening News

Member of English Heritage

Trustee of Le Paradis Massacre Memorial Appeal

Trustee of Norfolk Family History Society

My Favourite Things

As if you haven't had enough of me, I promise I'm getting to the end of this autobiography. Before I finish, I thought I would just list some of my favourite things. I have to say that I've always avoided watching The Sound of Music but in the spirit of a song from that film entitled "My Favourite Things" here are a few of mine.

Favourite Colour: Blue (the colour of my eyes when they aren't bloodshot).

Favourite Number: 6 (it seems to be nicely rounded and of course is the number of balls bowled in a cricket over).

Favourite Book: Great Expectations by Charles Dickens (I never saw the twist coming the first time I read it). Big mention also for Wuthering Heights and the Mayor of Casterbridge

Favourite Film: It's A Wonderful Life (ok James Stewart is rather over the top but the moral of this story is very strong).

Favourite track/song: Mockingbird by Barclay James Harvest.

Favourite Album: Once Again by Barclay James Harvest.

Favourite Group: A tie between Barclay James Harvest and the Beatles.

Favourite solo artist: Harry Chapin.

Favourite piece of classical music: Vltava by Smetana.

Favourite country to visit: Switzerland (all those lakes and mountains and all that snow).

Favourite City in the UK: Liverpool, closely followed by Belfast (both because of their history).

Favourite City in the World: Berlin (modern, brash and colourful).

Favourite meal: Beef Wellington (it's a long time since I had this).

Favourite Football Team: Norwich City (because I come from Norwich and not for their footballing ability).

Favourite Sports Person: Roger Federer (for being sheer class).

Favourite Television Programme – Coronation Street (has to be as I remember the first ever edition and it's been going for well over 60 years and I'm still watching it).

Favourite Son – Both of them (almost caught you there as you thought I was going to pick one)

Favourite Grandchild – All of them (same reason as above).

Favourite Wife: Anne (I've only had one so sorry to disappoint you again. But at least my humour still seems to be intact).

FINALE – THREE THINGS
AN OPEN LETTER

I spent some considerable time editing this book. As I did so I was also reading an autobiography by Gyles Brandreth entitled "Odd Boy Out". It's about his days at school, his early years as a celebrity and his family. Gyles Brandreth is one of those people I suspect you either love or hate. I find him very entertaining and the kind of person I would like to have a lunch and a pint with and I'm sure the conversation wouldn't flag and would take in many facets of life. Of course, I doubt that lunch will every take place although I'm rather tempted to send him a copy of this book.

Towards the end of "Odd Boy Out" Gyles writes an open letter to his beloved father whom he refers to as Pa. I think it's a nice way to conclude a book. So, I decided to do a similar thing and write an open letter to my beloved mother to say some of the things I have always felt but probably never told her during her life. So here goes, but before I start, I would just like to say a heartfelt thank you to you for reading this book and having the stamina to get this far. I hope you have enjoyed it and mainly I hope that you have been entertained by it. I have tried to be honest in it and hope you feel that it has come from the heart and that you have been able to truly see that I have lived "A Charmed Life." The bad news is there are other volumes being prepared.

Do contact me if you have enjoyed it and do follow my daily blog which is available at

https://www.facebook.com/groups/486377568989294

My website is at: www.peterowensteward.weebly.com

And you can catch me by e-mail at petersteward@sky.com

Here is my open letter to my mother:

Dear Mum

I have long known that I will never be able to speak to you directly and I don't necessarily subscribe to the idea that one day we will be together again.

As you know I'm not a religious man and I'm not sure that I believe in an afterlife. You of course could tell me if there is one although if there is you are unable to communicate that fact to me.

I did go with a friend to a spiritualist church once and they had a medium. It was shortly after dad died. I was picked out and told that somebody by the name of Arthur who had recently passed was trying to get through to me. He was with somebody called John which I thought might be Uncle Jack. Anyway, the message I received didn't make much sense although I was spooked when the name Arthur was picked out, but this is more about me and you anyway.

I suppose that the mere fact that I'm writing this open message to you must mean that I have some belief. So, whatever my views are let's pretend you can receive this message in some way and that you are truly looking down on me and still guiding me.

It seems hard for me to grasp that I'm now 10 years older than you were when you died. Of course you may know everything I'm going to write.

I don't think that I've turned out badly and much of what I am today is down to you. I hope that I have inherited your patience, your kindness and your spirit. I can only remember you getting angry once and it didn't last all that long. You were probably under pressure at the time.

I've just written my autobiography and I know that fact will amaze you as you never showed any interest in literary pursuits at all. I have no idea where I get my love of literature, history and writing from, but I really don't have to analyse it as it's just there.

It's difficult now to remember just what I was doing when you died. I'm sorry but I don't remember your funeral. It's as if I've erased it from my mind. I can't even remember the date when you died as remembering you is what is important to me and not dates, although I always remember your birthday - June 10th and that of your mother, my grandmother, which is December 5th. I can't remember whether I called your mother nanny or grandma but that doesn't really matter. I do remember that she was as kind as you.

I am very much into genealogy and have carried out a lot of research on the Dew and Sandall families. I have traced the Dews back to North Norfolk and now regularly wander around churches in places like Blakeney, Cley, Wells and Salthouse. After all they are your ancestors as well as mine.

But this isn't really about the older family. This message/letter is about getting you up to date with what has happened since you passed.

I got the idea from a book written by Gyles Brandreth who wrote a similar letter to his father. You won't have heard of Gyles Brandreth but no matter as he isn't important to us apart from being the catalyst for this message.

Do you remember the day when you compared me to the girl who lived next door. I believe her name was Debbie. We were roughly the same age, but she had just gone out for the day with a boyfriend and I was coming back from the park after having a kick around and I was eating a Zoom lolly. Those were the ones with different flavoured/coloured ice and they were long and thin. I think you thought that compared to Debbie I was still a child. I have never been sure how eating an ice cream to cool down made me a child but it's just one of those crazy but irrelevant things that I remember and which I've now put into this book which is already well over 100,000 words long.

But I'm now going to turn the clock back. When we knew how ill you were back in 1981, we tried desperately to keep you alive so that you could at least see your first grandchild. We didn't know whether it was a boy or a girl. Nowadays couples find out well before the birth but more of that later.

I remember you going away for a few days with dad but having to come home because you felt so unwell. And from there the cancer really took hold. You died in November, and I remember those last few days when you lapsed onto unconsciousness and your breathing became laboured. You will know that I'm not good with illness and I really struggled to deal with yours at the time.

I wanted to remember you as a happy smiling vibrant person and not as that empty shell dying in your bedroom.

From memories that I have dredged up and from writing this book I realise that your relationship with dad was at times difficult through his selfishness. I have tried throughout my life not to be selfish and always to put others first and I hope you don't think that I'm being boastful when I say that by and large I think I have been successful with that aim.

Writing my autobiography has made me realise the sacrifice you made to ensure I had a good education. It was something I didn't always realise at the time and for that I apologise. You must have gone without many things to support me with my piano lessons and other pursuits.

Your first grandson Christopher Owen was born in February 1982, just three months after you died. Yes, we included the name Owen as my grandfather had and as you had with me. You never explained where the name came from and why it was handed down through the generations. I assumed for a long while that it was Welsh connections but now realise it was the surname of an ancestor before she married.

I am always sad that I never knew my maternal grandfather, your father. He died five years before I was born. I believe it was from a heart attack. I am sad that you never talked about him. I regret not asking you about him but back in the 1960s people didn't talk so openly about their lives. It took me a long time to realise that when I was born in 1952 the second world war was still fresh in people's memory and had only been over for seven short years. It also took me a long time to realise that when you were born the First World War had only been over for less than four years. To me that makes you sound very old, although I always remember you as being young.

You will have grown up in a city still scarred by bomb sites and still being rebuilt, although I'm not sure whether you were born in Great Yarmouth or Norwich. I always assumed the former but now my research suggests the latter. We used to visit Great Yarmouth an awful lot and I didn't realise until a few years ago that town's importance in our family history. We still visit Yarmouth, often now with our grandchildren (your great grandchildren) and I'm always drawn to the town as well as to North Norfolk where our family roots are. But I'm going off at a tangent here and need to get back on track.

It seems ridiculous in my mind that if you were still alive you would be 103. That may sound an unobtainable age to you, but I have to point out that your sister-in-law, dad's sister lived to be 105. Dad lived to well into his nineties although you will already know that. You won't be surprised to know that dad and his sister didn't speak to each other for many years. As a family we often visited Aunty Vera as she made us very welcome, but we never told my father that we had been round.

Twenty-three months after Christopher was born, we had another son who we called Matthew David. This ensured that the Steward name lives on.

You would have to ask the boys whether we were good parents. I like to think we are/were. Of course they are now men, both in their forties which scarcely seems possible. You will be pleased to know that they have both turned out fine and I firmly believe that a part of you lives on in them, although you never met them and they never met you. They would have loved you as much as you would have loved them.

Both the boys picked up my love of sport and both have children of their own - your great grandchildren. I'm sorry if you already know all this but I can't be sure, so I'm going to tell you anyway. Matt met Emma when they were both working at a local hotel. Their first son Oliver was stillborn. Their second son Elliot was born on what would have been Oliver's first birthday. Then along came Poppy under three years later. By my reckoning she was the first direct female descendent since Aunty Vera was born. Elliot and Poppy are bright, happy and a delight and again carry some of your character within them.

Chris got married but it didn't work out but in 2023 he got married again and towards the end of the year he and Alicia presented us with another granddaughter - Lyla.

When I write the word daughter or granddaughter I can't help but remember the angst that has caused in our family. Vera always openly said she wanted a sister and was very unhappy when she was informed that she had a brother (your husband and my father). Similarly, when Vera and Jack had a daughter Jack wouldn't have anything to do with her for some considerable time because he desperately wanted a son. As for us, well we are just delighted and blessed to have grandchildren and couldn't care less whether they are boys or girls. I always joke about this with the words "as long as they aren't ducks." So far no ducks have been born to any of us!

Well, I suppose I need to tell you about myself, although it's all down in my book. I guess you may not get copies of books wherever you are.

I was just 29 when you died. I had quite a lengthy career on local newspapers before joining the police and working in public relations. I'm not sure you will understand just what public relations or pr is. I'm not sure I understand it myself. But I don't want to go on about work as that's all very dull. I retired quite a few years ago but am busier than ever with my writing and voluntary work of many kinds.

I hope that I've made you proud of me and I hope that a little of your character has rubbed off on me. I truly believe that it has.

Do you remember how you would talk about people with "letters after their name" as if this made them special, which in your eyes it probably did. Well now I have letters after my name. They are called post nominals. I went to university when I was working for the Police and got an Advanced Certificate in Education and then a master's degree in professional development.

So now I'm Peter Steward MA, Adv Cert Ed. How about that?

I've also been very fortunate in winning a number of awards which have include a lifetime achievement award from South Norfolk Council. I am very proud of this.

I will tell our children and our grandchildren and who knows maybe our great grandchildren if we live long enough about you, about the shop where I was brought up but mainly about the love you always showed me and how this love has helped to make me the person that I became after losing you.

Dear Mum sleep tight wherever you are. I love you now and I have always loved you.

Your affectionate son

Peter

And Finally –

Back to the Beginning

I would like to finish this memoire or autobiography if you prefer by returning to the beginning.

Late Spring 2024, I had this idea of returning to some of my old haunts and having what I refer to as a "poke around."

I wanted to see how Hellesdon had changed over the past 60 or 70 years and whether anything still looked the same. They say you should never go back but this wasn't something I was about to subscribe to.

Technically it wasn't my first time back. I have been there a few times, either to the library or the community hall but I had never retraced the steps of my youth which was what I was about to do.

I wrote what I found as one of my daily blogs and so here is that blog which was posted on May 1st, 2024.

"Can we ever relive our past and does it just grip us so tightly because we feel safer there? I found my journey uncomfortable, not because everything had changed as you might expect but because so many things were practically the same in some kind of strange way.

"My journey into the past started in Tombland at the bus stops just down from Norwich Cathedral Close. This is where I caught the bus every day to go home from The Norwich School. The bus numbers have changed, as have the routes. Yesterday I was looking for either a 36 or a 37. Back in the sixties it was an 84 or 86 down Reepham Road or an 85 or 87 down the Cromer Road. The 84 and 86 took me to Berkeley Close which was just a few yards from the shop where I lived. When we moved to Middleton's Lane it was best to catch an 85 or 87 which terminated in Windsor Road, again a short walk to home.

I used to get the first bus to come along as it was a very short walk from any of them. When we lived in Reepham Road my parents had to pay my bus fare to school and back as you only got a free bus pass if you lived more than three miles from the school as the crow flies. When we moved just round the corner to Middleton's Lane, I got a free bus pass despite the fact that I often got the bus to and from the same place as before.

As I write this, I'm sitting on a bench on Hellesdon Recreation Ground. In the distance I can hear children's voices. It's 11 am and there goes a whistle which must indicate the end of what we called playtime and what is now known as morning break. The noise from the children will have come from Kinsale Avenue Infant School - My old school.

I sit on the bench watching dogs run for tennis balls. Nobody is playing football or cricket or tennis today as it's a school day. There are quite a few small children with their mothers on the swings, a reminder that our darling granddaughter Lyla isn't far short of being five months old. Soon we will be able to take her to the swings.

But enough of this reverie. Back to the present in search of the past. Trips rarely go to plan and I got slightly the wrong bus. I say slightly because it allowed me to retrace my past ok but in a slightly different way.

The 37 went down Cromer Road and onto Horsford rather then in the past when the service turned left down Middleton's Lane and terminated in Windsor Road. On the way we passed Buxton Road where I had piano lessons on a Tuesday and Mecca Bingo Hall which used to be the Norwood Rooms, Mecca of entertainment.

I got off opposite what was formerly The Firs pub, but which now isn't and I walked through what will forever be known to me as The Firs - the place I spent many happy hours watching Norwich speedway.

As I walked, I tried to hear in my mind the roar of the bikes and the smell of the track. I tried to conjure up the ghosts of Ove Fundin and Ollie Nygren, the twin Swedish spearhead that made Norwich famous in the speedway world. Fundin is still alive so perhaps I shouldn't be surprised that I couldn't conjure up his ghost.

I think I failed anyway as the houses that replaced the speedway stadium are packed so closely together as to destroy memories. Architecturally I have always thought them to be awful. Many have two floors with the upper floor sloping alarmingly from the front to the back. I was glad to get out of the development and just remember the days when we rode our bikes around the outside before being chased off by the speedway team manager whose name was Len Parkin. The things I remember from all those years ago.

As I exited the Firs, I took note that there is no longer a bus stop in Windsor Road. I walked the route I had walked many times before which took me from Midleton's Lane to number 122 Reepham Road where my grandparents lived. On the way I passed Chapel Court which is a housing development with a church that was built on land sold to developers by my grandfather for a pittance - prime development land in a major suburb of Norwich.

I walked past the dentists on Reepham Road where I had so much pain inflicted on me as a boy. It's still a dentist but I hope the treatment is a little more modern today. No, I hope the treatment is a lot more modern.

I passed the house where Robert Votier lived. He had the nickname Bubs for a reason I never knew. And there it was 122 Reepham Road. The bungalow I have so many happy memories of. Saturday night watching television with my grandad who always called me Old Petner which was obviously Norfolk for partner. The bungalow where I went so often for Sunday lunch. My grandmother did the biggest roast potatoes known to man (or woman).

And across the road was number 157 where I was born. The old windows of my bedroom have been replaced and what was the back garden is now a concreted car park "they paved paradise, put up a parking lot" as Joni Mitchell once said. If I had taken the car, I could have boasted that I parked it in my old back garden.

Inside Dixon's, it felt dark and soulless and on this Tuesday morning there was hardly anyone around. I didn't fancy a cup of coffee as the cafe seemed lacking in charm as well. I climbed up a floor to try to get as close to my old bedroom as possible, but it was just a maze of corridors. My mind was in overdrive, but I couldn't imagine it as it once was and gave up.

As I exited the shops, I glanced at number 155 where Elsie Watson lived. It's now a shop entitled Heart of Norfolk. Many is the time I went searching in her garden after kicking a football in or hitting a tennis ball so hard against our wall that it ended in her garden. She never complained about me going in or breaking her flowers and plants as I probably did on many occasions.

So next on my walk was to go down Links Close to the little cut through that would take me to Kinsale Avenue School. It was a six-minute walk. How on earth did we take an hour to get home from school?

"It's only me," I would announce as I entered the shop.

One thing I did establish was the name of our shop. I have always believed it was called Northgate Fruit Stores but never been able to nail it down.

But there on a road sign was the word "Northgate." It wasn't the main name of the road which ran alongside Dixon's, but it did confirm the name of the shop.

So back to my walk.

There was the house where Karen Magee lived and close to the school was the house where my friend Eric Xuereb lived. His parents were Maltese, hence the unusual name.

Next, I walked down to the park/recreation ground.

Well, I've been sitting on this park bench writing for almost an hour so it's time to move on with the walk before I seize up.

I went to the library and it was an unstaffed day but, as I have what is called open access, I was able to get in for a brief look. It's very different from the days of high counters and only four books per person with all the shelves in rigid rows. Now it's a much more welcoming place although Hellesdon Library isn't as pleasant as either Hethersett or Wymondham. It still feels a little dark.

I walked down to have a look at my former home in Middleton's Lane. It's down a small cul de sac off the main road, so I felt a bit conspicuous trying to have a crafty look whilst going absolutely nowhere. It's now a strange place. They have erected large boards in what was the front garden, and it looks as if there's a large extension in the back garden. I didn't hover too long, I had seen enough anyway.

I did think about going back to Dixon's for coffee and lunch but didn't fancy it. I decided I had had enough and achieved what I came to do. Maybe the past is best left there. That's probably why I didn't take a single photo despite having a camera and mobile phone with me. I wouldn't be able to re-create what I remembered. I did think about my life though and how the days I was reminiscing about were days before my life's adventure had really begun. Days before college, days before marriage, days before work, days before children and grandchildren, days when the future stretched out ahead before it began closing in.

It did make me think about the support and good education that my parents made possible for me, primarily my mother, and how grateful I truly am that today I am able to write reasonably coherent blogs and books and that I feel I can genuinely call myself a writer. A writer at home, a writer on buses, a writer on a park bench, a writer in a library and sometimes just a writer.

Somehow, I felt that a day that had promised so much actually delivered little and do you know what? I wasn't too unhappy about that. I had assuaged my curiosity. From now I will keep my memories in my mind or for my writing. I feel no need to return to the places of my youth. Been there, done that and got the T shirt as they say.

I got a number 37 bus (this one did go along Reepham Road) back to the City centre and then a second bus back to Hethersett, realising that more of my past memories are in this South Norfolk Village rather than in the Broadland suburb of Hellesdon and there must have been a reason why when we decided to return to Norfolk from the Midlands we didn't even consider living in Hellesdon.

And as I shut the door in Hethersett I realised that once and for all, I do know where my home and where my happiness is.

But before finishing this part of my story I have to tell you that as a result of my visit and the above blog I was contacted to speak to a Hellesdon group about my memories of growing up there. I was also contacted by the clerk to Hellesdon Parish Council, who just happens to be the daughter of a good friend of mine, offering me the chance to peruse parish council minute books from the 1950s to the 1970s and I took up this opportunity to help with this book and give me an even more rounded view of the place where I was born.

After a day of reading through documents and minutes I had more of a handle of what some of the issues were around the time that I was born.

First and foremost were the efforts to set-up a Recreation Ground and community centre in Hellesdon with the Rec bursting to life in 1953, just after I burst into life.

The problem about reading minutes some 70 years later is that there is no descriptive matter. It always assumes that the documents are being read contemporaneously (blimey that's a big word) and not seven decades later when people like me want to find out about things. There's mention of the Welcome Home Fund and the Coronation Celebrations in 1953 but only that they took place, while what I want to know is where they were held and what the entertainment was. I will probably have to look up archive newspapers to find that kind of thing out, although Hellesdon Parish Council was forever moaning about lack of press coverage, something that is certainly still the case as parish pump stuff rarely makes the news today and it should do. That I feel is where local magazines come in. Perhaps in 70 years' time somebody will want to find out what happened in their area in 2024 and get a reasonably rounded picture from a small publication.

So the parish council minutes I viewed just gave me the bare bones of everything that was going on all those years ago and the discussion between people who are no longer with us and that is a sobering thought in its own right.

But reading through the minutes you do get a feeling for the issues which in this case included the unacceptable noise from St Faiths aerodrome, something that culminated in a petition to parliament and enlisting the support of the local MP of the time.

Then there was the closure of Hellesdon Railway Station although this only warranted a passing mention.

There was opposition to the new proposed civilian airport and which obviously failed because Hellesdon is where Norwich International Airport is.

There were desperate pleas for a roundabout at a busy crossroads. That took a few years to achieve but I crossed it twice during the day yesterday.

Then there were school overcrowding issues, noise problems, parking issues, street lighting and the fight not to be subsumed into Norwich with a desperate attempt for the parish to keep its own identity (something it managed to achieve then and also now).

"We would point out to the Minister that we are not and never have been part of Norwich," the council told Government.

The council even went as far as writing to individual groups asking them to make their views on the subject known and they organised a petition and had a public vote on the matter with over 3000 voting against and only 50 for joining Norwich. Then there was the controversy over council membership that is unlikely to exist today.

Reading through the minutes it is obvious that at election time there were always more candidates than seats available. I can remember when this was the case in Hethersett as well but not as marked as in Hellesdon when on one occasion there were 25 candidates for 15 seats.

The problem arose one year when there was a vacancy and the council filled it by co-opting somebody, something they were legally entitled to do. But it caused a furore because members of the public and some councillors felt the vacancy should have been filled by the person with the next highest number of votes at the previous election provided, of course, that person wished to be on the council. That story certainly did make the newspapers.

I had to laugh at one complaint from the council which was with regard to the loading of stock cars at Firs Stadium and the late-night noise this was creating. The response from the stadium manager was placatory and apologetic. It was easy for this to happen as the stadium closed and demolition began just a couple of months later. No mention of this major event was to be found in the minutes.

*   *   *

And that as they say is that. I've given it my best shot to write something reasonably coherent about my life. I've dredged up some memories from the back of my mind and along the way I've relived my childhood (even more than usual), relived growing up, relived my working life and relived my life of volunteering since I retired. I have probably left out more than I put in and I'm sure that long after this book is published many more memories will come to mind. At least I have my blog to allow these new memories to come to the surface.

As I have written about "My Charmed Life" I have had periods of joy and periods of sadness. There have been things in it that made me feel happy, there have been things in it that made me laugh out loud and there have been things that made me feel sad and things that brought more than one tear to my eye. Yes I don't mind admitting that some passages made, a mainly unemotional man, cry. Above all I have found the strength to write down as much as I can remember. I have mentioned people and places I thought I had long forgotten about.

I hope you like my efforts and I hope they have at least given you an hour or so of entertainment. If they bring out the same emotions in you as they have done in me then I will be well pleased. I have thoroughly enjoyed writing this and I would sign off by thanking you so much for taking the time to read it.

The End

Printed in Great Britain
by Amazon